READING RURAL LANDSCAPES

A FIELD GUIDE TO
NEW ENGLAND'S PAST

READING RURAL LANDSCAPES

A FIELD GUIDE TO NEW ENGLAND'S PAST

Robert M. Sanford

With illustrations by

Michael Shaughnessy

With foreword by

Mark Lapping

Tilbury House Publishers
Thomaston, Maine

Tilbury House Publishers
12 Starr Street
Thomaston, Maine 04861
800-582-1899
www.tilburyhouse.com
Text © 2015 Robert M. Sanford
Illustrations 2015 Michael Shaughnessy
Photographs © 2015 Nathan D. Hamilton, Gary Salmon, Robert M. Sanford
Foreword © 2015 Mark Lapping
ISBN 978-0-88448-366-3

Library of Congress Cataloging-in-Publication Data
Sanford, Robert M.
  Reading rural landscapes : a field guide to New England's past / Robert M. Sanford ; with illustrations by Michael Shaughnessy and a foreword by Mark Lapping.
     pages   cm
  Includes bibliographical references and index.
  ISBN 978-0-88448-366-3 (alk. paper)
  1. Historic rural landscapes—New England. 2. Land use, Rural—New England. 3. Historic agricultural landscapes—New England. 4. Agriculture—New England. I. Title.
  HD266.N36S26 2015
  643'.120974—dc23
                        2015007289
Printed in the United States
15 16 17 18 19   MAP   10 9 8 7 6 5 4 3 2

To the memory of
Richard Selden Sanford, 1926–2013.

Contents

Acknowledgments

The mistakes and quirks of this publication are mine alone. This is despite the advice, assistance, and support of many people. In particular, I would like to acknowledge and thank Robin A. Sanford, my wife, librarian, and friend; my dad, Richard S. Sanford, who first inspired me with walks in the woods behind our dairy farm with my sisters and brothers (Dave, Suzanna, Liza, Jennifer, and Andy), all of whom tolerated and even liked talking about historic landscapes with me; and my children, Corey, Daniel, and Morgan. Tilbury House Publishers brought this book to life; I am grateful to them, especially Jennifer Bunting, Jon Eaton, and Fran Hodgkins.

In alphabetical order, my appreciation also goes to Virginia Barlow; Edward L. Bell, Senior Archaeologist, Massachusetts Historical Commission—thanks for the review comments; Dr. Libby Bischof—thanks for your helpful suggestions; Nikkilee (Lee) Carleton, who read and commented on an early draft; Dr. Mike Cline; Dr. Ann Dean; Beth DellaValle; Dr. Phyllis Deutsch; Dr. Kevin Doran, Maine Forest Service educator; archaeologist Dr. Kenny Feder; James L. Garvin, New Hampshire State Architectural Historian; Roberta Gray, University of New England reference librarian; Dr. Nathan D. Hamilton, archaeologist and colleague; Kerry Hardy, with whom I had many talks about landscape history in graduate school; Harry Hoyt, retired surveyor with hundreds of tales; Don Huffer and Nina Huffer, Vermont consulting foresters; Rosemary Hunter; Dr. Bob Kuech; Dr. Jane Kuenz; Dave Lacy; Dr. Mark Lapping, inspiring planner, agricultural historian, and colleague; Katherine (Kate) McBrien, Maine Historical Society; Paul F. Miller, with whom I roamed the woods as a child; Christi Mitchell, Maine architectural historian; Tom Mulrey, artist; Dr. Tom Neumann, my former archaeology consulting partner and fellow "reader" of historic landscapes; Whitney Parrish; Giovanna Peebles, former Vermont State Archaeologist, source of particularly valuable criticism; Will Plumley; Patricia (Pat) Potter, University of Southern Maine reference librarian; Gary Salmon, Vermont forester; Katie Ann Shapiro, USM environmental science student and talented photographer; Dr. Travis Wagner; Christina Walker; Tom Wessels, ecologist and author; and Dan Yates, my son-in-law and fellow appreciator of family history.

Finally, Sebago Brew Pub and its employees—sources of inspiration in more ways than one (including its Gorham restaurant being an adaptive reuse of the old railroad station)—deserve my thanks and acknowledgment for their support.

Foreword

I grew up in the Northeast and most especially in New England. Over years of roaming its woods I came to know the birch, beech, maples, pines, firs, and other tree species that came to define much of the northern forest. After time I could identify barks, leaves, nuts, and seeds with some confidence. Some years later I moved to the edge of the Ozarks to teach forestry and land use planning. I needed a field guide to the region's trees to know with some degree of accuracy how to identify oaks, hickory, walnut, dogwoods, redbuds, and others. I am also a "birder" and I have used Peterson's and several Audubon Society field guides to help me to identify what I was seeing and hearing in my forays into the woods. Field guides are teaching aids and they help us to understand in more specific ways what we are sensing and experiencing. Rob Sanford's book, greatly enhanced by photographs and Michael Shaughnessy's drawings, is a field guide to the landscape of America's first region, New England, and more specifically the northern portion of the region. Unlike most field guides, however, Rob's work tells us not only about what is but also about what was. In a sense, then, *Reading Rural Landscapes* is something unique in that it is a guide to what we are seeing but it is also a retrospective field guide that helps us to appreciate the forces that shaped the region, its people, and the landscapes which, in their turn, helped to define the modes and manners of living in northern New England. What might initially appear "natural" in the landscape has, in fact, been a shaped and created set of places and sites. When I coined the phrase "working landscapes" now over three decades ago, I meant what Rob has so well elaborated and explained. He has, in a sense, put the "meat on the bones" and in doing so I and all those who will use this book will profit from and deeply appreciate. This is a book that will bring insight and clarity, and not a little pleasure.

—Mark B. Lapping, Distinguished Professor
Edmund S. Muskie School of Public Service
University of Southern Maine

Preface

This book is for anyone who's curious about the remnants and features of the bygone New England countryside, particularly those places where the houses, barns, and outbuildings are gone and only ruins remain. It is for history-minded people who drive along rural roads, hike through forest and field, or enjoy the views from their back fences. The geographic focus is northern New England—Vermont, Maine, New Hampshire, and northern Massachusetts—and the historical focus is on how the rural landscape reflects the past several hundred years of people making a living on the land. What clues to their agricultural and industrial activities did they leave behind? And how can we explore and experience the common (or "vernacular") ways in which the landscape we see today was shaped by their endeavors?

My goal is not to replace the many fine books and maps that can guide you to and through specific places, nor have I tried to create an exhaustive inventory of historic rural features. Rather, I hope to share with you the language of the land so that you can interpret rural landscapes much as an archaeologist or environmental historian might. The descriptions in this book are short, intended to spark your interest and point the way to more in-depth references. I invite you to look closely at the landscapes that unfurl before your eyes in New England, and to find the clues to the past that are hidden within them.

—Robert M. Sanford

Author's Note

Throughout the book, two spellings occur for this word and its variants: *archaeology* and *archeology*. Both are correct, but my personal preference is for the former, which you'll see in the narrative unless it is spelled the other way in a title or the name of an organization. In addition, all websites provided were accurate at time of publication.

—R.M.S.

1 Change in the Rural Landscape

To-morrow to fresh woods and pastures new...
—Milton

Life is simpler when you plow around the stump.
—Old farmer's saying

Perhaps when you come upon the remnant stone walls and foundations of a long-abandoned farm, you wonder about its past—who lived there, when, and what did they do? Maybe there are no stone walls or foundations, but you see old apple trees or other indicators of a past and are curious how they got there. If you own property in the country, perhaps you have found historic resources on it, things left behind or things built in or on the landscape—items that can help you understand or appreciate the past. Knowing more about the significance of these historic remnants can help you manage a woodlot or other rural property. It can add value to your land and enrich your understanding of the landscape. Or it can simply help you enjoy your experience in the country.

This book is intended as a guide to "reading" rural landscapes[1] that hold clues to New England's agricultural past, whether you are merely curious about the countryside you ride through or want to know more about a particular plot of land or type of feature. Interest in and speculation about the past are hardly new. Hayward's 1839 *Gazetteer* points out a puzzling aspect of the landscape in Francestown, New Hampshire: *On the north side of Haunted Pond, there is a bar of 20 rods [1,230 feet] in length, 6 feet high, and 3 or 4 feet through; but for what purpose or by what means this barrier was raised, is a matter of conjecture only.*

People have always been interested in stone walls, and there is a growing number of publications covering everything from their geography to how to build them[2]. Likewise, you can find many publications dealing with specialized or particular historical and cultural features of the rural landscape, such as barns.[3] But what if the barns and houses are long gone, the stone walls are in ruins, and the site is overgrown with trees? What can you tell from such meager remnants? As it turns out, even in landscapes that have been long abandoned or put to different uses, we can read features that tell us about the agrarian past—an environmental history. *Reading Rural Landscapes* is designed to help you gain an immediate sense of landscape history from what you see during a walk, drive, or paddle in the countryside. The book's many illustrations of meaningful features will help with your interpretations. You may want to take photographs of the places you visit for later interpretation or simply to document your discoveries. You might also provide a measurement scale and GPS coordinates for future reference. The US Geological Survey has a free mapmaker (http://www.usgs.gov/pubprod/). Whatever approach you take, begin by looking around the common countryside.

Anyone—from the curious onlooker to the professional researcher— can look at the landscape and extract meaning about the past. Historical resources in the landscape include the places containing evidence left behind by people who once lived in an area, whether a Native American village site from 1,000 years ago, a charcoal kiln from the eighteenth century, the remains of an 1890s logging camp, or an old farmstead.[3] These historical resources preserve information about where people lived and what they did. The ability to understand such resources comes primarily from association: their relationship with objects and features around them. Resources that are kept intact are preserved for the future. Reading landscapes enhances our appreciation of our surroundings.

Everything you see in a landscape—each component—is part of a mosaic of local, state, and regional historical contexts for who, when, why, and what happened there, a full understanding of which requires documentary research about the historical geography of the location in question.[4] Think, for example, of the progressively larger geographic scales, each one culturally meaningful, that establish the context for a single farm: the home-lot is surrounded by the farm itself, which is contained by the immediate neighborhood, the town, the county, the state, the region. An iron-making enterprise requires the mines and mining settlements, the woodlots for charcoal, the dwellings of workers and management, industrial support buildings, and other elements in hinterlands and village. The functional purpose of a feature (say, a cold-storage cellar) and its part in a working farm is one way of looking at the historical landscape. Another way is from social and economic contexts. In such cases, the material remains will disclose more about social tensions, ideologies, and class issues of the cultural geography, and reveal the social landscape.

To evaluate changes to the New England landscape, we can imagine its appearance long before Europeans arrived. New England was covered with vast forests for centuries. Native American inhabitants of the region practiced a hunter-gatherer lifestyle that included horticulture but not the intensive agriculture that developed in the southeastern and midwestern regions of the country; thus they changed the forests comparatively little. This does not mean that the New England wilderness was "primeval." It had been home to native peoples for perhaps 13,000 years before Europeans arrived, and through their activities, inventiveness, and traditions, native peoples were landscape transformers. European fur traders and fishermen cruising New England's shores in the sixteenth century noticed that the native peoples had altered the coastal forests by clearing land for cultivation. Still, it was nothing like the amount of land cleared by European settlers into the mid-nineteenth century, when the forest cover was reduced to about 20 percent of northern New England—

almost the exact reverse of forest coverage at the start of the twenty-first century. The 1860 census reported that 32 percent of the land in Maine was in use as farmland, and New Hampshire and Vermont had 63 and 84 percent, respectively.

Forests now grow where once stood farms, factories, mills, and villages—Maine is the most forested of the states (about 90 percent); New Hampshire, at 84 percent, is second only to Maine, and Vermont is about 78 percent forested. Massachusetts might surprise you because although it is the third most densely populated state in the nation, it is the eighth most forested at 62 percent (http://masswoods.net/forests). Even as the forest returns in some places, it recedes in others. New residential subdivisions and commercial strip development are spreading out from urban areas and the landscape is again undergoing change. Multiple land uses over time create an interesting dynamic and we can "read" old and new changes by looking at the rural landscapes around us now. The land near the edge of roads provides a lot of information, as do short walks into the forests and fields surrounding highways and waterways.

Everything is a potential clue to the past, even small plants. Most of the plants we see along our roadsides are not native to North America.

Common plant species found in disturbed areas

Evening primrose (*Oenothera biennis*)
Day-lily (*Hemerocallis fulva*)
Chicory (*Cichorium intybus*)
Yarrow (*Achillea millefolim*)
Gill-over-the-ground (*Glechoma hederacea*)
Goosefoot (*Chenopodium*)
Green amaranth (*Amaranthus retroflexus*)
Plantain (*Plantago*)
Stinging nettle (*Urtica dioica*)
Burdock (*Arctium minus*)
Common tansy (*Tanacetum vulgare*)
Fireweed (*Epilobium angustifolium*)
Dandelion (*Taraxacum officinale*)

They are escaped invasive or exotic species brought over from Europe either intentional or accidentally. Plants that grow in waste areas—abandoned lots, roadsides, the edges of construction sites, power corridors—are the hardy early colonizers of disturbance and quickly move into old farm sites and other unmaintained spaces. Once we determine that the land was disturbed, other questions arise. When did the disturbance happen, and what was its nature? The plants provide clues. Field guide books[5] indicate many common species that thrive in disturbed areas, as shown in the accompanying table.

amaranth

The disturbance leading to the presence of such plants often derives from farming or the construction of homes, roads, and other development (Figure 1.1). Many of these plants were useful as food or medicine to people in the past, and were tolerated or even encouraged. Settlers brought tansy from Europe for medicinal gardens; many other plants escaped from earliest colonial times. Some sun-loving plants move in quickly, only to be displaced by later invading plants that shade them out. Some plants spread more slowly but are harder to displace.

burdock

dandelions

Over a quarter of a million miles of stone walls are in New York and New England. At one time or another, most woodlots were used for pasture or cultivated fields, leaving more clues than just stone walls. Foundations of houses, barns, outbuildings,

nettles

Figure 1.1. *A few of the common plants that indicate some type of recent disturbance from farm animals, land clearance, or other alterations often associated with farming or construction. These hardy invaders include amaranth, burdock, dandelions, nettles, thistle, and yarrow. Shrubs and trees will move in from the edges and replace these sun-loving plants.*

thistle

and wells might remain. The farmer had to do all kinds of things, and a farm might include a small factory, a kiln or forge, a millrace, and a sugarhouse. Old logging roads and farm roads may have left their mark. Tiny family cemeteries dot the landscape. Log landings, abandoned horse-drawn farm equipment, and surface scatterings of broken glass, ceramics, nails, horseshoes, railroad spikes, and bricks bear testimony to past lives. All these clues may reveal a surprising amount of information about the land's history. And they also raise questions: What *are* these things we see? How did they get there in the first place—and when? Who lived here before? What is the pattern of change and interaction between people and the environment?

Landscapes do not stay the same even if they are left alone. Landscapes undergo a sequence of events that in New England always tends to return former forest land back to forest. This means that undeveloped land in most of New England is on its way back to being forest. This journey back may be fairly rapid if the land is abandoned, left undisturbed, and has good soil for growing trees. Or it may take hundreds of years or longer if people live in the area or have altered the soil in a way that discourages forest regrowth. Either way, there will still be a natural progression of vegetative change back to woodland.

How do we look at a present-day forest and determine its environmental history? An undisturbed path of succession (a progression in which one type of plant community gradually changes to another) leads to an "old-growth" forest. Not much of this original forest type remains—maybe several hundred acres in Vermont, more in New Hampshire and Maine, perhaps 1,120 acres in Massachusetts, mostly in the western Berkshires.[7] The response of a forest to severe land-use changes, such as fire or clearing for agriculture, may change the types of trees and plants. Other changes may include alterations to the surface of the land—piles of stone, a flattened landscape, plowed field edges, cow paths, empty excavation pits, cellar holes, and other signs and byproducts of its use. The result can be a "signature" in the subsequent plant community, a feature chronicled by May Thielgaard Watts in her classic work, *Reading the Landscape*,[8] and more specifically described for New

England forests by Tom Wessels in his *Reading the Forested Landscape* and *Forest Forensics* books.

In comparing potential changes in the landscape, it helps if we can tell what regular processes (stages of succession) and eventual outcomes would exist without direct human influence. This is discussed in Chapter 2, which begins with the forest that originally covered most of New England and explores the interpretation of vegetation: how trees and other plants reflect the environmental history of past agrarian

Figure 1.2. *Worth a second look, this rather common roadside view of a thicket at the top of a hill surrounded by field provides a fleeting vision to someone zooming by on the highway. A closer look yields clues that this is the site of a farmstead. The thicket indicates where plants have moved into a "disturbed" area. The disturbance was the existence of a house, and the small fieldstone cellar hole is visible up close. If cows still roam the countryside, they will keep the forest from filling the surrounding field, but the thicket brambles keep the cows out and allow woody growth in the cellar hole. Someone has filled the hole to make it safe just in case the cows do get in. Much of the stone has been taken for reuse elsewhere, perhaps by the frugal farmer, or perhaps someone just helped themselves. The hilltop location provided fresh breezes, good drainage, warmer temperatures, and a view of both the rising and setting sun. Expect trees of this size growing up within the cellar hole to have been there for more than half a century.*

landscapes. Chapter 3 focuses on vegetation from old houses, barns, and outbuilding sites. Subsequent chapters deal with translating information from other common landscape features associated with farming and rural life: foundations, roads, walls, fences, rivers and streams, and cemeteries. Plants and other environmental aspects of a setting are treated in context; for example, some plantings are more likely to be associated with house foundations and others with barn foundations, with the distinctions being rather subtle. Perhaps there is no one best way to organize this by subject matter, but that is also the charm of reading landscapes—they are hodgepodges of information—hints and clues—sometimes conflicting, but all pointing to a linked but jumbled agrarian past (see Figure 1.2). The result is a landscape with history to be read in it.

2

Trees and Plantings Associated with Forest and Field History

Look for a tough wedge for a tough log.
—Publilius[9] Syrus, 42 BC

"The time to cut hay," he said firmly, "is in hayin' time."
—E. B. White

Feb 10 1896
The Boys are loging
Halling them to Mr buneys John & John Egen
are chopping them Frank and Mr Morgan are driving team
—Mary A. Hall, *Ledger and Daybook*,
Maine Women Writers' Collection, University of New England

Up until shortly before the Civil War, the typical New England farm supplied just enough to meet the needs of the family (a "subsistence farm").[10] This included taking trees from the woodlot for firewood and construction. The original forests in northern New England tended to be northern hardwood (various species, with large amounts of beech, birch, and maple), northern coniferous (diverse, but mainly spruce, fir, and hemlock), central hardwood (primarily oak, some hickory, and other species) in southern parts, and pine forest types throughout much of the region. Most of the forestland in New England has been and remains in private ownership and most is classified as commercial timberland. The large amount of forestland only hints at the pastoral landscape of a past with greater amounts of cleared land dotted with farms.

Some coastal and river-valley forests were already cleared by the Native Americans, but most forestland in northern New England (except in the far northern parts near Canada) was first cut in colonial times to make way for houses and fields, and to supply wood for construction and fuel. A second major cutting of these forests began in the late 19th and early 20th centuries, but was not as intensive. This cutting was more extensive, moving deeper into the valleys and higher up the mountains to get wood for pulp and paper mills. This second cutting slowed down considerably during the Great Depression, shortly before World War II. The New England forests are still being harvested for a wide variety of forest products ranging from high-quality saw logs for lumber to low-quality logs for wood chips, pellets, and firewood.

A few pockets of old-growth trees have escaped all past harvests. Elsewhere, a significant amount of forest grew back between the first and second cuttings, and even more so between the second cuttings and the present. The evidence regarding the first and second cuttings is largely limited to written documentation, but the signatures of logging within the past century can be seen in the remains of stumps (from the most recent cutting and perhaps as far back as 20 to 30 years, and longer for some pine, hemlock, and other species in the right places), old logging roads, log landing areas, loading ramps, logging camps, railroad lines, forest management practices, and in the resultant economic activity. There are other signs of change. Intentional plantings ("soldier rows") of single-species trees (mono-crops) have replaced some of the clear-cuts—there have been far less of them than the clear cuts that created the first agricultural fields, forests have regenerated, skid trails have turned into roads, and rural communities have developed (Figure 2.1). The trees left behind in some forests that were not clear-cut are the result of logging for a particular species (e.g., pine and spruce in earlier times, and, in more recent times, oak, sugar maple, or white birch for specific markets). The present New England forest is based on a more tempered harvesting regime from over a century of "selecting" trees for a variety of reasons within the scope of management plans created by the emerging profession of forestry in the very early 1900s and continuing to the present day.

Stumps are among the most obvious indicators of tree harvesting and land clearance. When a tree falls naturally, it pulls up roots and tips over, leaving a depression and a mound, sometimes with rocks that had been in the root ball, but no stump. When a tree breaks—be it from lightning, a storm, stress, or rot—it falls, too, but leaves a jagged, broken-off stump, usually higher than the foot or so above the ground height of the typical sawn tree stump. However, stumps cut during a deep-snow winter might be higher than a foot above the ground. Looking at the condition of the stump gives an idea about when it was cut or bro-

Figure 2.1. *Intentional plantings of "soldier rows" of a single species of tree have replaced the original forest. The compressed soil of the old logging road has caused the forest to grow back more slowly than it has in the surrounding land.*

ken. A flat stump with moss, softening wood, and mostly complete bark on it may have been cut only 5 to 10 or 15 years ago. When the cut stump is still fairly flat on top but has mossy, shaggy surfaces, loose or missing bark, and abundant fungus, it may be in the 15- to 20-year range.

As a rule of thumb, stumps last no more than a few decades, gradually becoming shaggy mounds resembling compost. Stumps from before the late 20th century disappeared from the forest because they could not survive exposure to air and rot. Stump survival varies greatly, depending on soil conditions, moisture, climate, biological activity, and what kind of tree originally stood there (Figure 2.2). Spruce and hemlock, for example, have hard, durable branches, and their stubs may still be sticking out of an old stump. Chestnut stumps left over from the early 20th century chestnut blight can survive for a very long time.[11] Hardwood species tend to rot fairly quickly from the inside to the outside. Elm rots fast, but sends up new shoots nearby when it can. Maple stumps get a black, mis-

Figure 2.2. *Pine stumps and mound from old logging site. The stump on the left is a conifer, about 30 years old when it was cut approximately 20 years ago. The height suggests it was cut in winter when the snow was high and skidding logs was easier by bobsled. How fast the stump deteriorates depends on the species, soil conditions, moisture, sunlight, and weather. Conifers rot from the outside to the inside. Hardwoods tend to rot from the inside to the out. The date of cutting is inferred by the stump condition and by the growth of surrounding vegetation. On the right is a mound from an old logging operation in a hardwood forest during the mid-20th century. Early logging efforts prior to mechanized equipment had little direct impact on the surface of the land itself.*

shapen fungus on them that breaks them down. Conifers will rot from the outside to the inside. Birch rots very fast because the bark keeps the water in the wood from escaping. Moist environments will accelerate rot and deterioration of trees and their stumps, but if conditions are too wet, the lack of oxygen slows down bacterial action. As a result, submerged stumps in rivers and flooded dam reservoirs survive longer than their counterparts on land.

The Original Forest

Mature forests existed in much of New England when the first colonists arrived. Some land had been cleared by Native Americans, but primarily for villages and fields along the coast[12] and rivers, and not in the high-country areas.[13] The great swaths of trees were an amazing sight to Europeans from denuded countries. The British quickly realized how important the tall, light trunks of the Eastern White Pines were for constructing masts, enabling the British fleet to keep its dominion over much of the seas. White pine was even called King's Arrow Pine. By 1691, all white pine bigger than two feet in diameter and located within three miles of water was designated property of the king and could not be cut by colonists. The king's surveyors marked trees with an axe or hatchet, making three slashes fanning out like an arrowhead, but looking similar to a turkey track. New Englanders being what they are, more than a few of these reserved trees found their way out of the forests and into local ships and houses.[14] The king's agents inspected log shipments and sawmills for wide pine planks to be sure the law was being met.[15] Moving these giant pines was a massive job, and the logging continued well after the Revolutionary War nullified the king's claim. Judge Sewall noted that 40 oxen were needed to haul a large mast pine in Salmon Falls, New Hampshire.[16] Even in the late 20th century, foresters and loggers recited legends of how a few of the arrow-emblazoned trees still remained if you knew where to look.

Early logging efforts directed at specific forests were aimed at species that were concentrated, fairly easy to cut and move, and easily converted into usable lumber; these were the white pine and red spruce stands. Much of this work was done by professional sawyers who often built small sawmills at adjacent rivers and tributaries.[17] Beers and other 19th-century atlases show many hundreds of sawmills all over northern New England. By the mid-19th century, most of the large stands of spruce and pine had been felled. The Civilian Conservation Corps (CCC) and the Works Progress Administration (renamed Works Project Administration in 1939 and known as the WPA) programs associated with the Depression in the 1930s created plantations of trees in a major reforestation effort. Paper companies in the northeast did not have large plantation programs, but in some small plots, those interested in management of the resource planted desired species in "soldier rows," as shown in Figure 2.1. The farmer was more likely to manage by cutting individually selected trees in small woodlots rather than by replanting.

Many northern hardwood and mixed hardwood–softwood forests were cleared by the early to mid-19th century to accommodate farms. After the Civil War, farming declined but logging efforts expanded north-ward. Significant amounts of forestland had come under farm ownership as woodlots. The US Commissioner of Agriculture reported in 1887 that 22.4 percent of forest area in Maine belonged to farms, as did 43 percent of forests in New Hampshire, 79 percent of forests in Vermont, and *all* of the forests in Massachusetts.[18] Forests in harvested woodlots gradually reclaimed much of the landscape when the farmland was abandoned, but did not necessarily consist of the same kinds of trees. This "second growth" forest now provides the basis of comparison for past land uses. A few scattered examples of "original" forest survive (Figure 2.3), indicating the true size and composition of trees in the early landscape—such as The Cape in Goshen, Vermont. (See the Vermont Natural Areas Registry for a complete list.) According to the Maine Tree Foundation, Maine has 93 old-growth stands.[19] The Ancient Forest Exploration & Research organization has a report available online that lists the old-growth red pine forests in the United States and Canada,[20] and other resources for learning about old-growth forests. Some Native American cultures call these venerable old trees "standing people." How old can these trees get? A red spruce in the White Mountain National Forest is more than 400 years old. A black gum (*Nyssa sylvatica*) in Rockingham County,

New Hampshire, is more than 690 years old—perhaps the oldest tree in New England.[21] Eastern OLDLIST, maintained by Columbia University's Lamont-Doherty Earth Observatory, lists maximum tree ages for eastern North America.[22] Old trees do not necessarily mean big trees, and big trees are not necessarily old. Each state has a register of big trees,[23] and the American Forests organization maintains a national list of the biggest trees by species.[24]

If the trees have been removed and new trees have grown back, we can look at the age of the new trees to see how long it has been since the land was last cleared. The majority of mature trees in forests today are between 50 and 150 years old—well below the maximum ages of tree species that occurred in the early forest communities (see Table 2.1). The first step is to know what trees are on the site. You can use a reputable Internet site[25] to determine the scientific name of the tree if you know the common name. If you do not know the common name, you can use one of the tree guides such as *Trees of North America*,[26] *Bark*,[27] *The Book of Leaves*,[28] or *Master Tree Finder*,[29] which can fit into a pocket, or the National Arbor Day Foundation tree identification materials.[30] Most states also publish a tree list that includes what trees live in the state, their scientific names, and common characteristics.

Figure 2.3. *Old-growth trees represent a very small part of New England forests. These giants, spared by the native peoples, original settlers, and subsequent farmers and loggers have been in existence for hundreds of years as "primary forest."*

Table 2-1. *Some common trees and their age range in old growth forest*[31]

Tree	Scientific name	Old-growth age
Oak	*Quercus*	200–600 years
Eastern hemlock	*Tsuga Canadensis*	500–900 years
White pine	*Pinus strobus*	200–450 years
American beech	*Fagus grandifolia*	300–400 years
Sugar maple	*Acer saccharum*	200–300 years
Yellow beech	*Betula alleghaniensis*	150–200 years

The forest floor reflects the dynamics of the vegetation. Trees die and fall over, pulling out their root balls and leaving holes in the ground that may gradually fill in. Rotting logs build up organic material in other areas. Thus, the floor of a mature forest is not nice and flat; it tends to be hummocky, with lots of small irregularities. Most disturbance in a mature forest is small, localized, and part of an ongoing natural process—as in the case of a dead tree finally falling down. But what if the disturbance is wider, more significant? The type of severe disturbance that might cause a natural forest stand to be replaced might only occur every 100 to 800 years. So what can we learn about past disturbances from what we see in the landscape now?

Forest Disturbances

Ecologist Tom Wessels describes six common forms of major distur-bances that are either natural or human-caused:[32] fire, pasturing, logging, blights, beaver, and blowdowns.[33] He tells how to read the ecological history of an environmental setting to determine the type and extent of the original disturbance. These are useful themes for looking at how forests change, and we can draw upon them as we explore individual set-tings of former farmland (this chapter owes a strong debt to the work of Tom Wessels). Each form of disturbance has unique characteristics. For example, fire usually destroys the understory (the lower trees) more than

Estimating Tree Age

Estimating the age of a tree is just guesswork unless you can take a core sample or someone happened to record when he or she planted it. Can you tell by how tall or wide the tree is? If the soils and growing conditions are harsh, even a small tree can be quite old. The spacing between trees affects their competition for sun and food resources, which in turn affects their growth. You may find some tree age patterns, especially true if you are looking at a single-species plantation. If you can relate the diameter or the height of the tree to age, then perhaps you can make rough estimates of age. If the tree is on your own property you might want to use an increment borer to take a core sample (Figure 2.4). Just measure the diameter in centimeters of the tree 4½ feet (about 1.3 meters) above the ground (diameter at breast height, or dbh) and divide by two to find the radius of the tree. Bore to the heart of the tree and count the rings. Tree dating is one tool for understanding how the forested landscape changes. Other tools include looking at overall patterns in vegetation and researching documents and local histories.

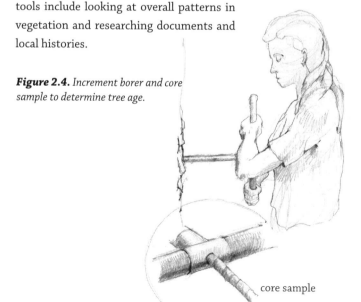

Figure 2.4. *Increment borer and core sample to determine tree age.*

core sample

it does the main forest canopy.[34] Fortunately, severe fires are rare in New England, especially compared to wind events and human disturbances.

Human disturbance in the form of creating pasture leads to old-field succession after abandonment, with characteristics influenced by the pasture's history. Another human disturbance, logging, tends to remove the taller trees (the "overstory"), leaving the understory free to take over. Blights affect particular species and what happens after depends on the role and niche that species occupied. One animal species, the beaver, is a major change agent; pretty much extirpated by the late 18th century, they began a comeback in the mid-20th century, altering streams, ponds, and other lowlands. Blowdowns tend to remove the canopy and initiate secondary forest succession by kicking up the soil (Figure 2.5). If the soil is completely removed and the land has to start bare, a primary succession will begin. Land can be stripped of topsoil by humans or by nature and can take a long time to recover. Old quarries and landslides can remain bare and sparsely vegetated for many decades. Usually, though, the land changes much quicker because there is some soil left, particularly when the initial uses were related to agricultural development.

Figure 2.5. *A wind storm ("blowdown") has stirred up the soil, uprooted trees, and re-set the vegetation growth pattern. This one occurred about a dozen years ago, as indicated by the saplings.*

In addition to the vegetative changes associated with houses and other buildings (addressed in Chapter 3), patterns of change are associated with four common initial agrarian activities: cut-over land, bared or stripped land, pasture, and plowed cropland. If the land grows back into a forest, it may differ from other forests in species composition on the basis of its past land use.[35]

What happens to the land at one of these starting points depends on what people did and for how long, in addition to natural conditions such as soil and climate. A farm would likely have undergone all these starting points because its space would radiate outward from the farmhouse in terms of energy usage and intensity. This means that cropland would be closest, followed by hayfields and mowing areas, then pasture—where the cows or sheep were let loose in forested and cut-over land too rocky, steep, or wet for hayfields—and finally the woodlot, land left aside for the farmer to cut wood or hold in reserve for the future. Some of these uses would overlap because, for example, cows could use forestland that also had open meadows and hayfields could be alternated with corn or millet. However, you can see this general pattern in farms that are still operating. Variations in the pattern today are greater than in the past, reflecting economic factors, the parceling out of land into noncontiguous plots, and the availability of roads and modern agricultural equipment. The environmental patterning of the overgrown or abandoned farm will likely reflect various aspects of these historical land uses and starting stages, even if the land has grown back to forest. *(Plate 1)*

When the land is cleared, whether intensively by the farmer or lightly by the herd, be it through plowing, cutting, grazing, or other use, tree coverage is reduced. More sunlight comes in and new plants appear. The plants available to move in on new open space reflected a European palette (a few are listed in Table 2.2). Many weeds and cultivated plants came over from Europe, providing a long-term experiment on the land: What would happen as these plants were intentionally or accidentally introduced into newly created open space? It did not take them long to become common on the farm, and the American rural landscape was forever changed.[36] The 1869 Maine Board of Agriculture Report describes common invasive plant species and their effects on agriculture—these weeds would have had a similar impact in other New England states.

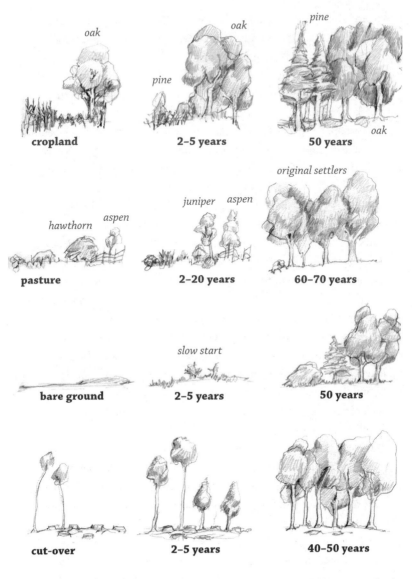

oak

oak

pine

pine

oak

cropland   **2–5 years**   **50 years**

original settlers

hawthorn   aspen   juniper   aspen

pasture   **2–20 years**   **60–70 years**

slow start

bare ground   **2–5 years**   **50 years**

cut-over   **2–5 years**   **40–50 years**

Figure 2.6. *Four agricultural origins of change to the original forest: cut-over land, bared soil, pasture, and plowed cropland. The stages show how the land might have changed; each launches a pattern. By looking at the characteristics of a site, you may be able to make a good guess about which of the starting points most likely applies, and how much change has occurred. (Figure based on Neumann & Sanford, 1987.)*

Table 2.2. European invasives
Many of the common, invasive plants of New England originated in Europe and moved onto old farmland.

Dandelion (*Taraxacum officinale*)

Goat's beard (*Tragopogon duplius*)

Elecampane (*Inula helenium*)

Common plantain (*Plantago major*)

Wild mustard (*Brassica kaber*)

Field bindweed (*Convolulus arvensis*, in the morning-glory family)

Common mullein (*Verbascum thapsus*)

Ox-eye daisy (*Chrysanthemum leucanthemum*)

Sow thistle (various species in the genus *Sonchus*)

Common tansy (*Tanacetum vulgare*)

Clover (*Trifolium repens*)

White sweet clover (*Melilotus alba*)

Alfalfa (*Medicago sativa*)

St. John's wort (*Hypericum perforatum*)

Common barberry (*Berberis vulgaris*)

European elder (*Sambucus nigra*)

Transitions After the Forest Has Been Cut

After timber has been harvested and the land allowed to rest, reverting naturally, forest regeneration follows patterns based on environmental factors of climate, soil type, and soil moisture. Each region will have its own pattern and each setting will have its own variations. The degree to which the remaining vegetation tolerates shade will affect regeneration patterns, including species composition. The intensity of the cutting practices will also affect regeneration patterns.

Early farmers were as much loggers as anything else, augmenting their living by supplying lumber not needed directly on their farms.[37] Once most of the trees were cut, the farmer in a marginal holding would have to move elsewhere, so he would think carefully about what he cut

(Figure 2.7). In the main, farmers managed their land for the long term, similar to foresters, and it's possible to look at a forest and tell if it has been managed. Infrequent cuttings over long periods of time create a forest characterized by greater ranges in tree diameters, smaller ranges in number of species, and greater shade tolerance than any other type of cutting practice. The many thousands of acres of northern hardwood forest composed mostly of sugar maple, beech, and yellow birch found today are the result of infrequent cuttings carried on over the last century and a half. Without human intervention, things still happen in the woods—the forest experiences fires, blowdowns, ice storms, and other events that create large-scale openings—but this is not the same as what happens when people start cutting trees.

Logged-over areas, whatever the degree of logging, leave direct evidence in addition to changes in the vegetative pattern. This evidence is usually in the form of stumps, scars on bark of existing trees, log roads and landings, and lumber camp sites. Under certain conditions, some

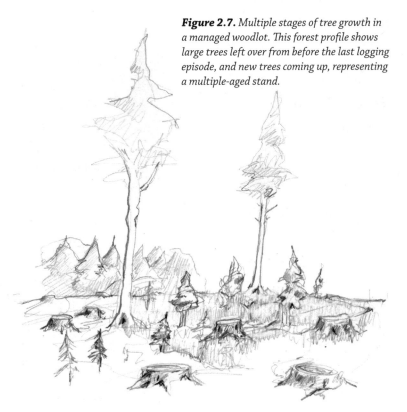

Figure 2.7. *Multiple stages of tree growth in a managed woodlot. This forest profile shows large trees left over from before the last logging episode, and new trees coming up, representing a multiple-aged stand.*

stumps may last 50 years or more, so a tract may contain evidence of more than one cutting. Logging road systems can survive for many years (see Chapter 6). In general, they differ from other forest roads because they tend to funnel inward and downhill toward one or more common areas where the logs were concentrated (Figure 2.8), and these log landings may still be discernible. The exposed soil will sometimes cause the abandoned landing area and logging road to completely seed into trees, resulting in a young, dense stand of trees along much of the length of the roadbed. Lumber camp sites may contain remnants of tree species not common to the area (e.g., apple), in addition to cultural features such as abandoned equipment, old foundations, pieces of wire rope, and the dump from the cook shack. Broken bobsled irons might also be found near the old logging roads.

Nature also shaped the forest with large-scale weather events, including the 1938 hurricane along coastal New England, the 1947 forest fires (over 200,000 acres of land burned in Maine), and the 1998 ice storm (millions of forestland acres in New England and Canada were

Figure 2.8. *This recent "log landing" in Castleton, Vermont, has been stripped of topsoil, compacted by heavy equipment, and exposed to the elements. Left alone, the sumac, birch, and other hardy pioneer species will move in. The presence of older trees with healed scars can suggest whether or not the landing area had also been used as such in the past.*

affected). These events had the effect of creating cut-over land, as did the need to treat the forest after waves of spruce budworm and other disease and insect manifestations.

Forestland tends to develop a "pit and mound" topography as trees fall down and their roots pull out of the ground, or stumps and debris develop into mounds. Remember, the "natural" forest has a hummocky look to it. Land that has been logged regularly might look a little less lumpy. Land that has been bared or stripped will look even flatter or have other changes that reflect usage.

Transitions After Land Has Been Stripped of Topsoil

Bared or stripped land in northern New England usually results from large gravel pits, quarries, topsoil removal projects, borrow pits, landslides, severe fire sites, log landings, and in other places where the ground was severely disturbed. Land that has been bared or stripped generally follows a secondary succession path. However, severe soil disturbance may result from a large abandoned excavation site, or an extremely hot fire can start a primary succession path. For example, the 18th-century destruction of the red spruce forest atop Mt. Monadnock in southwestern New Hampshire triggered the following stages: moss meadow, aster/fireweed meadow, hairgrass sedge meadow, willow/birch thicket, aspen forest, and spruce forest.[38]

Even if the ground has been severely disturbed, generations later it will look like succession on a former plowed field. If the top layers of soil have been removed or covered, the succession will be more easily distinguished from that on abandoned cropland. The presence of stumps should help to distinguish bared or stripped land from logged land, unless the logging took place more than several decades ago, making it unlikely that any stumps remain. Logged land may also have skid trails in which the topsoil layer was bared, with a resultant successional change.

During the initial five years or so after the land is bared or stripped, vegetation tends to be dominated by pioneering plant species such as goldenrod (*Solidago* spp.), horseweed (*Erigeron canadensis*), goosefoot (*Chenupodium*),[39] Queen Anne's lace (*Daucus carota*), chicory (*Cichorium intybus*), aster (*Aster* spp.), raspberry (*Rubrus odoratus*), and grasses. Depending on the proximity of seed sources and the degree of soil disturbance, aspen, paper birch (*Betula papyrifera*), white pine, northern white cedar (*Thuja occidentalis*), sumac, and willow establish themselves in clumps within a few years. White pine reproduces best when the seeds get in direct contact with soil, as when the land is scarred by equipment, or just by turkeys scratching in the duff.

Sometimes we can tell what happened to the land by the pattern and type of trees that get reestablished quickest. For example, pure paper birch stands on the upper slopes of steep hillsides are pretty good indicators of fire influence. After the fire-damaged trees have fallen over, the new birches will crowd together, exhibiting the closed-canopy descriptions associated with clear-cuts, and getting the jump on other tree species. Gray birch (*Betula populifolia*) is another hardy species that can grow on inhospitable sites. It is short-lived, though, seldom reaching 50 years of age.

Figure 2.9. *This site has had the topsoil stripped from it to supply local gravel needs. The lack of topsoil has slowed regeneration and the hardy pioneer species of birch, sumac, and moss have persisted for many years.*

Trees and shrubs regenerating on stripped land tend to remain in clumps. Trees exhibit closed-canopy growth traits in the interior of their clumps and open-growth traits about the edges. In old quarries and other places where the exposed land or fill has low nutrition, the mix of scattered trees and shrub clumps and hardy pioneer plants may persist for decades (Figure 2.9).

Severely disturbed land will often have the top organic layer of soil partially removed in areas, revealing exposed light-colored patches of subsoil. This land may also have irregular features such as small earthen mounds called berms and scooped depressions, or pits, along with buried leavings from human residents. The vegetation can be used to estimate what happened and when, as well as the extent of the disturbance and when it stopped. The age of trees growing on the fill or in depressions helps date the disturbance. The composition, size, and general health of trees also reflect a response to the disturbance.

Transitions After Pasture

Except for the Maine north woods, the majority of northern New England has been pasture at one time or another, but this history is not always clearly discernible because so much of the land is reforested or has been changed through sprawl and urban development. On a working farm, the pasture was usually the least valuable agricultural land—too rocky, steep, or infertile for crop use—and therefore is often readily identifiable as such due to its physical characteristics even if it is no longer in use as a pasture. Prior use of land as pasture can be recognizable if the land was abandoned or if it later was converted to housing with open land around it. Cows, sheep, and horses would eat the hardwoods but not the spruce and white pine, making it easy for an old pasture to turn into today's conifer forest.

The dominant vegetation in abandoned pastures changes from a variety of grasses and forbs to grasses with a scattering of seedlings avoided by cattle, e.g., hawthorn (*Crataegus* spp.) or juniper (*Juniperous communis*). Sheep are less discriminating than cattle in their grazing and, when kept in large flocks, will remove the woody, thorn-bearing

Table 2.3. **Farming stages in northern New England**

Farming stages in northern New England. The Native Americans had small subsistence fields in coastal areas and river valleys. Early settlers had subsistence farms. New Englanders grew large amounts of corn and wheat until this function was assumed by large farms of the Midwest. Sheep became popular in the early 19th century. Dairy farms sprang up in the late 19th century and declined in the late 20th century. A resurgence of locally produced, small-scale agriculture may be occurring in the early 21st century.

Stage	Dominant period	Characteristic
Subsistence	Native American and colonial	Small land areas, stone walls.
Local and regional crops	Early 19th century	Shade tree in center or edge. Stone piles, stone walls.
Sheep	Mid-19th century	Sheep, and the goats kept with them, eat nearly everything—after sheep, open reclamation.
Dairy	Civil War to 1970s	Cow trails. Fences to keep animals in.
Sustainability resurgence	Late 1960s–1970s, revived again in early 21st century	Back-to-the-land movement. Ecologically diverse.

plants. In 1811, William Jarvis brought Merino sheep to his farm in Weathersfield, Vermont, launching a massive production of sheep in Vermont, New Hampshire, Maine, and elsewhere.[40] By 1830, approximately three million sheep were in Vermont, New Hampshire, and Maine—many more sheep than people.[41] Hayward's *New England Gazetteer* (1839) lists the number of sheep in each town and provides clues about the agriculture. Andover, Vermont, with its 975 people, had 4,500 sheep; Andover, New Hampshire, had 1,324 people and 4,000 sheep; Amity, Maine, had no sheep listed, but had "fine soil for wheat." Sheep farming slackened by the late 1840s with the decline of favorable tariffs for American farmers over Europe, but persisted until the late 19th century, when dairy cows took over.[42] It may be possible to tell what type of pasture—sheep or cow—existed based on the appearance of the land and what plant species recolonized the field.(Goats are even less selective about what they eat than sheep; they eat just about anything, but were seldom kept to any large extent in New England except for occasional use to keep poison ivy down or, less commonly, to maintain cemeteries.)

The more particular nature of cows means that we can sometimes tell the difference between abandoned sheep pasture and abandoned cow pasture. Sheep, for example, will eat wild carrot (*Daucus carota*), and were sometimes let into hayfields to help keep down weeds after the harvest.[43] After the animals are removed, widely spaced trees will grow from seed that comes in from surrounding forests, and the forest boundaries will creep across the fence lines. The plants ignored by the cows have a head start. In either case—sheep or cows—the tenacious nature of tree regrowth through continual seeding eventually ensures that a full forest emerges.

Abandoned pasture also provides the sunlight for white pine and white cedar (and, in some southern areas, red cedar) to quickly move in among the hawthorn and juniper. Hardwoods such as red maple, aspen, and white birch will also move into the newly abandoned pasture, but the white pine will have a head start because the farm animals would have done a good job chewing up the hardwood sprouts right up until the time of abandonment. In tracts of land developed for residential subdivisions, there may still be groves of pine, hawthorn, and juniper at the fringes of the landscaped areas; these indicate a former pasture. Residential hillsides that still have grass and juniper may also contain visible remnants of old cow paths. Mullein (*Verbascum thapsus*), orange hawkweed (*Hieracium aurentiacum*), wild carrot, Canada thistle (*Cirsium arvense*), raspberries, burdock, and other common agricultural weeds show up in the old pasture and croplands. The US Department of Agriculture Report of 1886 expressed concern about the problem of buttercup (there are many species of buttercup in the genus *Ranunculus*) taking over "large fields of pasture-land."[44] The 1897 *Report of the Secretary of the Maine Board of Agriculture* describes the pervasive problem of hawkweed and wild carrot, which had invaded in the 1880s, reducing the nutrient value of both hayfield and pasture.[45]

The presence of thorn trees amid grasses and the presence of widely scattered open-growth trees are both indicators of an old pasture. The open-growth trees often got their start from an existing hedgerow or "seeded in" under the shade provided by the thorn trees. Once trees gain a foothold, a forest can begin. The resulting stand will contain the open-grown early invaders (Figure 2.10), the dense closed-canopy trees that came later, and, for a few years, the remnants of the thorn trees. The age of invading trees helps indicate the date of pasture abandonment.

Figure 2.10. *Forest that grew up around an old pasture oak. The branches begin low on the trunk and sprawl out to the side, suggesting this oak got its start in an open setting and the forest grew up around it. Open-growth maple, elm, and other shade-producing trees from old pasture or field might also survive in the regrown forest. The presence of scattered large rocks suggests the open setting was used as a pasture or field rather than a more carefully groomed cropland.*

A farmer may have let a potato field or hayfield go, turning it into pasture. Pasture converted from cropland can be occasionally determined by the presence of a large, open-growth tree, such as an apple, oak, maple, or pine, standing well above the encroaching hawthorns. This conversion is more likely to occur on low-quality cropland that may still contain a fair amount of rocks. The absence of rocks on upland sites indicates that the original cropland merited the effort of their removal. They will probably be found in a pile or in nearby stone walls.

American elm (*Ulmus americana*) often marked fence or road boundaries. Elm is a hard, cross-grained wood that is tough to split and process for firewood. (My dad used to send my brother and me out with a cross-cut saw to scrounge free wood from dead elm trees—it took *forever* to process one.) Elm is also an effective seed propagator. Accordingly, these trees tended to survive land clearance if they stayed along the edges of fields. Their high canopies provided shade and helped define the rural landscape. The persistence of the elm helped root it in the American mind as a symbolic tree; by the 1850s, elm was commonly planted along streets in villages and cities.[46] But by the 1930s the fungus *Ophiostoma ulmi* (also known as *Ceratocystis ulmi*), transmitted by two species of bark beetles or by root graft, began spreading Dutch elm disease, and the trees began to die. Now, most of these elms are dead or are young trees soon to be caught by the disease. The elm is hardy and takes a long time to die, and the base of the stump will keep sending up sprouts. You can pick out an old dead elm silhouetted in the landscape by its light color and characteristic vase shape—even more apparent in live trees with their full foliage (Figure 2.11). *(Plate 2)*

Sugar maples and oaks are also pasture remnants. Trees that grow out in the open spread their branches out much more than trees growing in crowded areas where they have to grow tall to compete for sunlight. An open-growth oak made a picturesque shade tree for the farmer and the animals. These trees suggest either past use of the field for crops in the days before tractors, when the plow horse could use respite from the sun, or use as a pasture, with a natural "awning" for cattle (hardier sheep had less need of shade). If the oak has been cut, the stump may have visible ray lines perpendicular, like a star shape; no other tree will have this

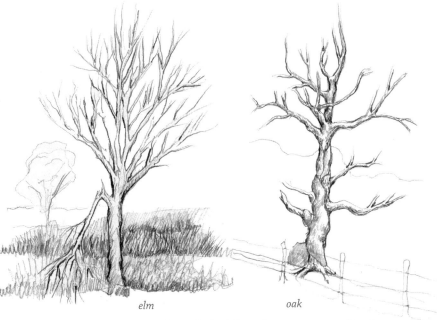

elm   oak

Figure 2.11. *The distinctive shape of a dead elm makes it easy to spot. Live elms have a characteristic umbrella-like appearance. Elms often mark old fence lines, former shade spots to protect the plow horse and cattle from the sun, and the edges of fields and other ecosystem boundaries. Compare with the dead oak.*

Figure 2.12. *The edge of old pastureland shows juniper moving in, followed by maple, aspen, and birch. In other edges of this same field, thorn apples grow and white pine leads arrival of the forest into the field. The young trees and shrubs hint at fairly recent abandonment, perhaps just a generation ago.*

characteristic. Some fields may have red cedar (*Juniperus virginiana*) come in and start growing, but the sun-loving red cedar will lose out to white pine and other fast-growing trees. If the soils are relatively moist, white cedar will move in (Figure 2.12).

Black walnut (*Juglans nigra*), an indicator of good soil, was also an excellent shade tree for cows, and the leaves seemed to discourage insects that would otherwise harass the animals. The black walnut provided useful nuts, and, as a popular colonial wood, represented an investment for future cabinets and other domestic products.

Transitions After Crop Fields

Some agricultural fields dated to long before the European settlers arrived. The Native Americans began clearing land for crops in southern New England a thousand years ago; fire was the main tool for clearing. Samuel de Champlain (1567–1635) noticed the cleared fields along the coast of Maine on his voyages in the early 17th century. His 1606 map of Plymouth, Massachusetts, shows villages and gardens.[47] Portuguese fishermen, sailing off the coast in search of cod, also saw cleared lands. Many of these fields lasted hundreds of years because settlers took them over or, far more rarely, because agrarian Native Americans survived European settlement. In some places, "Indian cornfields" were still discernible as late as the 1930s.[48] But once abandoned, the land begins to change. Cropland is under different successional pressures than either cleared land or pasture because all the invading plants have an equal start on the open ground. A plowed field will establish a meadow after two years, which may be succeeded by pine or poplar, and red cedar may also appear before the hardwoods begin to move in. A hayfield will also go to meadow in two years.

The early invasive plants include crabgrass, ragweed, goldenrod, aster, goosefoot, Queen Anne's lace (wild carrot), and, occasionally, horseweed and raspberry (Figure 2.13). Usually there are no more than a few thorn trees, if any. In some areas, a stand of aspen or white birch will become established five to ten years after abandonment and may remain

Figure 2.13. *A former vegetable field. The field was too small to have needed a shade tree in its center. As a vegetable field, the large rocks would have been removed. Similar to abandoned pastures and fields, abandoned cropland is marked by early invasive plants such as ragweed, thistles, ironweed, goldenrod, aster, goosefoot, and raspberry. These plants suggest this site has been left alone for only a few years. Longer abandonment would be indicated by shrubs and small white pine, birch, and other trees, especially along the boundaries.*

as the dominant vegetation for the next several decades until replaced by more shade-tolerant and longer-lived northern hardwoods, or, depending on the location, spruce. If aspen or white birch is established early after abandonment, the forest that results will be closed-canopy and even-aged, similar to that resulting from a clear-cut. If the initial sequence is characterized by goldenrod, aster, and such, the pattern resembles the change undergone by old pastureland.

As in a pasture, a large crop field might have an older, open-growth tree—an oak, maple, or maybe a dead elm—somewhere near the center. These trees served as shade for the farmer and draft animals. An open-growth pasture pine (a "lone wolf" tree) might have been left, but the farmers did not like to keep anything under pine because the sap gets on equipment and the needles drop into things.

On cropland, the boundary characteristics will be similar to pastureland, including fence lines, hedgerows, and stone walls. But without grazing animals, former cropland is more likely than pasture to have well-developed trees along the stone walls. These trees may have gotten their start after the cropland was abandoned—you can make a guess by seeing if the trees would have blocked the sun, because the farmer would have cut down whatever kept the sun from the crops. However, some trees may have gotten their start while the land was farmed, particularly if they were useful sugar maples, ash, or cherry, and could occupy the area between the plowed field and the stone wall unreachable by plow or harrow. A large pile of small rocks suggests their collection from a field so that the land could be used for a root crop such as potato. Another indicator of a plowed field is a "step-up," a transition line between the edge of the plowed land

Figure 2.14. *The "step-up" is a transition from the crop field to the adjacent land. Numerous turns of the passing plow over the years can leave an indelible mark, whether the plow be tractor-pulled or animal-powered. The field is slightly lower than the surrounding land, leaving an edge along its border about the height of one or two steps, depending on whether the edge is upslope or downslope. If the ground is revegetated, there is little force to act on the step, and it will remain visible for many generations. Look at the vegetation to get an idea of how long ago the last plowing might have been. In this case, the presence of young pioneer trees suggests this has been about 20 or 30 years.*

and adjacent land. The last "dead furrow" is usually downslope and where the annual plowing created a final ridge that could not be reached by the harrow to smooth it down. An increase in height of a foot or more might mark this boundary; an observer can sometimes detect this change generations after agriculture ceased on gently sloping or relatively flat fields (Figure 2.14). A light dusting of snow often shows old furrow lines and edges. On steep crop slopes, the erosion will go down the slope, and if a wall is there, the soil will build up against it and trees will grow.

When you are exploring, keep in mind that everything a farmer did served more than one purpose. When the forest was cleared to create field, the farmer gained wood for construction and fuel, stumps for fences, and an open area to put crops. The walls around land cleared for crops tend to have more cobbles and small stones in them compared to other walls. Farmers growing root crops had strong motivation to remove rock. Sometimes there were simply too many stones to move out to the sides, and they were piled right in the field—getting them out of the way while saving time and energy.

Local place names also can reflect past agricultural activities, including the existence and use of fields.[49] For example, Potato Hill in Chester, Vermont, was an area where potatoes were grown. The potato fields contain large piles of cobbles and rocks of all sizes (Figure 2.15). Potatoes were the dominant root crop in 19th-century northern New England. A former field or garden that had lots of stones would probably have more than one pile of them, and the piles would be far enough apart for convenient throwing as the farmer cleared the area. Long after farming of the root crop stopped, the stone piles would remain and harbor trees that got an early start among the rocks. Years later, the mound of rocks might be partly disguised by the buildup of organic material and by denser, larger trees than might exist in the former field surrounding the stone pile.

By 1820, Maine's major crops were, in order: Indian corn, wheat, oats, barley, rye, peas and beans, potatoes, flax, hops, and hay. Crop amounts are not known, but Greenleaf reported the Maine Legislature's 1820 inventory of the amount of capital in tillage, mowing, salt marsh, fresh meadow, pasture, and by type of livestock and crop.[50] Interestingly,

Figure 2.15. *This stone pile is in the middle of a former potato field in central Vermont. Effective use of root crops such as potato meant the need to clear stones and rocks from the plow zone. Thus, a large center or edge pile of stone suggests a possible old crop field. Vegetation around the pile can provide clues to the age of abandonment of the field. The size of the stone might also suggest how long or how thoroughly the field was worked. Over the years, ever-smaller stones might be removed and tossed onto the pile. Trees that could grow on the rocks would have a head start over the trees that would sprout in the rest of the cropland after it was abandoned. An older even-aged group of trees on a rock pile in a forest of younger trees is an indicator of former cropland.*

emergence of the local food movement in sustainable agriculture may lead to a new emphasis on these crops.

The apple crop

Although apple orchards are now fairly common in New England, such was not the case in early New England. If a farmer had the space and the energy, the apple (*Malus pumila*) might be grown for more than just family use. However, commercial orchards were not the norm initially—early orchards were mostly seedling trees.[51] These trees produced mostly mediocre apples, good for cider and related products rather than for eating. Better varieties came with nurseries. Still, an apple orchard could provide an important market crop, especially after the Revolutionary War.[52]

The orchard would be near the house. If it was too far away, it would be harder to keep the deer away from it,[53] and because deer can leap nine feet or more, a fence or stone wall would not be sufficient unless it was a wide, double-wall structure. Large orchards would be further away, usually on the side of a hill away from the valley bottom where the cold air and frosts settled. Cleared land was precious, and most New England farmers did not set out nice square orchards like we have today. Instead, the fruit trees would be placed along fences, near house and barn, along cow lanes and rock piles—areas that could not be readily cultivated. An orchard might be set up on steep, rocky land that could thereby be working for the farmer. After the trees got a good start, the farmer might keep sheep among the trees because that would reduce weeds and provide pasture space.[54] Sheep would also eat the windfalls and keep the grass short.

If the farm prospered and the land allowed, blocks of formal orchards might be added. Annual spring plowing and cultivation was recommended for a block orchard, according to the Maine State Board of Agriculture (1901). Such an orchard would not be in a pasture; it would be a cultivated field in which a market crop was raised. The trees would be trimmed to allow the horse-drawn plow and the cultivator to fit between the rows. This trimming also stimulated apple growth. Such orchards may still exist today because they were large and more likely to be commercially viable. Small subsistence orchards could more easily disappear into the forestland that crept up around abandoned farms.

Row patterns of apple trees—remnant orchards—can still be found in the woods today. Some of the trees are still producing small, hard fruit. An apple tree in the woods has often been overtopped by white pines, aspens, red maples, or other trees that moved into the relatively open spaces of the orchard (Figure 2.16). In older woods, maples and other trees that can grow in shade have replaced the white pine and aspens, while the apple struggles on. Residential housing developments in former orchards usually contain some surviving apple trees, which may resume producing fruit after they are pruned and freed from the overstory trees. A restored tree provides food for wildlife and helps perpetuate the old varieties.

Figure 2.16. *This apple tree survives in the woods, but it has had to send some branches up high to compete for sunlight, losing the pruned look of the open-orchard apple. Maples and other trees that grow well in shade have outcompeted it, but it still survives and can even be restored by trimming the trees around it ("release cutting") and through careful pruning.*

Hay and wheat fields

Old fields are a testimony to our agricultural history. Writing to John Jay, Thomas Jefferson, a lover of all things agrarian, stated: "Cultivators of the earth are the most valuable citizens...they are tied to their country and wedded to its liberty and interests by the most lasting bands."[55]

Wheat was a major crop in northern New England. Springfield, Maine, with its tiny population of 398, produced 9,429 bushels of wheat in 1837. China, Maine, produced 12,953 bushels, with a population of 2,641 people. Farther south, Cumberland County produced 37,803 bushels.[56] Aroostook County in northern Maine was still producing wheat in 1939, but hay and oats were more important. Hay crops in Vermont, New Hampshire, and Maine increased after the Civil War and remained high until the 1920s.

Upland hayfields were well-drained if possible,[57] and relatively free of large rocks that would damage the haying equipment. Small rocks could stay in the ground, though they would emerge and increase in number when the field was plowed. The hayfield would not usually have shade trees left in the center as would a pasture—good land for hay was simply too valuable, and the plow horse could rest near the shaded stone walls.

Not all hayfields came from original forestland. In coastal areas, salt hay (*Spartina patens*) was harvested from salt marshes that had been in existence for thousands of years. In Figure 2.17 you can see the remains of the "staddle" that stored the hay above the high-tide level prior to moving it by wagon or flat wooden boat (gundalow) to the barn. Salt marshes are

Figure 2.17. *Wooden crib (staddle) that held the harvested salt hay* (Spartina patens) *above the high-tide level of Scarborough salt marsh in Maine. Because the remains are still visible, this staddle is probably early 20th century. Some coastal farmers continue to use salt hay, but most salt-hay harvesting ceased shortly after World War II. Salt marshes are now generally protected as important natural areas with critical wildlife habitat.*

rich biotic communities, and the hay stored well. Farmers in the late 18th century and the 19th century constructed ditches to expand the salt hay areas. They also filled in upland areas to create new fields for fresh hay, which reduced the environmental effectiveness of the salt marsh.

Hayfields may be used for generations after the original farm has folded. This land is comparatively fertile and can help support the few remaining dairy farms, which have likely had to greatly increase the number of cows in order to survive. The hayfield may also be used by the farmer who markets hay to others. Still other hayfields are converted to horse pasture. When the hayfield is abandoned, stinging nettles, daisies, buttercups, clover, pea, and other open-space coloniz-ers move right in, and sumac, juniper, and white pine will begin to feather in from the edges. The emergent pine forest might be termed "pasture pine."

Woodlots and sugar bushes

Every farm needed a woodlot for firewood and logs. Before the inven-tion of the closed cast-iron stove, a typical farm family consumed 30 to 40 cords of wood per year for cooking and heating.[58] This is a massive amount of wood—twice what was used per household in the late 19th and 20th centuries. Further, the woodlot could provide an extra source of income to the farmer who sold wood to the many brick manufacturers and other consumers of wood. The small woodlot owner and the farmer held much of the timberland in the United States, and even by 1909, the amount was still 45 percent.[59]

The woodlot could also supply nuts. Beech (*Fagus* spp.), black walnut (*Juglans nigra*), butternut (*Juglans cinerea*), chestnut (*Castanea dentata*), oak (*Quercus*, especially white oak, *Quercus alba*, which is lower in tan-nins), and hickory (*Carya* spp.) provided high-energy food for humans and animals. Every tree had a use of some kind. For example, hickory and American hornbeam (*Carpinus caroliniana*) made great tool handles. Elm, while hard to work, can make beautiful furniture, and perhaps was most commonly used as barn floorboards where moisture from animals was going to be a factor. White cedar, red cedar, honey locust, and chestnut made fence posts and rails. The chestnut blight arrived in the early 1900s, and by the mid-20th century had wiped out almost all the chestnut from its habitat in southern parts of New England, so if you come across chestnut in old telephone poles, railroad ties, fence posts, or stumps, you can estimate that it pre-dates this era. White cedar made shingles, and ironwood (*Ostrya virginiana*, also called Eastern hophornbeam or just hornbeam) made hard, durable rake teeth, wedges, and small tool parts.

The tree management practices of the farm extended to the villages. Leaving small thickets of regularly trimmed trees ("coppices") encouraged the growth of certain species, especially hardwoods. Cronon notes: "Coppice cutting was a major reason that chestnuts, which were prolific sprouters, increased their relative share of New England forests following European settlement."[60] But by the early 20th century, a fungal blight was destroying all the chestnuts. Nevertheless, small forested hummocky areas may mark the original locations of these coppices, and their wood can be found in old barns and houses.

If they could, New England farmers had sugar bushes or "sugar lots" consisting of sugar maples (also called "rock maple" or "hard maple")—the quintessential New England tree.[61] This tree was ornamental and practical, producing shade, sustenance, and strong wood; even if there was no land for a farm, people still liked to have sugar maples in their yards. Sugar bushes can last for well over a hundred years, and current sugar bushes have often been worked for generations. Abandoned bushes might have "monarch" sugar maples still surviving on the site near the top of a ridge or hill. A grove of young maples may be below the ridge, seeded in from the old trees. Some areas may have the fieldstone foundation of an old sugarhouse, or the bricks that held up the arch for boiling the sap. Old metal bucket remnants may be found (Figure 2.18), and wooden ones might have rotted away leaving an iron band or an "ear" of sheet iron, which seated the spike for anchoring the bucket on the tree. Given the immense amount of wood needed to fire the arch and boil the sap, charcoal deposits and staining of the soil around the boiling site may be visible. Old boiling-pan and firebox fragments may also be found, perhaps even some old metal pipeline, the predecessor of modern plastic tubing.

The forest or woodlot landscape is much different from that which surrounds houses and buildings and which represents a much more intentional manipulation of the environment. Some trees, like sugar maple and oak, can be found in multiple places and make good landscaping. In the next chapter, we will focus on trees and other vegetation more specifically associated with houses and other structures.

Figure 2.18. *The condition of these buckets and sap boiling pans from a sugarhouse in Vermont indicates abandonment was relatively recent. The holes in them have probably prevented them from being removed by souvenir hunters. The corrugated tin is from the collapsed roof of the sugarhouse. The firebox door was left behind probably because it was too deteriorated to be used elsewhere. The iron grates are lying in some ash, with brick rubble behind them. Slate shingles, asphalt, and cedar shakes were also used to cover sugarhouses. Many farms had their own sugarhouse.*

3

Vegetation Common to Houses, Barns, and Outbuildings

When life gives you scraps, make quilts.
—Old farmer's saying

*...that big New England landscape quilt that generations of farmers
wove and stitched together across the countryside.*
—Kent C. Ryden

The sites of houses and farms are often marked by the foundations themselves, by altered landscape features, and by the arrangement and type
of plant communities influenced by the pattern of use. Similar to a quilt,
the patterns tend to be intentional and therefore predictable. Even when
the house and related buildings are gone, the pattern can be interpreted
to help figure out what was likely there and when it was there.

Typically, a residential site will have begun with one or more
structures or foundations of some sort, a yard, a garden, and ornamental or orchard trees. The larger, older ornamental trees may roughly
correspond with the date of the structure's construction (Figure 3.1).

Figure 3.1. *The presence of a non-native tree such as this black locust (Robinia pseudoacacia) indicates a nearby homestead. Sure enough, within a few dozen feet is the site of a house. The cellar hole had been filled in and has raspberries growing in the center. An old lilac is in the background. Reddish fire-cracked rocks in the foundation suggest the house had burned, although the soot has faded away. Probably the hole was filled in to prevent animals from falling in. Black locust is not native to northern New England but was popular at old farms. It gets its first growth fast, and provides good wood where water and soil contact occurs. Notable uses include fence posts and planks for boats and troughs.*

Non-ornamental trees in the yard often correspond to the time of abandonment. Cellar holes often have trees in them whose age can be estimated. Sugar maple trees were commonly planted in pairs ("husband and wife," or "coffin" or "marriage" trees; see below) or rows to mark residential yards and rural industrial or manufacturing sites (many 19th-century businesses copied the style and appearance of residential yards). The trees provided shade, a place for children to climb, sap to make maple syrup, and perhaps a year's worth of firewood apiece when they died.

Most abandoned farm or house sites will contain only a few large yard trees or their remnants. A cultivated tree helped ease the experience of living in the wilderness or on a rough farm. The most popular large trees by a house were usually sugar maple, often bearing the markings of taps and climbing children (Figure 3.2), but sometimes white pine and oak were in the yard. Many smaller, early successional-stage trees such as poplar, birch, and cherry, along with sumac, can be found near late 20th-century foundations. If originally planted, a black locust or its offspring may be hanging on; though not native to northern New England, they were popular imports and naturalized quite well. Some berry bushes may persist at remnant open-space boundaries. Grasses are abundant until trees and shrubs take over the yard area. Due to continued disturbances, the boundaries between forest and road may have grasses, daylilies, and shrubs long after other sites have been taken over by trees.

If the foundation of a house, barn, or other building has been left to nature, the first several decades follow a fairly typical pattern. Introduced

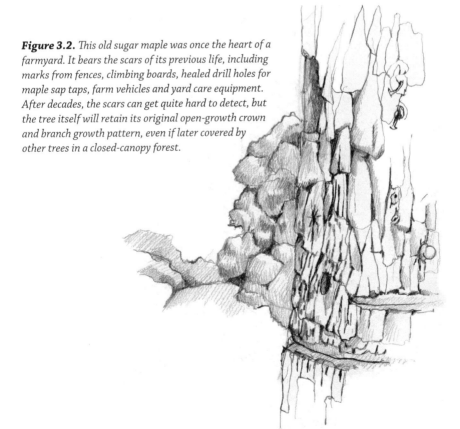

Figure 3.2. *This old sugar maple was once the heart of a farmyard. It bears the scars of its previous life, including marks from fences, climbing boards, healed drill holes for maple sap taps, farm vehicles and yard care equipment. After decades, the scars can get quite hard to detect, but the tree itself will retain its original open-growth crown and branch growth pattern, even if later covered by other trees in a closed-canopy forest.*

ornamental trees and shrubs eventually give way to traditional New England plants and trees (or some hardy plant invaders). However, a large ornamental tree (locust, poplar, or spruce) may survive abandonment for decades. Sumac, raspberry, and other hardy pioneer plants quickly take over on exposed soil, especially if it has been disturbed. The yard, if relatively large and open, follows a sequence similar to that of pastures, although thorn trees are less likely to be found. If the yard was small and contained large trees, the yard area will be occupied by the offspring of the original yard trees along with whatever other tree species were adjacent.

The first trees into an open area tend to be the most abundant and the smallest. The distribution of trees, space, and vegetation is patterned. Fruit trees and isolated clusters (copses or coppices) of sumac or poplar flanked by large, open-growth, shade-tolerant trees are all cultural clues. Asymmetrical crown development in trees may indicate the former existence of an adjacent structure. Introduced species such as yew (*Taxus* spp.) and cedar (*Thuja* spp. and *Chamaecyparis* spp.) may be holdovers from foundation plantings. Some tree species represent particular periods of fashion. Horse chestnut (*Aesculus hippocastanum*) is an introduced

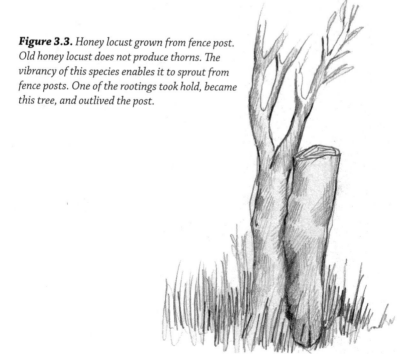

Figure 3.3. *Honey locust grown from fence post. Old honey locust does not produce thorns. The vibrancy of this species enables it to sprout from fence posts. One of the rootings took hold, became this tree, and outlived the post.*

species fashionable as a shade tree in the 19th century. Catalpa (*Catalpa speciosa*) was a popular suburban tree in the 1920s, with distinctive flowers, leaves, and seed pods, and many are still in good shape today. Lombardy poplar (*Populus nigra*, var. *italica*), another introduced species, was often planted along property lines, particularly in the 1950s.[62] Thornless honey locusts may represent rootings of fence posts taken from old trees (Figure 3.3).

The Yard Apple Tree

Even if there might not be room for an apple orchard, just about every rural house had an apple tree.[63] Having the apples close was handy for the cook. Apples were the main fruit that could be grown in northern New England, and there is quite a history to their cultivation, including the development of local varieties. The apple could be dried and stored in root cellars, playing an important part in helping the family get through the winter (see Chapter 4, Foundations). Apple pies are a New England tradition, but perhaps even more importantly, apples could be made into cider (and applejack or cider brandy). The fermentation process helped make it safe to drink—safer than water, which could be contaminated—and cider quickly supplanted beer as a common beverage for New England colonists.[64] A few of these old

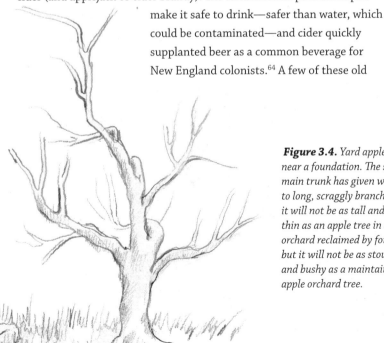

Figure 3.4. *Yard apple tree near a foundation. The short main trunk has given way to long, scraggly branches; it will not be as tall and thin as an apple tree in an orchard reclaimed by forest, but it will not be as stout and bushy as a maintained apple orchard tree.*

yard apple trees (and possibly a few other fruits in central or southern
New England) and nut trees such as butternut (*Juglans cinerea*) may be
found adjacent to 19th- and 20th-century homestead sites. If the yard
apple has been surrounded by forest, it might look like one of the scraggly orchard trees mentioned in the previous chapter. But if the house or
barn site has been surrounded by pasture or field, or kept open for other
reasons, the tree will be shorter, with a large trunk, often hollow, though
still likely in desperate need of pruning (Figure 3.4). If the site is still
accessible, people may have come to get the apples from time to time;
certainly the deer will have tried. Apple trees grow slowly, so a tree may
be quite old even if it is not large.

The first apple orchards in Vermont were planted by the French in
the Champlain Valley in the 1730s.[65] Apples quickly became a critically
important fruit in New England. There were hundreds of varieties, many
of which have been lost or are in danger of being lost. Fortunately, the
Seed Saver Exchange, Slow Food movement, Maine Organic Farmers &
Gardeners Association, and other organizations are working to preserve
heirloom types. An interesting thing to do if you find an old apple
tree that has fruit is to see if you can determine if it is an identifiable
heirloom variety. Some varieties were known for hardiness, and despite
their plain appearance may produce exotic flavors, especially if the tree is
restored by pruning it and by trimming adjacent vegetation.[66]

Shrubs and Brush

Shrubs near the farmhouse were the result of plantings for food, medicine, and ornamentation, or the consequence of invasive species taking
advantage of open, disturbed areas. Some plants were both hardy and
useful. Varieties of red raspberries (*Rubus idaeus*), dewberries (*Rubus
flagellaris*), blackberries (*Rubus fruticosus*) and other berries can be found
in old fields, growing around stumps, and at the edges of woods. These
berries are native to North America and were used by indigenous peoples
long before the arrival of colonists. By the 1820s, active domestication
of these berries had produced many varieties. The farmer liked to have

Figure 3.5. *Lilacs can indicate the site of an old farmstead. These lilacs have survived untended for a century.*

a variety of fresh fruits, so old farm sites tended to have a good range of berries that would ripen throughout the summer. Raspberries would come into season first, and as they faded away the blackberries would appear, followed by the apples. Blueberries would come in at different times from middle to late summer, depending on the variety.

Lilacs (*Syringa*) originated in Europe and Asia and were popular in colonial America. Lilacs can last for centuries. Thomas Jefferson and George Washington both told of planting them. In addition to gardens, lilacs were popular shrubs planted next to the house—so popular, in fact, that the purple lilac (*Syringa vulgaris*) was adopted in 1919 as New Hampshire's State Flower. Spring blooms of lilacs in abandoned countryside are a visible indicator of one or more nearby home sites (Figure 3.5). *(Plate 3)*

The Yard and Garden

The front yard is a relatively late addition to the farmstead, not appearing until the 1820s.[67] In the early 19th century, the front yard was a formal, fenced affair, which working-class and middle-class farmers had copied from the large estates of the elite. By the 1880s, the front yard had become a less formal and less defined space except in the landscapes of the wealthy.[68] However, there was always a dooryard and a barnyard because these were essential to any farm. Both these workspaces became well-compacted from years of use. When soil is compacted it is harder for plants to grow, and the hardy pioneer species have an advantage over more delicate plants. Sumac can grow on disturbed, compacted soils and is a common early invader of an abandoned workspace.

The front yard might be marked by "marriage trees," often sugar maples, planted at the time of construction for the new couple. Sometimes these trees were called "coffin trees" because they might be expected to last the lifetime of the couple and to be cut down for eventual manufacture into coffins for the family. (Perhaps what you called them depended on whether you were an optimist or a pessimist.) Whatever you call them, these maple trees might be found on a southerly side where they provided shading in the summer and allowed the sun in during the winter. Spruce was a common yard tree from the 19th century onward. A clue to a homestead site is the sight of a spruce in an upland environment where they are not native. As previously mentioned, one or more apple trees, separate from a formal orchard, may also be in the yard, usually off to the side so that the fallen fruit would not be underfoot, but close enough for the farm dogs to keep the deer away.

Common plants, both native and European imports, remain from old yards and gardens—periwinkle, daylilies, plantain, dandelions, chickweed, bloodwort, mulleins, mallow, nightshade, daisy, rhubarb, tansy, asparagus, horseradish, and many other species. Some plants were considered weeds and others were planted in gardens and survived after the homestead was gone. In the early stages of abandonment, the yard or garden will consist mostly of grasses and flowers. Depending on their hardiness and resistance to shading, the flowers can persist for quite some time.

Gardens provided more than just food. They provided herbs, medicine, and household products. Some plants were in formal gardens while others were edge plants around landscape features and foundations. The aromatic herb tansy, a perennial in the sunflower family, is recognizable by small, flat-topped clusters of button-like yellow flowers in summer.[69] Tansy is a medicinal herb common to many farmyards because of its hardy nature and its ability to mask the odors of household garbage— the sort of waste that might be tossed out the door for the chickens to scratch around in. Tansy is also a natural insect repellant, making it a desirable yard planting. It was an early European import to New England and radiated from there, surviving in old gardens, on roadsides, and in waste areas. In addition to plants brought over from Europe, the medicinal chest included many local plants, and New England settlers learned about them from the native peoples.[70]

Some gardens contained hops (*Humulus lupulus*), which can be very hardy and survive for one or two centuries after abandonment. In the 18th and early 19th centuries, Massachusetts produced the most hops of any state. In 1850, Maine produced 20 tons of hops, and New Hampshire grew 65 tons. But Vermont leaped ahead with 319 tons— more than Maine, New Hampshire, and Massachusetts combined.[71] The homesteader could either sell the hop flower heads or brew his own beer from them.[72] At the time, beer was safer to drink than water because boiling the water during the brewing process killed many pathogens and people noticed they were less often ill if they drank beer instead of water, although they did not know why until the scientific work of Louis Pasteur. Local hop production has undergone a revival with the microbrewery movement, which began in the late 20th century, and this may lead to further resuscitation of old farmstead hop sites.[73]

Another common farmstead plant is the daylily (*Hemerocallis* spp.).[74] These are not true lilies, but they are common, hardy plants that persist long after the garden is gone, though each bloom itself may be short-lived. Daylilies can be seen at foundations that have been abandoned for

Figure 3.6. *These daylilies are surviving near a cellar hole. The size of the adjacent sugar maples suggests abandonment occurred half a century ago. One can only imagine how many generations appreciated the daylilies while the house was occupied. Logging in the area has kept the forest comparatively open, and the daylilies are doing fine.*

a half century or more (Figure 3.6). Allegheny sedum (*Sedum telephioides*), also called "wild live-forever," lily-of-the-valley (*Convallaria majalis*), and periwinkle[75] (*Vinca minor*) are garden escapees that are also good indicators of cellar holes.

Rhubarb (*Rheum* spp.) is a vegetable with very large leaves. It was known to the ancient Chinese, brought to Europe, and then to the New World. By the early 19th century, it became popular in New England as a hardy food source with some medicinal value. *Dr. Chase's Recipes*, a popular 19th-century publication,[76] recommends it for diarrhea and other problems. A well-established bed of rhubarb can exist independent of cultivation for a long time. Rhubarb can survive a hundred years or more, and the plants may occasionally be found at the sites of old households. Valued as the "pie plant," the stems can also be made into a stew. However, the leaves contain oxalic acid and soluble oxalates, which makes them toxic. Rhubarb provided one of the earliest sources of fresh food at the end of winter, and was highly prized. Some farmers marked their rhubarb patch with low stone walls to keep the livestock out.

The young common burdock (*Arctium minus*) looks like fuzzy rhubarb leaves, but is edible (though the stems are not). Burdock is a hardy invasive pioneer that does well in disturbed areas—former gardens, pastures, and yards—and many of these weeds have been around for quite some time. Dandelions spread out from Boston in the 1770s, along with white daisy and buttercup.[77] Cows avoid buttercup, so it survived in old pastures. Parsnip (*Pastinaca sativa*) also escaped—the same parsnip we eat. However, its stem and leaves can give a chemical burn (phytophotodermatitis) because the sap reacts to the ultraviolet light in sunlight.

Along roadsides, the invaders tend to be hard, salt-resistant weeds. Except at high elevations and in the northern portions of the states, poison ivy (*Toxicodendron radicans* or *Rhus radicans*) and Japanese bamboo (*Fallopia japonica*)[78] do quite well. Poison ivy can help preserve some settings because people tend to avoid it.[79] Fewer than one person in a dozen is resistant to poison ivy, so if you venture from the roadside in rural or urban disturbed areas, it is wise to know how to identify it (Figure 3.7). In undisturbed areas, poison ivy is not widespread; with the increase in disturbance, however, this hardy plant grows in all but the coldest, most northern parts of New England.

Figure 3.7. *Poison ivy is a native invasive plant. Common at the edges of disturbed wooded areas, it occurs as groundcover, vine, and shrub. Everyone should know how to recognize it. "Leaflets three, let it be" is the old warning. The leaves have an oily or waxy look. Poison ivy contains the toxin urushiol, which, in addition to blistering the skin, can sear the lungs if it gets into smoke. Goats were used to clear out poison ivy, stinging nettles, brambles, thistle, and other undesirable plants so the land was could be put to other uses.*

A variety of the common plants and trees are associated with old house and farm sites—and many of them are particularly hardy. Some survive long after their original intended use and some are new invaders that move into disturbed areas and are able to gain a foothold there. Both the species and locations of vegetation can give valuable information about what was once there. But the foundation itself is an even more powerful clue.

4

Foundations

Stern Ruin's ploughshare drives elate
Full on thy bloom . . .
—Robert Burns

When the past no longer illuminates the future,
the spirit walks in darkness.
—Alexis de Tocqueville

Abandoned or deserted farms are not a recent phenomenon. The "year without a summer," 1816, sparked the abandonment of many farms as people sought better opportunities farther south and west.[80] A second wave of abandonment occurred in the last quarter of the 19th century and continued gradually through the 1930s. A third wave occurred in the 1970s with the decline of the dairy industry, but was largely balanced out by the migration of people from cities back to the countryside, though not necessarily as farmers. The markers of these trends dissipate with time. An unoccupied structure often does not last more than a generation, leaving behind only a foundation.

It is comparatively easy to interpret the history of a house, barn, or other building when the structure is still standing. More of a challenge is trying to infer this information when all you can see is a foundation. If it is going to survive for any length of time, the foundation must be made of stone, or maybe brick, and certainly concrete will last. A wood foundation is a short-lived foundation. Stone foundations will survive for centuries—they persist until something or someone comes along and moves them or takes them apart. Together with other landscape features, the foundation and surrounding vegetation provide clues to the past use of a site and of the buildings once on it. Sometimes, rectangular holes in the ground are all that is left, the surrounding stone having been removed or tumbled in.

The householder was interested in having a sturdy foundation and in presenting an orderly appearance. Consequently, large "dressed" blocks (usually granite) form the upper, visible portion of many foundations, underlain by locally collected stones and boulders from fields. However, such cut pieces of stone (dimensional stone) were valuable and therefore most likely to be taken and reused.

In addition to the foundation, there may be all sorts of cultural indicators, lost survivors of the old farm or business. Old wagon wheels often ended up leaning against a tree, and after years went by, the iron became incorporated into the tree and the wheels rotted away. Old dumps may exist, usually down-slope from the household or barn and away from where farm animals could get injured. Such remnants and sites should be viewed as nonrenewable resources and explored with care. They may be important to the history of the area but they can be hazardous, particularly hidden wells. Any exploration of the landscape should be undertaken with these cautions in mind, and with the permission of the landowner. But if you cannot go onto the site and must stay by the roadside you may still be able to glean information by looking and "reading."

Features associated with prior vegetation might be discernible in or near foundations. For example, there may be small paired mounds near a road, developed by the surface roots of large sugar maples and left after the trees were removed or died. Entire settlements came and went. A parallel series of cellar holes marks a failed 18th-century hamlet in Francestown, New Hampshire. In northern New Hampshire, after years of logging, the depletion of the spruce forest led to the abandonment

Native American Place-Making and Farming

Agriculture moved into New England from the south and west. By the Late Woodland Period (1,500 to 1,000 years ago) lowland Abenaki and other Native American peoples were living in settlements near their gardens. Some forestland had been cleared for plantings or to provide browse areas for deer.[81] Native people used both river valleys and upland sites, and encouraged the growth of multiple wild plant species. They also harvested blueberry, butternut, chokecherry, grape, elderberry, blackberry, and raspberry. Horticulture expanded to include corn, beans, and squash (in popular literature, this is sometimes referred to as "the three sisters"). Coastal resources were abundant for fisheries, including anadromous species such as salmon, which supported seasonal village sites at predictable resource locations.

Whole villages were eliminated through the spread of epidemics like the Great Dying of 1616–1618, causing massive abandonment along coastal and inland areas. Local populations of Native Americans disappeared or were reduced to a tenth of their original size. Almost nothing remains of these villages and seasonal occupations—no stone fortifications or foundations are known. However, some village and agricultural sites that were built in desirable locations, with fields already cleared, were assimilated into colonial villages by European immigrants. Others are known primarily to archaeologists and historians, with post holes and other evidence of dwellings encountered only through field excavation. Buried agricultural fields can also be detected with ground-penetrating radar.

While many Native American peoples in northern New England were pushed to the side by European-style culture, native traditions stayed alive through oral histories and practices passed on through generations. The visual landscape history does not reflect any particular features that would distinguish their farm sites from those of other working-class peoples. However, oral tradition and indigenous cultural knowledge about agriculture and farming persists among native communities.[82]   *(continues)*

(continued)

The Bureau of Indian Affairs lists 565 federally recognized Indian tribes, including those listed below. Vermont does not have a federally listed tribe, but Abenaki people do live there, and the Mohican maintain an active connection. Similarly, New Hampshire contains Abenaki and Pennecook Native Americans but no federally listed tribe. It should be noted that these are just the formally recognized and listed indigenous groups; people from a variety of origins and ethnic identities live all over New England.[83]

Maine

Passamaquoddy Tribe (Indian Township):
http://www.peopleofthedawn.com or http://www.passamaquoddy.com

Passamaquoddy Tribe (Pleasant Point): http://www.wabanaki.com

Penobscot Indian Nation: http://www.penobscotnation.org

The federal government also recognizes the Aroostook Band of Micmacs in Presque Isle, Maine (http://micmac-nsn.gov/) and the Houlton Band of Maliseet in Littleton, Maine (http://www.maliseets.com/index.htm).

Massachusetts

Mashpee Wampanoag Tribe: http://mashpeewampanoagtribe.com

Wampanoag Tribe of Gay Head (Aquinnah):
http://www.wampanoagtribe.net

Stockbridge-Munsee Mohican (now in Wisconsin, but maintaining a tribal connection): http://www.mohican.com/

Vermont

Stockbridge-Munsee Mohican (now in Wisconsin, but maintaining a tribal connection): http://www.mohican.com/

and un-incorporation of Livermore in the early 20th century. Abandoned hamlets and villages may be marked by old roads, plantings, cemeteries, foundations, and discarded equipment—mute testimony of past efforts and life in what are now mostly forestlands.

Historical maps are available to help figure out where foundations are—the United States Geological Survey maps show houses, as do the 19th-century Beers atlases. Maps are good for showing where roads went. Many town histories do not key buildings into map locations, and some research may be necessary to match names to individual farm sites. Increasingly, historical maps and other information about the past is becoming available for free or at modest cost on the Internet. Chapter 10 gives additional information on how to do research on landscape history.

Houses and Farms

New England states encouraged rural settlement and the development of houses and farms in the 18th and 19th centuries. Public land did not generate taxes, and the states were interested in generating revenue and in competing with the draw of western lands. Most rural houses were farms of some sort. With a large degree of independence from the outside world, many farms functioned like self-sufficient kingdoms with their own blacksmith shop, greenhouses, and other outbuildings for specific functions. A wide range of buildings were possible: carriage house/stable, milk room, cheese factory, kiln, woodshed, beehive, hop house, corn house, long barn, drying shed, manure shed, henhouse, granary, silo, sheep barn, sugarhouse, smokehouse, root cellar, springhouse, icehouse, and of course, the outhouse or privy. There would probably be an orchard and a woodlot, and various pens, fences, walls, and roads. The configuration of a rural household is suggested in the arrangement of its foundations. But many outbuildings had little or no foundations and their locations are harder to discern. We can still, however, get an idea of what they looked like. Many almanacs and manuals of the 19th century have been reprinted for centennials and other events, and these frequently give recommended layouts for rural living.[84]

Houses and their outbuildings were not necessarily fixed in the land-scape. Architectural historian Thomas Hubka summarized the extensive history of moving and connecting barns, houses, and other structures in 19th-century New England, noting, "Connected farm buildings were the manifestation of a powerful will to succeed by farming."[85] Small outbuild-ings and even large buildings could be skidded to a new location during the winter. Structures were also floated down rivers, moved by railroad or oxcart wagons, and, in the 20th century, by truck. We tend not to move buildings around now, so it is easy to forget how often they were moved in the past when there were no sewer lines, water lines, or other utilities to interfere with lifting the structure off its foundation.

There is another, larger pattern of movement, as well. Farmers tended to prefer hillsides to valleys. The soils might be stonier than in valleys, but they were more durable and less likely to be exhausted.[86] And it was easier to clear hillsides. Sanitation was easier on a hill than in a valley. The hillsides were well drained and less prone to flooding, and they got their fall frost later in the year than did the valleys. A few extra days before first frost can make a big difference in getting the fall harvest in. By the mid-19th century, the upland country farms gradually began to disappear as land became played out and opportunities were sought farther west or in manufacturing or commercial centers in the valley bottoms.

Prosperity after the Civil War fueled the development of a summer tourist industry—an influx of camps and cottages, with supporting services. New roads and the advent of cars boosted the arrival of tour-ists.[87] A second wave of tourist development began in the 1950s, with the wealthiest commanding the high ground, and this second wave continues today.

Some place names are remembrances of the original farm and its outbuildings. For example, Old Farm Road connects to Henhouse Circle in South Portland, Maine. Many towns had a farm that provided public support for low-income people and orphans, with a legacy of myriad Town Farm and Poor Farm Roads across New England. Some of the old town farms (also known as work farms, poor farms, and poorhouses[88]) have been swallowed up by development, but others, operating into the 1970s, may still exist as agricultural land.

Early cabins lacked foundations, as did the homes of the poorest people. Cellars kept houses warmer in winter and provided protected storage areas, so, if possible, a cellar existed, lined with field stones. The above-ground portion would have large "dressed" stones from a quarry, rectangular and more attractive than the hidden stones, in some of the more successful farms, and just fieldstone all the way up for the other farmhouses. The cellar hole might be all that is left, extending four to eight feet into the ground. Even after two centuries, the cellar walls may still be straight and true, while other walls show the signs of frost heaves and the pressure of soil and roots.

The house would start with a central chimney—a standard feature up until 1825 or so—that would be built up from the basement, if there was one. By the 1830s, cast-iron stoves made it more feasible to have side chimneys, which took up less space in the living area. The house would be expanded as the farm and family grew.

Today in the countryside you can still see some abandoned houses. But in the early settlement days, this was rare—houses were too valuable and they were moved or dismantled so the materials could be reused. If the entire structure was moved, the resulting archaeological "cellar hole" of a "salvaged" house is strangely empty in contrast to that of a house that burned in place and collapsed into the hole.

The foundation walls can give you a good idea of the size and shape of the former house, barn, or outbuilding. English traditional architecture dominated New England. A rod, about 16.5 feet, was the basic unit for road width and house layout, but there was certainly variation. By examining foundations, archaeologist James Deetz found that colonial Anglo-American rooms tended to be 16 feet by16 feet, with chimney sections being eight feet by eight feet.[89] These foundations are not as big as the ones we leave behind us today.[90] "Folk housing" is a term you might hear for these small houses, which were less likely to get the attention received by the dwellings of the rich and famous, but, perhaps as a result, can persist unnoticed in the landscape ready for us to rediscover. An interesting question is what you can tell about the people based on the foundations. For example, archaeologists have observed that prior to the early 20th century, low-income people were less likely to have foundations at all.[91] *(Plates 4 and 5)*

An overlooked stone stoop might be all that is left of an old foundation. It would define a dooryard or barnyard entry (Figure 4.1), but was often plucked for use somewhere else after the house or barn was abandoned or destroyed. A hot fire might crack the stone stoop, and a pinkish tint to the rock is sometimes an indicator of a past fire. If broken, the stoop was more likely to stay on site and avoid being carted away.

The first cabins were built with puncheon floors (split wooden post slabs dressed on top by a broadax or adz, then laid on top of pounded earth, anchored by end posts; in essence, a "sill-on-ground" floor[92]) and no cellar or foundation. But even a cabin would need a stone chimney base for a fireplace. An end chimney might be easier to build at first, because it incorporates into a wall. A center chimney is a more efficient heat source than a chimney built into a wall, and it is safer. By the middle 1800s, rural houses either had end chimneys or center chimneys, and larger houses often had multiple chimneys. The smaller house with only one chimney is called a "one-room deep" house, which is usually only 15 to 20 feet wide. A "two-room deep" house is significantly wider, usually 25 to 35 feet. Both house types would have a chimney base, as shown in Figure 4.2.

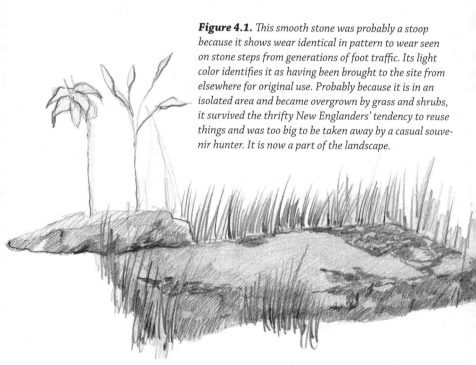

Figure 4.1. *This smooth stone was probably a stoop because it shows wear identical in pattern to wear seen on stone steps from generations of foot traffic. Its light color identifies it as having been brought to the site from elsewhere for original use. Probably because it is in an isolated area and became overgrown by grass and shrubs, it survived the thrifty New Englanders' tendency to reuse things and was too big to be taken away by a casual souvenir hunter. It is now a part of the landscape.*

Figure 4.2. *Top view of stone foundations for a one-room deep house and a two-room deep house. The base would be made of large stones, split or flat.*

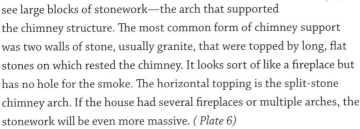

The structure was often larger than the foundation, due to kitchens, ells, porches, and other additions that sat on sills, footings, or low stone walls. The longer a structure was occupied, the greater the tendency to add on to it. If the foundation is not near a road where people could easily cart away the stone, inside the foundtion you may see large blocks of stonework—the arch that supported the chimney structure. The most common form of chimney support was two walls of stone, usually granite, that were topped by long, flat stones on which rested the chimney. It looks sort of like a fireplace but has no hole for the smoke. The horizontal topping is the split-stone chimney arch. If the house had several fireplaces or multiple arches, the stonework will be even more massive. (*Plate 6*)

Wood was both an ally and a liability on the farm—it was the universal product for New Englanders. It seemed limitless. But it catches fire and it tends to rot. Ultimately, any wood that got wet deteriorated. Sills and other wood parts from barns and houses in contact with the ground had to be replaced. Farmers knew all about different trees and what wood was best for a particular use. Dark soils can indicate the presence of rotted wood and other organic material, some of which may be found in middens (trash dumps).

Trash heaps

Another evidence of the old farm is the trash midden or dump—every farm had one. It took about 20 years for the 18th-century household to produce the amount of waste we produce now in one year, but it does accumulate over time. Most middens contain discarded materials from historical times—old bottles, tin cans, washing machines, and other debris tend to accumulate downslope from houses and other structures. The more recent materials will be on top and at the base of the slope, but most such dumps were abandoned by the late 1960s. The old dump will be in a convenient, accessible location behind or beside the house or barn (Figure 4.3).

A particular type of trash dump found near rivers and coastal areas is the shell midden. Large shell middens—piles of clam and mussel shells left over from harvesting the meat—can be seen today in coastal areas. The calcium carbonate in the shells tends to make the midden alkaline,

Figure 4.3. *Abandoned dump. The type of debris in it indicates whether it was associated with a house or business. The household dump is usually in an accessible downhill position from the house site. This dump has fewer trees than the area immediately around it. Newer trash is scattered at the base. Older material is higher up on the hill and underneath the more recent material. The dark soils indicate decomposition of organic matter, which most likely included wood. Food waste would have been given to farm animals and never placed in a dump, due to concern about attracting scavengers.*

Figure 4.4. *Shell midden in coastal Maine. It consists of mostly clams, but some mussels and periwinkle snail shells can be found. The bleached white shells and the mounded shape may make it easier to spot such middens. The locations should be kept confidential to protect the sites, but some are simply too noticeable to be a secret. Explorers of the rural landscape should take care not to disturb the middens.*

which enhances preservation of organic materials within them, and therefore the midden might be older than the organic material might otherwise suggest. Some middens were made prior to the early 20th century by settlers and fishermen taking shellfish to use as bait for cod fishing. Others were made by coastal tribes and date back hundreds or even thousands of years before Europeans came to the New World. The shell midden (Figure 4.4) is likely to exist on ledge material near the ocean or on any type of soil along rivers like the Connecticut River. Inland middens might be very small, perhaps only a few feet in size. Some coastal ones can be several hundred feet long and a dozen or more feet wide.[93] Many hundreds of middens exist, but they may not be immediately detectable. However, they all are vulnerable. Periodically, erosion and storm events expose previously hidden middens and make the new feature easily recognized. But even an old midden will have some indicators. For example, the bleached white shells will be quite noticeable, and daisy, poison ivy, and other tolerant, invasive, open-growth plants that do not mind the lack of soil will grow on the mound.

Barns

Barns and their ruins are classic indicators of an agrarian past. Some are still in use—a continually occupied barn lasts much longer than an abandoned one, and can serve area farms long after the original house associated with the barn has become a cellar hole. Even after abandonment, barns are slow to give up the ghost. Some sit like squashed giants, sinking into the landscape, their mortise-and-tenon beams holding up the sagging shell. Today, many of them have been taken apart and the beams used in upscale housing. The old barns had numbers carved or stamped inside the joists and connectors so that the barn could be reassembled if necessary, a testimony to 18th- and 19th-century craftsmanship.

Several excellent references are available to help you identify standing barns and their associated buildings (such as *The Field Guide to New England Barns and Farm Buildings* by Thomas Visser and *Barns: Their History, Preservation, and Restoration* by Charles Klamkin). Armed with such references, it is fairly easy to make sense of barns that are still standing. But what can we tell about the barn if only the foundation is left?

Barns in the 18th century were small, perhaps slightly larger than the main house. Expect the stone foundation to be wider, taller, and more substantial than the house. Usually, these barns would be of the "English style," with the barn door on the side of the building, opening into a central threshing room. A bay would be on either side of the central room and there would not be a cellar or below-grade room. The 18th-century log structures in the more remote sites might be gone, but if the stones were large enough and not needed elsewhere, you might be able to spot them.

Barns of the 19th century tended to be quite large, needing to hold animals, food, and farm equipment. If the farm was near a railroad line, the barn would be even larger, in response to the opportunity to ship milk. Barns with three stories were most popular between 1820 and 1950. Usually, the barn would have the main doors on the gable ends, and a central passageway through the entire length so that wagons could be driven though either door. Standing barns may be tied to ethnic identity—Dutch barns are quite distinctive with their gabled roofs,

widely spaced rafters, and end doors, for example, and may still be seen
in southeastern Vermont.[94] But when the barn is gone, the stone foundation is less likely to yield cultural information[95] beyond whether or not
things were prosperous when the barn was built, enabling the farmer to
afford large, dressed quarry stone. (The choice to use quarried stone was
also a function of the age of the barn and the availability of the stone.)
This might be granite, or even marble or slate. Stones were necessary
for at least the corners of the barn. Fieldstone was a handy source for
most New England farmers, but by the start of the 20th century, many
farmers were using molded concrete blocks that look like stone. The US
Department of Agriculture's *23rd Annual Report of the Bureau of Animal
Industry for the Year 1906* provides drawings and specifications for dairy
barns, silos, and other dairy farm structures; foundations can be matched
to these specifications to see if the site features match these early 20th-
century recommendations.

Many barns were built on split levels with a ramp to access the second floor. The ramp would consist of tumbled rocks and fill, which might
remain visible as a hummock or raised area near the foundation. The
ramps were buttressed with stone, and later with concrete. Occasionally,
dry laid stone marked the edges of the ramp. The post–Civil War barn
might have a cellar for storage of manure or root crops, in which case it
might also have a massive stone foundation step or a series of stone steps
leading up from the cellar. These steps would be bigger than those that
might be in a house foundation.

Barns in New England were more likely to be connected to the house
than in other parts of the country. Improved fire protection through formation of mutual assistance fire brigades and the addition of water tanks,
fire ponds, and other measures made the connection a little safer. By the
late 1800s, many farmers had moved their barns to be connected, or built
new attached barns. This made it easier for the farmer to get to the barn
to do chores in winter—an important feature, especially recalling that
the blizzard of 1888 killed people who were simply trying to get from the
house to the barn. Connected buildings saved energy and lives. If the barn
was moved, it will be quite hard to tell where from without archaeological

sampling or historical research. But everyone would have known at the time because moving a barn was a collaborative social event.

As discussed in Chapter 3, vegetation can provide some hints about barns and the date of abandonment. Thistle, burdock, and nettles are just three of the many plants that grow in recently abandoned fields. These plants like lots of nutrients, and manure, straw, and hay dump sites created rich soil. Thus, the vegetation will be rich on an old waste pile. In addition to plant indicators, changes in the ground topography, such as large bumps or mounds, may suggest the location of old dump sites.

Because red maple is toxic to horses due to an oxidant in its leaves, the growth of this plant was discouraged in horse pastures, near barns or in other places where horses might encounter it. However, red maple is a vigorous sprouter. If you see red maple growing near a barn foundation or overgrown horse pasture, you can expect that it got a start immediately after the abandonment of the farm when there were no longer horses around to be at risk. Similarly, black cherry is toxic to many animals because its leaves, when damaged, liberate cyanide.[96] On the other hand, sugar maple, oak, and other shade trees would be desirable in a pasture or near a barn. Any trees growing *in* the foundation, of course, suggest the age of abandonment.

Hints about the age of a barn foundation may come from its placement in the landscape. Early barns (before the 1830s) were likely to be facing south (Figure 4.5). These barns were generally part of a subsistence pattern for a self-sufficient farm, with little or no need to transport crops off site. The warming sun was more important than road and highway connection back then, and most machinery was handheld. With the development of market-based agriculture, barns were usually placed near roadsides and oriented to face the road, making it convenient for machinery and animal movement.

Setbacks from main roads increased in the late 19th century as roads improved and individual farms grew. Larger herds, haylofts, and better construction made it easier to keep the barn warm in the winter. The increase in farm size meant the need for silos to provide winter animal feed. The first silos were square, with stone foundations and walls. By the late 19th century, the silos still had stone foundations but were round

Figure 4.5. *Old barn foundation site, probably 18th or early 19th century. The small rectangular shape is oriented toward the south. The foundation is similar to a house foundation, so finding both makes it easier to tell which is which by comparison.*

with wooden walls. Round concrete and block foundations may be left over from 20th-century silos.

In the days before concrete,[97] some barns had flat, dry-laid stones in the floor, particularly if the barn was in an area prone to flooding or other sources of water. This helped reduce mud and was healthier for the animals.

Henhouses and chicken barns

Poultry was not big business for most of New England history; most people kept chickens and other poultry only for their own use.[98] The hens ran around the yard, eating waste and keeping ticks down. Unpenned, they were safe for the most part—even the dogs guarding the farm would have been brought up with them—and at night they roosted in the trees. Toward the end of the 19th century, people were shipping eggs to urban markets and becoming more scientific about breeding chickens and raising them. By the first part of the 20th century, people were more likely to have a henhouse. It might start as just one henhouse on the farm, but if there was any money in it, soon there would be multiple chicken coops just far enough apart to reduce the risk of communicable disease. Soon after,

with medicated feed and larger indoor flocks, the chicken barns began—
large structures that contained hundreds of chickens. But even better
transportation and the rise of corporate farming led to a shift south and
west in the market and the decline of most poultry operations in northern
New England. Abandoned chicken barns and the ruined foundations of
them are all that remain of most operations. These barns are identifiable
by their multiple rows of windows and the remnants of large ventilation
systems. The structures are often sided with corrugated tin or other metal
and do not include barnyards. Some have been converted into apartments
or renovated for commercial use. Once the structure is gone, the foundation sites look just like the rectangular foundations of other barns.

Outbuildings

Most small outbuildings had no foundations so that they could be moved
around the farm and reused. When they were abandoned, they rapidly
receded into the landscape (Figure 4.6), with nothing left, or perhaps just
half-buried large stones or boulders on which the four corners had rested.
Yet farms had many outbuildings, each associated with a particular
function. Farming social organizations (especially the Grange) and gazet-
teers/encyclopedias (for example, the *Farmer's Almanac*, and Periam's
The Home & Farm Manual) provided advice on many aspects of farming,
including dimensions, building materials, and types of outbuildings for
the farm. Byron D. Halsted's 1881 *Barns and Outbuildings and How to
Build Them* (reprinted most recently in 2008 by Lyons Press) shows many
building designs. The US Department of Agriculture's "Designs for Dairy
Buildings" (in the *23rd Annual Report of the Bureau of Animal Industry,
1906*) specified ideal configurations. The remains of old structures in
the landscape can be matched to these sources to determine potential
matchups. This may help you figure out the type of structure and how it
was used. It may also help in determining the period of its construction.

Indoor plumbing took a long time to arrive in the rural countryside.
Naturally, every house would have needed a privy or outhouse. A stone
foundation might remain, often about a four or five-foot rectangle or
square, frequently between the house and the barn. Many barns also had
a privy at one end.

Figure 4.6. *This farm outbuilding foundation has been filled in. The cement suggests early 20th-century construction, which generally means association with the dairy industry. Comparison with other foundations can help indicate the original configuration of the farm, including the uses of the various structures.*

Root cellars and stone enclosures

Among the many buildings associated with farming were stone structures, sometimes quite impressive in size and appearance, but also sometimes just a few feet wide. Occasionally, the origins of root cellars (Figure 4.7), lime kilns, and other stone structures are mistakenly attributed to ancient Celts and other Old World peoples.[99] Careful archaeological research and ample evidence have demonstrated that northern European immigrants and their descendants built these structures within the past several hundred years for agricultural and domestic uses.[100] Perhaps because they were such a common occurrence in agrarian society prior to the 20th century, people just did not tend to write much about them, causing a later generation some confusion about their origins, despite their mention in farm journals and almanacs.[101] Other structures are less easily assigned to agricultural use (see *Cairns*, Chapter 7).

Figure 4.7. *This small stone enclosure was a root cellar in Vermont in the 19th century. The rock material is found locally and splits easily into thin sections, making it ideal for roofing. The sturdy stone gives it an antiquated appearance, but it was quite efficient for temperature control. Its proximity to the household and the matchup with the stone in the nearby house and barn foundation suggest it was built at the same time as the farm. Because it is outside of the house, it was most likely used to store feed for the farm animals, which would require many times more food than would the family members.*

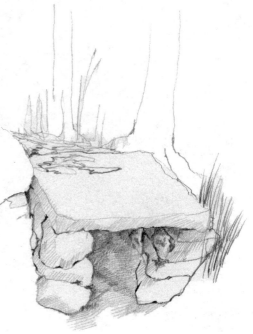

Prior to the mid-20th century, the necessity of keeping animals and storing vegetables, meat, apples, and other food contributed to the existence of many stone-lined cellars, outbuildings, and other features. The opening of the land increased the apparent harshness of winters by removing windbreaks and made food storage more critical. Stone was a handy and inexpensive material for storage chambers, a fact long recognized by people living in New England.[102] Stone worked just right for the required humidity and temperature for storage of apples and other fastidious crops.[103] Most structures were designed to be functional. But there was room for variation in style, and whimsical structures also existed, seemingly even more mysterious to those trying to discover their original use. Susan Allport provides an example of a dry-stone beehive-shaped structure[104] built by a hired hand in the 1920s. Contemporary artist and craftsman Dan Snow has built beehive sheds for clients and found that other people have mistaken them for ancient structures.[105] There seems to be a natural human tendency to pile rocks, and small cairns sometimes appear in streambeds when the water is low—although they might look like historical structures, they are as likely to be testimonies to folk art and a natural mound-building instinct, as they are to be footings for crossings, navigational aids, or fishing weir/dams. (Fishing weirs, discussed in Chapter 8, are usually V-shaped fish-trap remnants of stone or wood, and were quite common in the 19th and earlier centuries.)

Natural root cellars or storage areas also exist. One property along the Saco River in Maine is called "Indian Cellar" in reference to the bedrock walls reputed to have provided indigenous populations with cool storage for foods in summer. Bedrock formations are fairly common in northern New England, and when there are steep, sheltered rock faces, it is logical to imagine past cultural use, especially with local names like Indian Cellar. Figure 4.8 shows an example of a stone confinement, possibly an animal shelter, built into exposed bedrock, and a large boulder left over from the retreat of the glaciers.

In conjunction with figuring out the original use of a stone structure, you can also get a rough estimate of when it was built. "Lichenometry"[106] is a method for dating stone substrates—in this case, stone walls and gravestones—by evaluating the growth of lichens. Lichens—the three main types in New England are crustose (Micro-lichens), foliose (flat and "leafy"), and fructicose (branch-like)—tend to grow at regular rates. Of course, they vary by condition, temperature, and climate, but the ones that grow slowest are easier to use for age approximation. Crustose lichens are flat and "crusty" in appearance. Some species of these slow-growing lichens increase by about one millimeter per year under average conditions. One method is to measure the growth in centimeters from the center to the outside edge of the largest colony. Do this for the next four largest colonies. Take the average measurement of the five colonies and multiply by five to get an age estimation of the lichen. Since lichen takes a few years to get established, that age represents the newest that the stone wall (assuming the stone did not already have lichen) or gravestone could be.

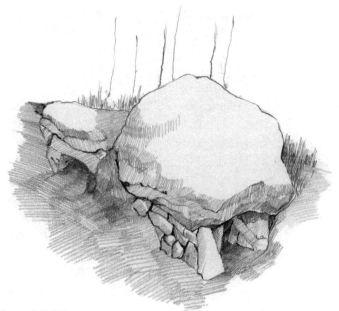

Figure 4.8. *This stone structure in northern coastal Maine (Camden) is in the middle of the forest about ¾ of a mile up the mountain from the nearest road—which would be a good way to ensure that your pigs weren't doing any damage to your neighbor's corn. The narrow entrance would have been appropriate for keeping bears out, and there were certainly plenty of bears in town before 1800. Built into a large boulder (a glacial erratic), it sits in a bedrock area covered with oak trees, which probably provided the bulk of the pigs' food; perhaps in November the owner would just go up the hill and fetch a pig or two for the winter larder.*

The stonework has been there long enough to grow a good patina of lichens, so it is clearly of some antiquity. However, the location and arrangement of some of the lichen suggest rock has been moved in a 20th-century reconstruction of the upper walls. Local history has it that livestock was grazed way up on Mount Battie, and even on Megunticook above it, so that British soldiers during the Revolutionary War and the War of 1812 couldn't come slaughter the pigs and cows to feed the troops. Maybe this structure dates from that time.

Wells, springs, water pipes, and troughs

Every house had a well or spring lined with stone. Round wells provided greater strength and stability than square ones. Most early wells were not very big, perhaps just a few feet in diameter. If possible, the house and barn were downhill from the well so water could flow, and to reduce the likelihood of contamination. If the barn was not near the house, it would likely have its own adjacent well or spring. Some stone foundations of houses and barns had built-in wells—a potential hazard to anyone wandering around them. Many old farm wells were covered with wood to keep people and animals from falling in, but the wood may have rotted away so it is particularly important to spot these things before an accident happens. The well cover might be a large round stone, or, more likely, fragments of one, looking similar to an old grindstone. Later well covers from the 19th century might be made from slabs of concrete. The hole in the center would be to raise and lower a bucket through. Vegetation may be taller around the location of a well.

A spring house was a common feature of the 19th century. Built over a pebbly bottom of seeping water, it could keep milk and milk products cooler than the surrounding temperature in summer. The spring house might contain a concrete storage pool with a deep area for coolest temperatures and channels to add or drain water. Spring houses could be rounded domes, similar to small silos, or square sheds, or faced into a hillside.[107]

Comparatively tall green vegetation might indicate the presence of a spring, a naturally surfacing supply of water. Some 19th-century houses had a stone-lined or brick cistern in the basement to store water. A cistern might be an external structure, too, especially if it collected rainwater from an outbuilding or was spring-fed. A drywell in an old foundation will not have any standing water in it. Nineteenth- and early 20th-century houses might also have drywells in the yard, used to get rid of "gray water." These disposal areas were hand-dug, shallow underground stone structures that were either completely buried or fed by a pipe or trough from the house or barn, or they would have a surface ring of stones to mark where buckets were carried and dumped into the disposal area. If it was simply abandoned rather than being reclaimed by conversion into a 20th-century septic system with leach field (as happened rather frequently), you might be able to detect a drywell site by its circular depression in the ground. A recently active drywell may have slightly greener vegetation in it as a result of the water discharged into it. Cisterns and wellheads of springs are easier to discern because they are less likely to be completely buried and covered up, and springs are more

Figure 4.9. *Small shallow well from a house site abandoned in 1912. It may not be much to look at, but it supplied water year-round at less than a tenth of the rate at which we use water today; it met the needs of a typical family of a hundred years ago. The ferns growing at the site reflect a moist, shaded environment, and a look at the well shows it still has water in it.*

Figure 4.10. *This small filled-in area may have been a well or the site of a privy. If it were bigger, it might have been a hole dug to get rid of material. The darker soil filling it in suggests an organic origin. Although not has clearly defined as a stand-ing well, small stones line its perimeter and there are some small ceramic shards mixed in with the fill.*

likely to have nurturing seeps around them that make them greener than their surroundings.

A levered hand-pump and stem may be lying around near the circular wellhead if nobody has collected it for a decoration. A modest circular arrangement of rocks might indicate either a spring or a well (Figures 4.9 and 4.10). If the soil is still moist and sheltered, the site might have some ferns on it.

Occasionally, metal, soapstone, ceramic, and even wooden pipe fragments can be found left over from the original water line. If the source was a spring and the water line was buried, the extra-green vegetation along the water line route may be discernible. Some historical settings may still have a linear depressed area of compacted soil and reduced vegetation as a result of generations trudging back and forth between the well and the house and barn. Fragments of old water pipes (Figure 4.11) might be visible between a house, barn, or industrial site and a well or spring.[108] The water line might be indicated by a linear depression in the ground between a building foundation and a water source, despite the passage of decades or even a century. Logs[109] were augered or bored for use as water pipes, and not just for farms, but also for towns—the Portland Water District in Maine maintains a display of old wooden pipe sections from its early 20th-century origins. Portsmouth, New Hampshire, had an underground wooden water pipe system in 1797. Boston and other cities had wooden pipes in the 18th and 19th centuries, many of which are still underground although no longer used. If the land is swampy, where conditions are not favorable for oxygen-dependent bacteria, wood from a water pipe might have survived. Water might be conveyed by metal, ceramic, or, less commonly, soapstone (steatite) pipes. The soapstone and ceramic materials will last forever, but the metal will deteriorate pretty quickly unless it is lined with lead. To avoid cost and maintenance, most people in the early days just carried water from the well or spring in buckets.

The Stone Structures of Northeastern United States website provides descriptions and photographs of wells, cisterns, related brick and stone structures, and pipes at http://www.stonestructures.org/html/wells-cisterns.html#Well. This site may help you determine the dates and nature of similar features you might find in the landscape.

Figure 4.11. *A wooden water pipe. The well-drained nature of the site, coupled with the natural resiliency of the rot-resistant wood, has allowed this pipe to survive over a hundred years after its original use. You are more likely to see such pipes in storage or after fresh excavations. Wooden pipe sections are occasionally recovered from urban renewal projects. Choices for wood included pine, cedar, and spruce.*

Schoolhouses

If you see a schoolhouse in what seems like relatively remote woods, you may be in an area that was once a cleared farming district. The rural schoolhouse was intimately associated with agrarian life. Schoolhouses were important community centers in small towns, villages, and hamlets. Their hours of operation were calculated to support work on the farm[110] and to allow participation by the parents, who would pitch in by supplying coal and wood, and by boarding the teachers. This way of life promoted local community identity, and children learned to interact with others older and younger because there were often only 10 to 20 students in the entire school for grades 1 to 6.[111]

In the early days, rural schools were usually rough shacks thrown up on the corner of some farmer's pastureland, if not simply using a room

Figure 4.12. *This road intersection once held a one-room schoolhouse. A quick check on one of Beers's late 19th-century county atlases (available online) may help verify the existence of the structure. The compacted play yard and scarred maples suggest heavy past usage.*

in the farmer's house. These schools were meager structures. But after the Civil War, schoolhouses became more significant. Periam's *Home and Farm Manual* of 1884 calls for the schoolhouse to be "the best building in the neighborhood...on high or well-drained land, near a public highway, and as near the center of the district as possible."[112] He recommends a 60-foot setback from the road and a 40 x 33-foot structure with belfry, and suggests that it also serve as meetinghouse and community center.

School consolidation was under way in earnest by the 1960s. Prior to that, small schoolhouses stood at the corners of central roads in villages and towns across northern New England. After consolidation, some of the buildings were converted to private homes, businesses, and civic centers,[113] and some buildings were moved to a preferred location. If the building was not in good enough shape to warrant conversion to another use or relocation to another site, it might have been burned by the local fire department for practice after it was salvaged for boards and other parts. The sites may remain if the community was not overcome by sprawling development from larger adjacent communities, or if the building was made out of stone (common in Maine) or brick. Consequently, you are likely to see either a building that looks reminiscent of an old schoolhouse—perhaps with the distinctive New England belfry—or you will see a mound that may or may not contain the remains of a foundation. Most of the 19th-century schoolhouses archaeologists have come across had rather meager or indiscernible foundations—perhaps a reflection of their rural, upland nature. Perhaps there is an old schoolyard tree, usually a sugar maple, that has survived generations of children playing in its boughs. The schoolyard itself would have been so compacted from recess play that the vegetative reclamation was much slower than elsewhere (Figure 4.12). The Beers atlases of the late 19th century label schoolhouses, showing a surprising number of intersections with them throughout the landscape.

Burn Pits

Fields were burned to help rejuvenate the soil and prepare for new crops. But the farms often had a specific area designated for a burn pile and used for getting rid of cleared brush and trash. Sometimes this would be done by reusing an old foundation—nothing like an old round, concrete silo footing to make a safe area for trash burning. Other times, it might be a ring of stones or perhaps just an open area. Repeated fires hardened the soil and slowed the regeneration of trees. Poison ivy and other highly tolerant plants made effective colonizers of old burn pits. Fire-cracked rock, particularly with a reddish appearance, ashy soil, and hardy plants might indicate an old burn pit. Twentieth-century burn piles are much more common than earlier ones—people had more to burn (Figure 4.13). However, by the 1970s most communities strictly regulated the burning of materials, and fires were supposed to be limited to natural materials.

Figure 4.13. *The fire-cracked, red/pink-tinted rock and hardened, dark earth suggest an old burn site. Regular use of such a site would usually be between the early 19th century and the 1970s, when environmental regulations discouraged open burning.*

We have summarized a few types of buildings and features that may have left their remains—or at least some clues—behind in the landscape. Most of these reflect an attempt by farmers to maintain self-sufficiency and to bring in extra income. The next chapter explores some examples of common rural commercial enterprises that also altered the landscape and left indicators of their presence.

5

Rural Industry and Commerce

The agricultural population, says Cato, produces the bravest men, the most valiant soldiers, and a class of citizens the least given of all to evil designs.
—Pliny the Elder

When we look at rural landscapes and the pattern of vegetation in old forests and fields, much of what we see is related to agriculture and the family farm. Often, a farmer did more than raise crops or animals to participate in the local economy. The farm required a diverse array of talents, and many farmers developed specialty trades of one kind or another. Land alterations, buildings, and structures that served nonagricultural industry were connected in some way to farming through shared markets, transportation, supply of goods and services, and through shared labor with the farmer and farmhands. The remains of these uses may be seen in old foundations, routes, and changed land forms.

Some structures represent factories rather than dwellings. This seems surprising to us now—the idea of small factories dispersed in the countryside—but since no electricity was available and there were no paved roads, it made sense to put an 18th- or 19th-century factory on site where the raw materials were—for example, brick kilns, furnaces, and clothespin, toothpick, and barrel factories. Many examples of cottage industry existed. All that was needed was a stagecoach road and perhaps a stream or river for water power. Large rivers could themselves be used by barges and other cargo- and people-movers. Smaller rivers blocked up by mills could still feed into an adjacent canal. In the second half of the 19th century, the railroads came and provided even better linkages, displacing canals and improving access to markets and urban centers. The thrifty New Englander was ever conscious of the opportunities to meet the needs of a growing country.

Many factories depended on water power, so the buildings were located near water and there were dams and millraces. If you do not see actual buildings or old ruins standing, perhaps there is the suggestion of foundations. Even if no structure or foundation remains, there may be site features associated with the former use of the site. These features may be the results of intentional landscaping or the accidental consequences of years of use. Features that might be recognizable include overgrown yards, loading platforms, cellar depressions, fence lines, and road alterations for driveways. The vegetation patterns will have been altered by the original use, with pioneering trees replacing shrubs and grasses. Once you see something you would like to identify, there are numerous sources available. The Society for Industrial Archeology has excellent resources on its website[114] and has regional sub-associations (chapters), including one for northern New England.

Creameries and Cheese Factories

Creameries became an important aspect of rural life after the Civil War, when refrigeration could help ensure freshness, and New England butter was on every table. In 1849, Vermont produced 12.1 million pounds of butter and 8.7 million pounds of cheese, and by 1900, that state led the nation in butter production.[115] But butter could not keep for very long. Cheese was one of the most efficient means for a dairy farm to convey its product to market, especially if there was any distance to travel. The farm might have its own cheese-making building for the family and local distribution. Farmers who had carved out land for their children's farms might work with them to make cheese at just one site, thus improving the predictability of the product. Cheese associations were formed that might include relatives and friends. Factory cheese production increased during and shortly after the Civil War, using raw materials from area farms. Small cheese factories dotted the landscape from the late 19th century to the mid-20th, when most disappeared. Some of these factories also made butter. The rectangular stone or concrete foundations of creameries or cheeses factories will be longer than those of houses and will not be in the classic barn location near the farmhouse. The Beers atlas or a local history may help verify the original use or type of building.

Gunpowder Mills

Most towns and cities had one or more "powder houses" near their muster fields (the working forerunners of some of today's urban parks) and maintained for mutual defense. Originally, gunpowder came from Europe, but it was logical to make it in the New World as soon as this could be safely done. Saltpeter, sulfur, and charcoal were processed by hand using mortars and pestles made of copper. Some New England powder houses produced gunpowder for the Revolutionary War, although most of it came from the French, who made a superior powder. Lesser-quality powder could be used for quarrying, rock ledge removal in road-building, and various industrial processes. As you might imagine, making gunpowder was a dangerous business. Mills were isolated from each other and from houses in an attempt to reduce damage from explosions (which happened with frightening regularity). Built of stone or brick, circular grinding mills and other buildings produced gunpowder. Making powder on a large scale was quite an extensive operation. There

Figure 5.1. *Gunpowder mill site in Gorham, Maine. This type of foundation differs from other industrial sites because, to reduce the risk of sparking an explosion, it has few metal features or artifacts. The grinding mill foundation shown here is round like a silo, but it is much more massive. For safety, the structures at a large gunpowder mill would be set far apart from each other. Small mills on other sites were a cottage industry, reflecting 18th- and 19th-century entrepreneurship.*

would be water for power, a charcoal house, a press mill, a kernelling or corning mill, and a dry house. The mills in Gorham and Windham, Maine, produced approximately a quarter of all the Union gunpowder used in the Civil War.[116] No iron or steel was allowed on the sites. Some copper was used, but almost everything—shovels, hoes, mallets, horseshoes, and wheels—was made of wood.[117] Looking like silo footings, mill foundations can still be seen along the Presumpscot River in southern Maine (Figure 5.1).

Tanneries

Very few tanneries exist in New England now, though small rural tanneries were scattered throughout New England near streams and rivers in the 18th and 19th centuries. Sometimes old place names indicate their presence: Tannery Lane, Tannery Road, and Tannery Brook are fairly common signs in the northeast. Tanneries provided a place for the farmer and trapper to bring hides. The farmer would bring mostly cow hides, and perhaps a few sheep. Leather had many uses on the farm and elsewhere, but making it was a messy, lengthy business.

Tanneries required a water source and a steady supply of trees, usually oak or hemlock, to produce the tannic acid used in preparing leather. Hemlock was the most common in northern tanneries due to its availability and tannin content. Leather and the means to produce it were an important economic engine of 19th-century New England. The Woburn area of Massachusetts alone had approximately 100 tanneries on the Aberjona River. Maine had 248 tanneries in 1820, and 395 in 1840.[118] Toward the end of the 19th century, the tanneries decreased in number but increased in size. Most tanneries were closed by the mid-20th century.

Beers labels the tanneries on its county atlases of the late 19th century, and some of the maps can be viewed online at various Internet locations. The rather toxic nature of tanneries would have affected local water quality, and abandoned tanneries were usually removed quickly. A number of old tannery sites have become EPA "Superfund" sites due to the high degree of toxicity found on them.

Bricks and Brickyards

If we see a brick on the ground while exploring, what can it tell us? Can we tell how old the bricks are? Bricks are a common indicator of historical sites and homesteads, and most brick was made locally. Bricks from Europe were preferred in the 17th and 18th centuries, but were available only to the wealthiest people, who could afford to import them. Fortunately, New England has many deposits of clay well-distributed in the landscape. Native Americans had made ceramics for centuries before the arrival of Europeans, and they knew where to get good clay. This knowledge was useful to the early settlers. A farmer of the 17th, 18th, and early 19th centuries might well be making his own bricks, or at least getting them locally. The Brick Farm Ice Cream Stand in Unity, New Hampshire, honors the history of the farmhouse built from bricks made on the property. In Buxton, Maine, round shallow clay pits in the back lots of several farmhouses suggest excavated clay for local brick-making, and perhaps also provided watering holes for farm animals.

After the clay is mined (a process called "winning" the clay), it is dried, cleaned, screened, and ground to powder. The powder is mixed with sand and water in a "pug mill" usually powered by a horse. The resultant "clots" of clay were coated in sand and pressed by hand into wooden molds, then placed in drying racks or sheds. These "green" bricks were baked for two weeks with salt to make them more resistant to water. (By the 1830s, coal dust was added, cutting the time to one week.) Steam-powered machinery in the 1850s meant that stiffer clay could be forced into the molds, resulting in greater regularity of shape. The three main types of machinery produced soft-mud, stiff-mud, or dry-press bricks. A guide such as Karl Gurcke's *Bricks and Brickmaking* (1987) may help you to tell the differences, though it will not necessarily tell you when the brick was made. Most bricks in the 18th, 19th, and early 20th centuries do not have makers' names or marks on them, but you can get an idea of whether or not the brick was handmade, and whether it was made prior to the 1880s, because of color variation and other differences (Figure 5.2).

Older brick are lighter in color—salmon pink. In 1884, makers began adding red ochre for a darker color. Old bricks would thus be pink or somewhat orange, irregular, and with more impurities than bricks in the late 1800s. Periodic episodes of fire through nearby cities and towns,

Figure 5.2. *A variety of common bricks. The one on the left is older, made by hand, and has more impurities than the others. It dates from the 18th century and was locally produced in a small kiln. In the center is a late-19th-century brick, also locally made, but from a larger factory. This brick has mold marks on it and is darker than the earlier brick. On the right is a brick from the 20th century. No longer locally produced, it is high-quality, uniform, and dark.*

particularly from the mid-19th century onward, would increase the demand for local brick. For example, after the fire of 1866 in Portland, Maine, much of the downtown was rebuilt with brick. And Portsmouth, New Hampshire, after the great fire of 1813, briefly had a rule that any new building above one story had to be constructed out of brick or stone.

The many different types of brick include paving bricks, sanitary brick (with enameled surface—easy to clean, and its hard, smooth surface resists contaminants), engineering brick, and firebrick (usually a light yellow). But most of what you will see is simply the common brick. The size of the brick does not necessarily tell how old it is, despite attempts at size standardization at various periods. Bricks made by hand are going to have less material in them and will be more crumbly than bricks made by machine. But soil condition and weathering will also affect the brick's hardness and durability. Bricks were also reused, so their age is not always a good clue for dating a homestead or other site. Some brickyards had slightly different color clays or added pulverized slate, and therefore made bricks of a slightly different color, which increases the chance that you could match a particular brick to its manufacturer.

The very earliest brickyards were at the site of the clay deposits and used a covered outdoor firing process rather than a kiln. Even if there was a kiln, it seldom survived unless the brickyard continued into modern times. The brick would have been reused as the kiln was disassembled.

A brickyard or brick kiln site will have lots of brick dust and broken bricks. It may also have the reject bricks, called "klinkers," in a dump pile. This pile may have settled over the years and have some hardy plants and trees growing on it, but it may still be a mound. The kilns were usually disassembled and reassembled for each firing, and may be gone except for a few iron parts and some brick rubble. Building material from drying sheds and other structures might be noticeable. Coal or wood ash may be left from the firing of the bricks. Most brickyards were more than several acres in size, and you might also see a route to the major source of transportation—wagon road, canal or river or lake, railroad, or truck route—depending on the eras. Heavy use of this route may have compacted the soils and slowed the regrowth of vegetation. If local clay was mined for the brick and the pits were not filled in for safety's sake, they might be discernible as small ponds because the remaining clay would have sealed the pit, allowing water to collect in it.

If the site is in an urban or developed area, all that may be left is a name, like Brickyard Cove or Brickyard Lane, and perhaps a reddish tint to the soil. As with other historical resources, the Beers atlases are handy references for locations of late-19th-century brickyards.

Mills

The first colonists quickly built mills powered by water. In northern New England, mills represented high technology beginning in the early 17th century. They enabled rural production of wood, grain, and other products. Many villages started out as mill sites along rivers and streams operated by early farmers and entrepreneurs. Later, professional millers served larger, more sophisticated mills, with major water impoundments, dams, sluiceways, and canals. Because of the importance of mills, the colonies passed "Mill Acts" that gave extraordinary power to the holders of mills—they could control the flow of water even on adjacent land, and they were deemed critical to the functioning of society; in some places, owners were even considered exempt from military service. But they also had civic and economic responsibilities.[119] By the late 19th century, the new steam-powered mills increased the flexibility of location—they could now simply be somewhere near a small stream that would be used to keep the boiler filled.

Sawmills appeared in the southern parts of Vermont, New Hampshire, and Maine fairly early in the 17th century, particularly in the 1630s.[120] Sawmills were the cornerstones of early towns and nurtured settlement in these water-rich states. There was a time when almost every stream had its sawmill, and dozens of sawmills lined major rivers. Taking advantage of the huge forests in New England, the sawmill was one of the first things settlers built, and they could be operated for a century or more (Figure 5.3). The mill would have a raceway to bring water to the large wooden wheel that operated the saw. It would have a sluice of some kind to bring logs in and out by water, in addition to wagon-drawn deliveries. By the 20th century, the number of sawmills had declined,

Figure 5.3. *This Vermont sawmill foundation has a water discharge hole at right. Built of dry-laid stone, it would have operated for much of the 19th century. Look for the remains of dams, culverts, raceways, and mill ponds when identifying the sites of old sawmills.*

but in 1909, there were still 848 in Maine, 570 in Vermont, 544 in New Hampshire, and 511 in Massachusetts.[121]

Like sawmills, grain mills were built at the source of water power. But a grain mill was less likely to be in a remote woods location. Grain mills tended to be near the sources of grain—the farms. Northern New England would have had billowing fields of grain in the early 1800s, waving across hilly fields. Wheat, rye, barley, flax, and other grains were

Figure 5.4. *Broken grindstone in the Maine woods. The disturbed circular area of earth in front of it makes one wonder if someone tried to lift it up and it tipped and broke. Every farm had small grindstones; a large one such as this would have been used by a mill.*

common, and many small grain mills dotted the landscape. Grain was locally produced and locally used until the railroads came in and large farms developed in the Midwest. Stone impoundments and sluices supplied water to turn the mill wheel. A grain mill, like other grinding mills, used thick, round stones (millstone or grindstone) to crush the seeds. Too heavy to carry away easily, they are still prized. You are likely to see them only if they are broken (Figure 5.4) or if you happen to be the first to rediscover them, or if they have been taken and now adorn a property entrance way.

Blast Furnaces and Foundries

The blast furnace was used to produce iron, which would be cast into parts for stoves and other products. These structures were small, independent operations beginning in the late 1700s. By the early 1800s, these furnaces were large structures 25 to 30 feet square and 30 to 40 feet high.[122] The solidified iron waste—heavy, black slag[123]—left behind is an indicator (Figure 5.5). Blast furnaces were located on dry ground but near a source of water, which would be piped or channeled into the site. A dry, well-drained site made it easier for the furnace to heat up. Built with brick or stone, the blast furnace featured an arch and hearthstones. There would be two walls with the space between filled with stone rubble. To see what these looked like, consult Victor Rolando's *200 Years of Soot and Sweat: The History and Archeology of Vermont's Iron, Charcoal, and Lime Industries* (1992). This is perhaps the single best source on the subject for northern New England. In addition to detailed descriptions of blast-furnace construction and operation, it provides photographs and drawings of blast-furnace ruins in Vermont, and these are applicable to other parts of New England. Anything reusable tends to get hauled away, but broken bits of large cast-iron cauldrons and other artifacts associated with furnaces may still be found in remote areas along with the remains of dams and water channels.

Saugus Ironworks is a National Park Service Historic Site in Massachusetts. A virtual visit (http://www.nps.gov/sair/index.htm) provides information about the beginnings of the American iron industry

(Saugus was in use from 1646 to 1668). Katahdin Iron Works is a Maine State Historic Site, and the website http://www.mainerec.com/katahdin. asp?Category=204&PageNum=204 contains information about the iron industry and the iron furnace that operated there from 1843 to 1890. Katahdin also operated over a dozen charcoal production camps to produce the significant amounts of energy needed to make iron. General information on this technology can be found through links provided by the Society for Industrial Archeology: http://www.sia-web.org/.

The iron that came from a blast furnace was processed by a foundry. Many products were made, including tools, farming equipment, machinery, turbine wheels, rifle barrels, stoves, plow irons, railroad-car wheels, printing presses, anchors, and steam-engine parts. Sometimes the foundry was located with the furnace, but usually it was separate in ownership and location.[124] A large firebrick-lined cupola with a steel jacket was the primary feature. Sometimes an air furnace was used instead of the cupola. An air furnace would use a heavy rectangular box.

Figure 5.5. *Blast furnace in Dorset, Vermont. This small site is similar to other rural industrial sites, but the chunks of dark slag, a heavy byproduct of the blast furnace, are a key indicator of its original use. The iron was melted by heat from charcoal, coke, or anthracite coal, which may also be lying around. Birch and aspen are growing over the pile of rubble from the furnace, and sugar maples have moved into the background. At the site, the walls are barely discernible unless you walk around it.*

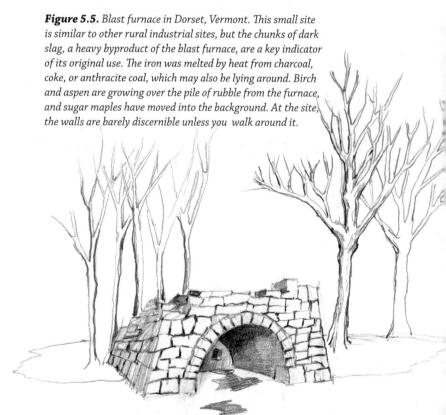

Both types of foundries had grates, hammers, tongs, rollers, and other tools for iron production. The site of a foundry would contain firebrick, metal fragments, slag, coke, charcoal, and hard coal.

If you think you have a site that might be a foundry, consult Beers to see if one is identified in the atlases. Town histories may also yield information. In Vermont, consult Vic Rolando's book. Nashua and Concord, New Hampshire, have inventoried their old foundries, as have many other New England communities. Local historical societies are a logical starting point.

Lime Kilns

Limestone forms from sedimentary deposits of carbonate rock (dolomite) and has many uses. When it undergoes geologic metamorphosis, over eons of time, it becomes marble. However, many stoneworkers and builders consider limestone to be a low-grade marble. A major use of limestone is in making lime. For this prime example of local industry, lime kilns—circular or sometimes square structures of brick or stone—were common in the early to mid-1800s.[125] Limestone was placed in the

Figure 5.6. *This circular ruin suggests an old kiln was here. The light powdery substance on the ground is a "tailing" of burned lime residue, which, along with small white stones and the charcoal-stained soil, indicates this kiln was used to process limestone. The exposed sections of 1-inch iron rod indicate their use as stabilizers in binding the kiln together. Even if there were no visible remains of the kiln, the yellow and white birches, along with other colonizer trees, are apparent from a distance as indicators of a disturbed area. These hardy pioneer trees do well in the compacted soil.*

top of the kiln, a fire was built under it, and the limestone was heated until it turned to powder. (Lime kilns required a tremendous amount of wood, often several dozen full cords for a single firing.) The powder collected at the bottom of the kiln, where it was removed to a cart or wagon. Lime was used primarily for fertilizer or for plaster or mortar mix. Although much of the original kiln structure may be gone, there might be white limestone remains (tailings) on the ground, broken brick, and charcoal (Figure 5.6). Some coastal areas may show lime tailings where the lime was loaded onto ships for transport.[126]

Northern New England has significant deposits of limestone, particularly in Vermont and in coastal areas. Lime kilns built in the early 18th century produced lime for shipment to England, but by the mid-19th century, lime was of significant importance in local agriculture, and small farm kilns existed in addition to the large industrial ones. The presence of yellow firebrick, often with concrete but occasionally with stone, suggests a date between 1870 and 1920.[127] The high heat on the inside of a kiln causes glazing on the exposed surfaces, which may be found on some of the leftover stone and brick. A collapse of the kiln may obscure or destroy the original arched entry and make the kiln site look like other cultural features like stone wells or food-storage chambers. However, there may be enough clues left for you to infer the existence of an old kiln, and you can confirm it by checking a historical map or atlas or local history publication.

Potash

Potash (potassium carbonate) was used to make soap and glass, and Fuller's soap was used to prepare wool, a process that required large amounts of potash. It was a major commercial product from colonial times to the 1830s, and on a much smaller scale after that. A Vermonter, Samuel Hopkins, holds the first patent on record (Patent X1, granted in 1790) in the United States.[128] He invented a process to make potash by leaching hardwood wood ashes and boiling down the lye. Water and ash were boiled in giant cast-iron cauldrons and the potash was collected out of the bottom. The potash could be refined into pearl ash by baking at temperatures high enough to remove the carbon in it. Then it would be shipped off, usually to England, for significant sums. Broken cauldrons can still be seen in the woods. One sat on a hill in Springfield, Vermont, for many years, where it served as a convenient echoing device for making spooky noises in the 19th and early 20th centuries.[129] Smaller cauldrons could be hauled out and used to hold flowers in farmyards. There is a Potash Hill in Holden, Maine, and in other states, so you may see namesake reminders of this once-thriving industry.

Charcoal Kilns and Mounds

Charcoal was a product of the woods in the 1700s and 1800s. Vic Rolando, in his definitive monograph on Vermont industrial archaeology, noted that chopping wood for the charcoal industry provided off-season work for farmers up through the 19th century on their own woodlots or those of others.[130] Logs were stacked vertically in a conical shape and covered with dirt to keep the pile airtight except for a few vents to allow minimal combustion. The wood slowly burned until it became charcoal. The charcoal kiln was usually a circular structure, sometimes with a base of brick or stone, but often just a circular depression in the ground. Late-19th-century kilns might have been made of stone or brick; this would have been removed and reused, or it would have collapsed. The charcoal will last forever and you may detect the compaction and dark staining of the ground. Rocks exposed to high heat will have cracks and a pinkish tint to them.

The early abundance of hardwoods fueled thousands of charcoal production areas. A farm might supplement its income by providing charcoal for local industry (Figure 5.7), but charcoal production became more than just something a farmer would do in the off season. Some industrial furnaces operated their own charcoal kilns, and entire villages rose around them. Professional charcoal burners lived out in the woods, tending their 30-foot mounds of hardwood covered in leaves and sod while they burned for several weeks. Careful tending was needed to make sure the mound smoldered rather than erupted into flame. The hard-packed, charred ground would be a circular reminder of this act for many genera-

Figure 5.7. *The packed, dark soil in a circular shape in this old farm woodlot suggests a charcoal production site. It is too large and too far from the farm to be a trash burn site. The hardwoods have grown back and the woodlot looks much as it did originally.*

tions, although hardy trees will have grown back on the site. The remains of the charcoal mounds and kilns may be quite subtle, but the dark soil will persist for thousands of years, barring external forces of change.

When coal was not available to make iron, charcoal could be used. It did not heat as efficiently, but it still worked. Iron was produced in rural blast furnaces. Molten iron waste ("slag") may be a visible byproduct. The blast furnace needed water piped or channeled onto the site. Therefore, it was located immediately adjacent to a pond or stream, or it would have a flume or channel to bring water to it.

Quarries, Mines and "Borrow Pits"

Northern New England is mostly a rocky place. Early settlers, farmers, industrialists, and others used this rock material for walls, buildings, and manufacturing by opening hundreds of small quarries, mines, and shallow surface pits. Minerals, dimension stone, sand, gravel, clay, ore,

Figure 5.8. *Borrow pit for road construction. The idea was to get the material from a source as close as possible to where it was to be placed. Big borrow pits can be seen along the interstates, but there are many more small ones near secondary roads. The bared land has lost whatever topsoil it might have had and is colonized by hardy pioneer species such as aspen, birch, poplar, and white pine. The borrow pit may be recognizable by its square-shaped or "scooped" depression in the ground, usually with no side wall on the edge nearest the access road.*

and gemstones came from these sites. The ground yielded marble, slate, granite, talc, soapstone, lead, gold, iron sulfate (also known as copperas or green vitrol), and copper. Many small quarries existed up until the middle of the 20th century, along with some huge ones like Rock of Ages, which is still operating in Bethel and Barre, Vermont.[131]

Indentations along railroad tracks and roads are often from "borrow pits," and reflect the need to build and maintain as level a route as possible using local materials. Borrow pits are generally small rectangular or square openings that have not been reclaimed. Some were opened up by the Civilian Conservation Corps as part of Roosevelt's New Deal during the Great Depression. But most were used by local communities for building and maintaining roads. These borrow pits supplied earth material for trails, dams, culverts, roads, camps, and other outdoor building projects, and they were a way for the farm to augment its income or at least to save on outside expenses. The bared land exposed meager and depleted soils to hardy pioneer aspen, white birch, and white pine (Figure 5.8).

Many sources of information on the location of old quarries and mines exist on the Internet and in local libraries and collections. These sources include atlases, almanacs, United States Geological Survey (USGS) Quadrangle maps, county and municipality histories, and historical maps. Local families may have knowledge of old sites. Each state has a State Geologist, with an office containing maps and quarry information, and lists of publications. For example, the Maine Geological Survey publishes a collector's guide to sites.[132] The New Hampshire Department of Environmental Services maintains a list of geologic publications,[133] and Vermont even has an online rock identification guide.[134] Maps and documents can be found at many places, including town offices, libraries, and historical societies, in addition to Internet sites.[135]

The most accessible and safest way to read the landscape of New England is from trails, rivers, and roads. Going onto land that contains quarries and mines can be dangerous. Some of these mines, particularly the ones that produced ore, may be toxic. Fortunately, most quarries and mines needed to be near roads, railroads, or canals so the heavy materials could be transported. The Roadside Geology series, published by Mountain Press, are good, quick references. You might want to have on hand *Roadside Geology of Maine* (by D. W. Caldwell, 1998), *Roadside Geology of Vermont and New Hampshire* (by Bradford B. Van Diver, 1987), and *Roadside Geology of Massachusetts* (by James W. Skehan, 2001). Nineteenth-century gazetteers like the Hayward edition (1839) list some quarry resources by town; Francestown, New Hampshire, for example, had a "quarry of freestone." A complete 1857 version of Hayward's gazetteer has been digitized and can be viewed free online at Google Books.

If you find something that seems specialized, you can research it on maps and descriptions of specific mineral and stone resources. Noted period woodworker Roy Underhill gives the locations of whetstone deposits in Maine, New Hampshire, Vermont, and other states.[136] The New England states, like most other states, have places—often streams or ponds—named "Whetstone" or "Grindstone," a handy clue that there might be an old quarry site around. Grindstones were big business. Moses Greenleaf's 1829 *Survey of the State of Maine* reported that 800 tons of grindstones shipped annually out of Eastport.

The presence of things used to process quarry products may suggest the proximity of a quarry. Limestone kilns would be near old roads and old limestone deposits, which were often just ledges in the case of small kiln sites—the ones most likely to be relevant to local farming communities. The ledges may show drill marks and other signs of having been worked. For large operations, staging areas for loading marble and other dimension stone would be near old railroad sidings brought as close to the commercial quarry as possible.

Many a farmer benefited from having a small quarry close by to get rock for the farm, to contribute to church and civic projects, and to augment the family income. Quarry walls may contain marks that show where stone was split off the rock face. Usually, these marks will be from drill holes. You can compare the drill marks and determine if they were made by steam or by hand tools. In the late 17th century, stones were being quarried with hand tools.[137] Hand-drilled holes were irregularly spaced and seldom more than five inches deep. The most popular methods were the flat wedge technique and the plug-and-feather technique. Set in a row, two iron pins ("feathers") were placed in each hole as shims. Wedges ("plugs") were put between the pins. Working along the face to be split, each wedge was pounded in turn. Many granite stones for the upper portion of house foundations ("facing" or "dress" stones) came in this way from small sites in the woods, if not from one of the larger commercial quarries (Figure 5.9). You can also see these quarried stones placed along the tops of stone walls, and in bridge abutments beginning around 1830. Pneumatic drills came into vogue in the early 1900s and left nice round holes that tended to be at regular intervals (Figure 5.10). Once cut, the dimensioned stone represented an energy investment and would be reused whenever possible.

By the 18th century, iron ore was also being extracted and processed from small sites in New England. In 1837, northern New England towns

Figure 5.9. *"Dressed" granite blocks used in the upper portion of foundation walls. This is the stone that would be visible to the outside world. The rest of the cellar walls would be built of local stone in typical dry-laid fashion. The granite blocks also got the floor joists and wooden wall frame well off the ground and away from moisture. The placement of the small trapezoidal shallow marks indicated the stone was hand-split using the "plug-and-feather" method common in the 18th and 19th centuries.*

Figure 5.10. *Small abandoned slate quarry in central Vermont. Size and placement of the vertical drill marks indicate the use of a pneumatic drill, probably from the early-20th-century use of the site. Small quarries were common prior to the mid-20th century. Drawing based on photograph by Gary Salmon in Sanford, et al., 1994:39.*

Figure 5.11. *Towns with iron ore deposits in 1839. Maine: Parsonsfield and Winthrop. New Hampshire: Bedford, Bethlehem, Brentwood, Campton, Claremont, Haverhill, Hinsdale, Lebanon, Lisbon, Madbury, Moultonborough, Nottingham, Orange, Peterborough, Rindge, Seabrook, Somersworth, Swanzey, and Wentworth. Vermont: Barnet, Bennington, Brandon, Bridgewater, Monkton, Pittsford, Rutland, Shaftsbury, Swanton, Tinmouth, and Waitsfield. Source: John Hayward,* The New England Gazetteer, *6th ed. Boston: Boyd & White, 1839.*

were inventoried for iron ore deposits[138] (Figure 5.11). Small bog iron deposits may still be noticed today by the reddish-brown staining of the shallow waters. So-called "bog ore" and magnetic oxides were available for local forges. The ore would be screened and cleaned for refinement in a blast furnace.

Copper and iron mines were excavated by tunneling or via open pits and shafts, as is the case in Orange County, Vermont. The entry to a mine is a dangerous thing that should have been sealed upon closing of the mine. (If you locate an unsealed mine, contact the local town offices or the state geologist's office).

Native American Quarries

For 12,000 years, Native Americans quarried stone for tool-making and other purposes. However, their quarries are not easy to spot unless they are large and you know what to look for. Seventeenth- and 18th-century explorers, soldiers, and early settlers might seek such sites as potential sources of flint for fire-starting and for flint-lock weapons. Some large sites of high-quality material drew ancient peoples from hundreds of miles away, as in the case of the rhyolite in northern Maine (Figure 5.12), or Mt. Jasper rhyolite from Berlin, New Hampshire. Native people fashioned/manufactured stone (lithic) tools from local sources of quartzite, rhyolite, chert, or other material that would flake well, but chert was the most prized. In Vermont, Cheshire and Dalton quartzite bedrock outcrops are common, particularly along the western flanks of the Green Mountains and to the west and north through Addison County. You might be able to see some localized sites of tool production if you notice chips (flakes) and other stone debris near a boulder or other rock source (Figure 5.13). Prior to the arrival of Europeans, there were extensive trading routes for material goods. The native peoples traveled widely, going hundreds of miles for good sources of lithic materials or exchanging other goods for them. A top-quality source of stone material was worth the extra effort; the Munsungun Lake Formation in northern Maine contains numerous paleo-quarries, and their products show up as finely worked tools including fluted points (among the earliest worked tools in New England) all over Maine[139] and in parts of other New England states.

Figure 5.12. *Detail of stone flakes near quarry site. Some quarries were large and highly valued destinations for Native Americans. A beach in northern Maine is comprised of rhyolite flakes and debris from centuries of quarry use, dating to long before European settlement. There are so many flakes and other "lithic scatter" that you almost don't notice them and could easily overlook their significance as an indicator of stone tool quarrying.*

Figure 5.13. *This boulder of quartzite shows evidence of having been worked by humans. The scattering of stone debris (debitage) from the boulder is a clue, as are the pocked surfaces. Quartzite, though common, was not the best source of tools—seldom worth a long trip—so we might speculate that it was more likely to be selected by nearby people who needed something at hand. Lichen growing on the rock indicates the work was done more than fifty years ago, but we cannot tell how much earlier.*

Peat

Peat, a lightweight organic material from decomposed vegetation, is found in old bog sites throughout New England. Peat was not farmed to any great extent in northern New England except in Maine. A United States Geological Survey report, *Peat Deposits of Maine,* issued in 1909, describes peat resources and is available online at http://pubs.usgs.gov/bul/0376/report.pdf. According to the Maine Geological Survey, peat was quarried for agricultural and horticultural purposes in the 1940s. The Maine Geological Survey has peat resource location maps available online. A peat quarry site is identifiable by the layered excavations in old bogs, fens, and peat swamps, and by vegetation—cranberries, willow, larch, red maple, black spruce, sedges, bog laurel, marsh fern, and other water-tolerant plants. New Hampshire peat sites are indicated at http://extension.unh.edu/fwt/Peatlands.htm#Where. The Vermont Agency of Natural Resources has information about the location of peat sites in Vermont. Each state's Cooperative Extension office associated with the land grant university has further information, as do the respective departments of agriculture.

Industry and commerce reflected New Englanders' thrift and enterprise. You might see evidence of a great variety of endeavors from an era when electricity did not exist and businesses were small and rural. Farmers and other rural folk often pursued multiple sources of income in local markets. Small commercial operations, particularly those on individual farms, did not leave many clues to their existence and disappeared quickly into the landscape. Overgrown roads and routes may be all that remain as indicators of what once was there.

6

Rural Roads

The road was new to me as roads always are going back.
—Sarah Orne Jewett[140]

Centuries ago, prior to the arrival of Europeans, a vast network of trails already existed in New England, connecting it to external trade corridors. Many of our present roads developed through the continued use by settlers of these established Native American routes and trails. Like the original inhabitants, explorers, soldiers, and settlers depended on river corridors for transportation, using trails to connect watersheds and to travel adjacent to rivers when not actually on them. The original trails were narrow and seldom marked. Some have been documented by historians and archaeologists. For example, Chester Price (1967) described 24 "important Indian trails" through New Hampshire, including the Merrimack-Winnipesaukee Trail, the Connecticut Trail, the Androscoggin Trail, the Ossippee Trail, and the Abenaki Trail, which extends from Massachusetts to Old Town, Maine.[141]

During the French and Indian Wars and the Revolutionary War, armies followed old Indian trails. The Revolutionary War led to the building of military roads that later became transportation routes between developing communities. Military roads favored a defensible route, avoiding valleys and following the ridges, where it was easier to keep an eye out for enemies. The high country made it less likely that cannon and freight wagons would get bogged down in a swamp. Major military roads have been commemorated with place names that continue to apply to the modern route; these can be matched with old maps and historical information to infer the location of other, secondary military roads that might have intersected. New maps may still contain this information. For example, the Revolutionary War–era Bayley-Hazen Military Road built north through Vermont to aid in a possible invasion of Canada is still labeled on the DeLorme atlas of Vermont.[142] The Daughters of the American Revolution and other groups have placed square granite markers on some of these roads.

Indian trails and military routes were often the basis for roads that were still used into the 20th century. Other routes, like the 162-mile Cohos Trail, which ran from the Connecticut River through Montpelier and along the Winooski River to Canada, are preserved largely as hiking trails. Some roads were not ancient, but were developed from hastily cut logging and transport routes. It took a long time for some roads to be improved. Sloane notes that "even as late as 1870 many roads in New England were only clearings through forest, with few level stretches and often with stumps left in the middle of the road."[143] Whenever possible, the road was built in dry areas, or was segmented with drainage ditches or the filling in of lowland, wet areas. Military roads, like the Crown Point Military Road in Vermont, needed to stand up to the passage of horses, wagons, and cannons: having troops mired in mud slowed the transport of militia and supplies. Engineers who could design and build a good military road were valued and so were their products, so old military roads were desirable assets for postwar settlement.

In addition to military and logging purposes, roads linked communities and villages for trade and social purposes. Most communities

corduroy road

plank road

Figure 6.1. *A corduroy road and a plank road. Prior to the 20th century, many roads were built by local farmers and townsmen. In-kind service on road construction was one way to pay the local taxes. The natural materials used meant that little evidence remains after the roads are gone, but many of these original routes became the modern roads we now drive on.*

were quite independent, and the roads received much less use than they would if serving the same size communities today. The primary function of a road affected its construction and its characteristics. In some towns, residents were required to work on public roads as a form of tax, to ensure safe and efficient transportation; in others, they could get out of this work by paying a fee or offering the use of their animals. As a result, the average farmer and villager knew something about road construction. Towns built charcoal, corduroy, and plank roads—hewn and on "sleepers"—along with graded dirt and ice roads (Figure 6.1), but very little trace of such roads remain visible. The paths they followed may have been swallowed up by woods with only a few clues, or the road may have been converted to a modern thoroughfare for cars. In Bristol, Vermont, the name "Plank Road" lingers to tell of its past construction.

Toll roads (turnpikes) were common, often built by locally formed investment companies. The turnpike had a gate across it, and travelers had to pay to use it. The turnpike was an attempt to actively plan the organization and location of a road, rather than have it appear organically from old trails. Turnpike companies generally were not very profitable and did not have long lifespans. Empowered by state legislatures, they largely existed between the late 18th century and the mid-19th century.[144] But some of these "post roads" lingered on, becoming public and losing their toll requirements or having the tolls largely limited to river crossings. Route 12 in Charlestown, New Hampshire, has the old toll rates posted at the bridge to Vermont, right near the old Crown Point military road, which connected the 18th-century Fort Number 4 in Charlestown with Fort Crown Point in New York; a map of this route is on the Crown Point Road Association's website at http://www.crown-point-road.org/history.htm.

Many mill communities were connected by turnpikes, but these tended to bypass the old, small settlement centers and farm clusters located up in the hills. According to Wood's classic 1919 survey, Vermont and New Hampshire had turnpikes constructed, but no turnpike companies in Maine were successful. Thrifty New Englanders did not like paying the tolls, and networks of "shunpike" roads sprang up as alternate routes to avoid them.[145] A farmer using a toll road would be assessed so much per head of livestock, and if he could find a different path to the market, he would take it. There are many roads named "Shunpike" to be found in New England.

The transportation eras in New England began with the original native trails, later enhanced into roads by settlers, and often paralleling watercourses. Towns developed along rivers because water power was essential for operating mills and for transportation. Canals were built in the early 1800s, and along with rivers, they represented the next great era of transportation until the railroads took over. The railroads dominated from the mid-19th to the early-to-middle 20th century. After that, the automobile was king. But the remains of past eras and former dominant modes of travel left their mark in the placement of villages and patterns of development.

Characteristics of Old Roads

Although modern roads often follow 19th-century roads, some of which were developed from even older roads and trails, the sharp corners and tight curves have usually been rounded out and smoothed over to accommodate today's faster traffic. Look inside the curves for the original roadway alignments and other historical roadside features. Although wide roads obliterate most traces of the past, undeveloped adjacent lands can give clues. Old charcoal, corduroy, and hewn-plank roads will have long given way to more modern paving materials or been reclaimed by nature. Roads in steep areas may have had planks, which would facilitate the passage of vehicles (Figure 6.2). As much as possible, roads were built up so that water could drain from them and thereby keep the roads usable during mud season. This meant bringing in fill material from borrow pits in adjacent areas. Road fill was also a good place to put extra rocks. The rocks under the road could work their way to the top and cause problems, but they also allowed underground drainage, helping to keep the route dry.

Figure 6.2. *This hiking trail was once an old plank road. The clues are the steep, narrow, well-drained roadbed, leading down from a settlement. Plank roads were narrow, and, to reduce slipperiness and wood rot, needed to be well-drained and stable. Steep slopes benefited from the stability and traction provided by the planks. Other indicators may include place names, local histories, and old maps.*

There are many sorts of old roads linking houses and farms—town roads, private roads, stagecoach routes, turnpikes, shunpikes, farm roads, logging roads, military roads. The bed of an abandoned road will have been compacted by use, slowing the growth of vegetation. But after many years, the bed may be completely overgrown. Old roads were lined by trees, which protected the traveler and the road, and these trees may still be in place (Figure 6.3). If the road was adjoined by a crop field, there would be fewer trees along the road because the trees would have shaded the crop. Trees along pasture, meadow, household, or orchard would be less of a problem, and even desirable. Some towns passed laws in the early 1800s protecting shade trees. Writing in 1884, Periam recommended intervals of 30 to 60 feet, and not just in a line of single trees, but with a row breadth of 60 to 100 feet.[146] Some communities favored trees as windbreaks for the road, but others were concerned that

Figure 6.3. *This old road was abandoned in the mid-20th century as a result of highway realignment to accommodate faster traffic. The adjacent homeowners have appropriated the roadbed, converting it to lawn, but have kept the old sugar maples that once lined the road. A relocated driveway may also still have the trees that lined it, providing a clue to how a farmhouse or other building has been reoriented.*

the trees caused the snow to build up on the road and held the moisture in the spring. Having all that snow was not so much of a problem if the town regularly "rolled" the roads in winter, which packed snow on the road for travel by sled instead of wheel. But such a road would also need to be elevated and well-drained, otherwise all that melting snow would create a real problem during spring mud season.

If a stone wall–lined public road has been widened, or new drainage ditches added, the stone walls may have been moved back and reassembled. The rebuilt wall may look different—the moss and lichen on the stones may not have grown back the same way, and the wall may have a tumbled-together appearance. There will not be any large trees between the wall and the road. Old roads were narrow and property lines went right up to them. The very distance from the road will be a clue that the wall is not in its original location.

Figure 6.4. *"Ghost" curb cut, indicating where a garage of carriage-house driveway once connected to the road. The driveway has since been converted to lawn and a new driveway connects the road to a house with an attached garage.*

Sometimes, large boulders called "glacial erratics" (an example is shown in Figure 4.8) are encountered during road construction. Lord's Prayer Rock, with the entire Lord's Prayer carved into it in 1891, is along Route 17 in Bristol, Vermont. Too large to move, the boulder is right against the road. A Dr. Joseph C. Greene had it engraved, perhaps in acknowledgment of harrowing road conditions.[147] If the boulder was small enough to be moved, it would usually be pushed to the side. However, you might find a boulder placed at an intersection of the road with another road or cow path. This got the boulder out of the way and served as a marker or meeting point. The boulder may still be kept in place if it is not a hazard to modern traffic. Usually this means one or more of the following: the road has not been widened, the road is in private hands, or the road is in a historic area.

Curb cuts are places in the road where the curb has been beveled to allow connection to a driveway. This is the modern practice, and permits are required to connect, but there is a vested right of access for old houses and driveways. The curb of an improved road would still be cut away for the driveway even if there is no longer a house there—such curb cuts might be perpetuated in subsequent improvements, providing a reminder of an old house site or road connection (Figure 6.4).

Stagecoach Roads

Early roads that passed through private property might have been stage-coach roads laid out according to old maps or surveys, or developed from the original Indian trails. Pre-dating town roads, those stagecoach and wagon roads placed as logical connectors between still-thriving places developed into modern highways. Abandoned stage routes might look similar to a logging road, but with more development. The former routes may be bordered by signs of past settlements, including cemeteries, and the sites of old houses, taverns, farms, and rural industries. Place names might provide a clue to past use, as might historical maps that use identifying labels for structures. An ideal giveaway might be if that old cellar hole is identified as a stagecoach inn in a 19th-century atlas.

Farm Roads

Left behind by the retreating tide of farms are the remnants of old farm roads amongst cellar holes, walls, and foundations. These roads linked activity areas on the farm. Perhaps they were a simple set of tracks leading to a mowing field, or a beaten path leading from the house to the woodlot or back pasture; or they might be a road between two sturdy stone walls that would have kept the cows or sheep where they needed to

Figure 6.5. *This old road was for farming access. It is not in the deep woods of the logging forest for a timber company but instead is part of an old farm complex. The woods have grown back in an old farm setting. The lack of formal roadbed construction, the partial stone walls (openings in stone walls may indicate where an old road once passed), and the narrow width of the roadbed suggest its use by a local farmer. Younger trees have grown up shaded by the forest canopy along the path of the road.*

be. Even if the walls or fences have been removed, you may still be able to tell where the road was (Figure 6.5). When the road grows in, the trees along it might be smaller, representing a noticeable band perhaps eight or ten feet wide winding through the forest.

Logging Roads and Skid Trails

Roads for logging were designed as one-way routes to get logs from the stump to the mill. Accordingly, they were networked to connect lots of small roads and trails to bigger ones headed downhill toward a landing where they could be pushed into a river and floated to a mill. Later, with the advent of trains, the landings were located at railroad heads and sidings for transport by rail. Still later, trucks took over this job.

The woods of northern New England are now in the third major wave of logging. The current wave is much more management-oriented than were previous ones, and includes an effort to use existing logging roads rather than creating new ones. Skid roads were old trails that brought logs to larger "haul roads," although the terms can be used interchangeably. These old trails persist and can be indicated by evenly spaced sets of ruts that might look like parallel ripples instead of deep grooves. The skid road was usually only about eight feet wide. Pulling the logs out of the woods might have left wounds along the base (butt) of adjacent trees on the skid trail, especially on the downslope side and on the inside corners of turns. The earliest wounds were made during horse logging (although horse logging still occurs today), and then by bulldozers, and now by skidders or "forwarders." An injured tree grows new wood around the wound, the thickness of the callus an indicator of how long ago the injury occurred (Figure 6.6). Scarring five or more feet above the ground indicates the wood was hauled out in tree lengths, with large branches and perhaps the tops still attached.

If modern equipment is used, there will be a set of parallel tracks, each about a foot wide, on the trail. Water bars (ditches across the road to divert water) may be present. Blackberries and raspberries are often found in skid roads. If it is an old, narrow trail with no obvious clues, there may still be the remains of stumps to show the path had been

Figure 6.6. *Long recovered, this trailside tree still bears the marks of past bumping from logs hauled out on the skidder trail. To the right is the old loading ramp, which made it easier to roll the logs onto a truck or wagon. In the background is a closed-over barway that had once been open to bring the logging road across the stone wall.*

cleared to pull logs out. The horse skid trail is less obvious, and the old ones are harder to find. Horse trails are narrow depressions about four or five feet wide. The logs were dragged out by the horse, making the depression as they scraped along the trail. Since horses pull smaller loads, there will be less scarring on trees at the edge of the trail. Generally, you will not see any water bars on an old horse skid trail.

Wet areas may have corduroy sections, parallel logs eight feet long and placed next to each other, making for a bumpy but relatively stable ride. The corduroy sections are usually long gone[148] but there may be some old locust or hemlock log abutments where the skidder trail crossed a stream. The name "Corduroy" may be preserved in a street sign (e.g., Essex Junction and Stafford, Vermont; Nobleboro, Maine; and Amherst, New Hampshire).

Barways—openings in the fence or wall—would provide a way for the skid road to cross property lines and pastures bounded by stone walls. The barways might be filled with stone to match the wall if there were to be decades or more between loggings, or if the farm expanded into the former logging area.

At the end of the logging road or skid trail would be a ramp ("header") where logs were piled on stacked earth to they could be rolled onto a truck or wagon. The ramp might also be a bluff or small cliff above a place where a wagon or truck could be driven for loading. Most ramps were built into a bank with a level spot on top at the height of a wagon or truck bed. A log cabin style was often used to build the ramp, with the logs crisscrossed at their ends (Figure 6.7).

Haul roads were created in the woods to bring lumber to the railroads and rivers. "Dugway" roads were tucked into the mountainside for main haul routes. They were built in the summer months and had to be stable. Another type of road, an "upper," was built as a secondary haul road and was not as sturdy as the original dugways, many of which were eventually incorporated into modern roads. Belcher notes that "today's explorer, veteran or novice, will get to know the difference between a dugway and an upper after a few bushwhacks. The former will get him through and the latter will not."[148] You may see a "Dugway Lane" or other similar name currently in use, marking the historical roots of the modern road.

Figure 6.7. *These rotting logs have been uniformly stacked, indicating the remains of an old logging ramp.*

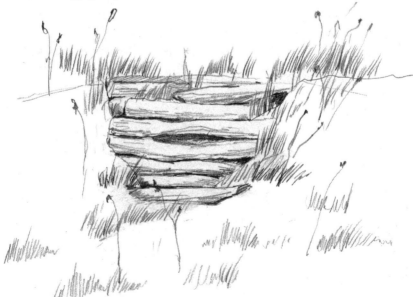

Landing platforms were used as staging areas for loading wagon freight and logging trucks. These landings were also at logging company railroad track sidings. An old loading platform may be visible as a large mound of vegetated earth incongruously protruding near former transportation routes. Look for a gradual slope on the back side of it where logs could be rolled up.

Trains, Tracks, and Trolleys

Railroads were important links for communities in rural states and New England had its share. Logging trains, freight trains, passenger trains, and trolleys left their mark in the landscape. Surveyors for timber companies covered much of the north woods, preparing for the logging railroads of the 19th century. Early morning trains would make the "milk run" from milk stations to the towns, waking light sleepers. *(Plates 8 and 9)*

Transportation in the past was not necessarily less efficient than today. Many places had even more alternatives than we have now. For example, in the early 1900s, you could go from South Windham to Portland, Maine, via road, canal, train, or electric trolley. Now there is just the road. But the memory of these other routes persists. The old trolley line left behind railroad spikes and faint contours. Trolley poles are shorter than high-tension-line poles, so if you see some along an old railroad bed, perhaps it was a trolley line. A trolley differs from a train by having its engine underneath, by running on electricity, and by being primarily in urban areas. The trains and trolleys had routes that connected the rural areas to hubs and eventually to the big cities. To determine these routes, you can consult old maps.

Railroad lines have to run pretty straight. When they cross a river or stream, they can't turn to make the crossing at right angles like a road does, so they cross at whatever angle they are already at. If you are canoeing down a river and you see footings or other evidence of an old diagonal bridge crossing, the chances are pretty good that it was for a train (Figure 6.8), and if not that, it might be a canal crossing, though there were far fewer of those.[149]

Figure 6.8. *The angle of this crossing suggests that it was for a railroad or, less commonly, a canal. The large cut granite stones on the embankment and now tumbled into the river would have provided the necessary support for the train. Perhaps there are old railroad ties strewn about, but even if not, a quick check of an old USGS map or other historical map can confirm whether or not a railroad crossed here.*

Some railroad tracks have been removed and the routes converted to bicycle and walking paths. Federally funded "rails to trails" programs helped support these projects, preserving the abandoned routes. Using these paths can bring a sense of history as we think of the trains from earlier centuries connecting towns and commerce. These routes may also reveal the location of railroad sidings and other features. Along Route 236, near the turn for Eliot, Maine, you can see the concrete abutments of an old railroad bridge. And not too far away is the large circular foundation of a roundhouse associated with the 1840s railroad and used for turning locomotives and railroad cars around (Figure 6.9).

Figure 6.9. *Small, rural trains needed a great deal of maneuverability. This old railroad roundhouse site was used for turning trains around. The grass suggests the site is maintained, perhaps due to its history, but the tracks are long gone, and the area trees suggest the site has been allowed to grow back for the past 50 to 100 years.*

Old USGS maps will show railroad lines. Large train stations in urban areas have had a difficult time surviving, but some small towns have been able to keep their stations by converting them to restaurants and other businesses. The old train station would be rectangular, with storage sheds, and located parallel to the tracks. Even if the station is gone, you may be able to tell where it was by seeing an old trolley or train route through town. There may still be a drainage swale along the edge of the railroad bed, and a green swath of trees (Figure 6.10).

Logging railroads plied the forested landscape. The subject has been popular among history buffs, with a good selection of books written for each state or region (e.g., Bill Gove's *Logging Railroads of the Saco River Valley*[150]). Between their ability to remove all of the timber from entire watersheds and to ignite giant forest fires in the late 1880s and the early 1900s from the resulting slash, logging railroads had a great impact on the structure of New England forests, especially where the vast stands of pine and spruce grew. The White Mountain National Forest was in part

Figure 6.10. *This ditch provided drainage for an old railroad line, long abandoned. Because the line ran right past the center of town, the drainage is still necessary to accommodate storm runoff, and is maintained. The elevated area behind it is where the old track ran. The elevation gave it a good line of sight for travel. The trees moved in and grew up after the roadbed was no longer maintained—their age of at least 40 years suggests when the tracks were abandoned. If you look around, you may spot some of the large coal chunks that fueled the train, and there will be gravel from the railroad bed. In areas where the tracks were removed, railroad spikes may still be found, too.*

established due to concerns from the citizenry about the logging and resultant huge fires in New Hampshire in the early 1900s.

Roads and routes are the lifelines of commerce into rural areas. Remains of these transportation corridors may exist long after the roads or routes themselves are gone or converted to modern highways. Along with changes in contours and vegetation in the landscape, fences and walls may be principal indicators of old roads. Fences and walls are also major indicators of rural agricultural and residential life. The next chapter focuses on "reading" old fences and stone walls.

7

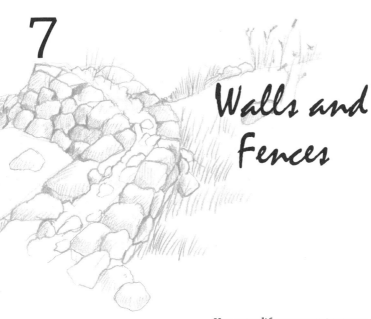

Walls and Fences

You gotta lift up every stone now sister
gotta lift up every stone now sister
gotta lift up every stone now sister
Gotta clear this field and build that wall . . .
—John Hiatt, "Lift up Every Stone"
(from the compact disc *Crossing Muddy Waters*)

Keep your fences horse-high, bull-strong, and hog-tight.
—Old farmer's saying

Perhaps the most noticeable indicators of human activity in the country are the fences and walls used in agriculture and in marking property lines. We interpret these features in much the same way we interpret cemetery fences and walls, which are discussed in Chapter 8. However, the original fences in New England were not made of stone; they were made of wood. Being practical, New Englanders wanted to clear their fields and have materials for fences at the same time, so they piled stumps and stacked logs on top. A fence made of dry pulled stumps can last a generation or more because the wood has had to be tough to survive in the ground.

Fences were serious business, denoting boundaries and keeping livestock out of gardens and new cropland. By the 18th century, most incorporated towns had established "fence viewers" as part of municipal government. Chestnut and cedar were preferred but often hard to find. Oak was a common material, but it does not last forever. Fences were hard work to maintain. Historian William Cronon quotes the 18th-century writer Michel-Guillaume Jean de Crèvecoeur: "Our present modes of making fences are very bad...they decay so fast, they are so subject to being hove up by the frost, it is inconceivable the cost and care which a large farm requires in that single article."[151] So why did we build fences?

A 1780 newspaper in London stated, "The stripping of forests to build fortifications around personal property is a perfect example of the way those people in the New World live and think."[152] Wood was a great luxury in England and much of Europe, yet forestland was widespread in the Americas—an invitation to the axes of an agrarian people. Fences were a good use for any wood that was not suitable for buildings. New Englanders appreciated being able to mark their boundaries and there were lots of fields to create. But more important was the need to separate animals from crops. So fences spread. The position of fence viewer (sometimes called "hedge ward") was a key responsibility in Canadian and New England towns, and it is one of the oldest municipal positions (Groton, Massachusetts, has had one since 1693). Good fences do not just make good neighbors, they make good animals. The 1858 *Farmer's Almanac* advises, "Poor pastures and bad fences make breachy cattle"[153] (a breachy cow is an unruly cow that is apt to "breach" or go through fences). The rise of the milk market and the shift from subsistence agriculture to market farming meant an increase in cattle and fences to manage them.

After the first generation of stump fences rotted out, it was comparatively easy to add wooden rails. If wood and land area were plentiful, the farmer might build a zigzag rail fence, sometimes called a "worm," "snake," or Virginia fence. Oak and ash were split into good rail material, spanning the nine feet or so between guide posts of cedar, locust, or chestnut. These posts could last quite a long time—when asked how long a locust post could last in neutral soil, one Vermont forester replied, "About an hour less than a stone post."

Cedar rails can also be found—their hardiness helped them to persist long after the need for the fence ended. By the middle of the 19th century, sheep farming made good fences a top priority. Thrifty New Englanders seldom built fancy ones, preferring the durable structures suggested in George Martin's 1887 manual.[154] An old zigzag fence might have its structure reinforced by stone, and gradually more and more stone was added (Figure 7.1). After the fence wood was gone, an incongruously zigzagging stone wall or jagged line of trees might be left behind to puzzle future generations. The zigzag fence also created a thicker fencerow. A fencerow is not just the land under a fence, but also includes the dense vegetation on either side of the fence—a hedgerow (and perhaps this nice, safe buffer is the source of the expression "hedging your bets"). But a wide fencerow meant more land out of production, so farmers were happy to switch to linear stone walls or barbed-wire post fences. Farmers today are more likely to keep a wide fencerow for wildlife conservation, a recommendation long endorsed by farm agents and cooperative extension services.

Zigzag fences require more wood than other fences, and they grew scarce by the end of the 19th century. In the early 20th century, an 80-year-old Vermont farmer stated:

Figure 7.1. *A zigzag (Virginia) split-rail fence stood here at one time. It had stones placed along its base as a way to get rid of excess stones from adjacent cropland. The wooden fence rotted away and the stones remain as a footprint. Vegetation has been allowed to build up here for over half a century, creating a thick, wildlife-friendly fencerow.*

You notice we have a good many zigzag rail fences around our fields, but we don't make any new fences of that sort. Rails are getting scarce nowadays. They're split out of cedar, and there ain't much cedar growing. It's a bother even to get enough cedar posts for wire fences. Every field, large and small, used to be fenced, and we had to keep a good fence along the road because people let their cattle run and feed in the highways. There'd be gates across the roads in some places that travelers had to open and shut.[155]

Property Boundaries

The earliest surveys were made along cardinal compass points. As land became further divided, the surveys might have gotten smaller, but they were often more complex. In any case, the property boundaries had to be marked. Congress set out a rectangular system of surveying in 1784. A typical township had 36 sections, and each section could be subdivided into plots of 640 acres (1 square mile). The boundaries of each plot would be surveyed and marked. Suspect a fence was a property line marker if it is built where there are no signs of past agricultural uses on either side and where it falls into the pattern described above. Building a fence just to mark a property boundary was labor-intensive and expensive; the typical farmer wouldn't do it or pay to have it done unless it also kept in sheep or cows.

If a fence did not mark a property line, other means were used to do so. Axe blazes on trees were a common method to mark these boundaries. An oval-shaped scar on a tree at breast height might be a visible reminder of a property line. Since people occasionally updated the boundaries, axe marks might even be recognizable, made in a way that distinguished the boundary line blaze from an ordinary tree wound. At the corner of a property, the tree might have sets of blazes on four sides. To ensure longevity of the boundary marker, more than one tree might be marked—these are "witness trees." If the actual boundary corner itself did not have a tree on it, a mound of earth or a stone cairn and post might be used to create a "post and stones" corner marker. The witness trees would be marked to let people know the corner was near.

Changes in the land might make these boundaries hard to find. One

Vermont surveyor told of following a stone wall boundary line until it disappeared into a pond. He found a second stone wall, which went into the pond, too. The surveyor got a canoe and paddled to where he could see the walls meeting underwater and saw the submerged cedar post embedded in a cairn of stones.[156]

Stone Walls and Fences

What is the difference between a stone wall and a stone fence? Height—the fence is taller. Thorson examined the Department of Agriculture's 1872 national census of fences, finding that a stone wall is "any accumulation that reached a height of two and a half feet, regardless of whether it was part of a fence or not."[157] A stone fence, he reported, had to be four and a half feet tall. Regulations in Maine and New Hampshire would accept animal fences of only four feet, but Vermont and other states required them to be four and a half feet. Meeting the height made things easier in court when people complained about animals escaping and damaging crops. Stone fences needed greater periodic maintenance than stone walls, particularly if they were thrown together ("tossed"), as were the majority of both stone walls and stone fences. Most stone walls and fences were dry-laid (no mortar). Mortar (wet-laid) was generally reserved for walls and fences in urban and suburban areas. Although there is a difference between wall and fence, for the sake of expediency, the terms are often used interchangeably (including in this book) unless referring to retaining walls (Figure 7.2). Retaining walls hold in the earth on one side and do not have open air on both sides as do fences.

About three feet is high enough for comfortably lifting large stones; after that, a ramp or lifting device becomes necessary. But the stone wall could be increased by other means. Compound fences are made of wood and stone: a stone wall could be raised to a fence by adding wood poles and rails (and later, barbed wire), a quick way to provide more containment or protection for horses or cows. In other cases where there was an abundance of rocks surfacing—cleared land increased soil dynamics, making it seem as if the land was growing rocks—the walls were gradu-

Figure 7.2. *Retaining wall at the base of a bridge. This retaining wall has granite blocks along the top, reused from either an earlier bridge on this site or from somewhere else. We can infer the reuse because the stone has 19th-century drill marks that are not associated with later 20th-century bridge construction, but do reflect timeless New England thriftiness.*

ally increased through the years even if the height was already sufficient. You might suspect this to be true if you observe one or more of the following: the fence seems unusually tall, the fence contains large stones at the top as well as at the base, or if the surrounding land seems to have been formerly used as cropland.

Stone fences were built in New England as early as the 1600s, though most were built in the 18th and 19th centuries—mostly between 1750 and 1850. Writing for the 19th-century farmer in America, Periam stated: "Fencing with stone walls is not to be advised in any case, except when it is absolutely necessary to remove the stones from the land."[158] In describing how to build stone walls, he further cautions the reader that these walls use up too much valuable space, occupying even more land than the zigzag (or Virginia) fence, and that they promote the growth of unwanted plants. But Periam knew how much stone we have in New England. Building with stone was a practical necessity because it helped clear the land and it provided permanence. Interestingly, this permanence is achieved in part by the mobility of stone—dry-laid walls and fences are flexible; they shift with the frost and the warmth, responding to the pulls of land and weather.

Practical farmers in a hurry may have just thrown stone together, but some stone walls have been built with great skill, becoming an art form. A classic New England saying is, "I don't know who built this, but I can tell what kind of a person he was." When not at the nation's capital, a typical day for founding father John Adams began with work on his stone walls, saying in a letter to Benjamin Rush, "I call for my leavers and iron bars, for my chisels, drills, and wedges to split rock."[159]

An appreciation for stone is timeless. In 1971, I worked as a stone carrier for a man who learned his stone wall building technique as part of the Civilian Conservation Corps work relief program of the 1930s. He had been offered the chance to apprentice with brick but preferred stone because no two were alike. Some 40 years after working almost every day in stone, he said he had still not seen the same stone twice and that he never would.[160]

Stone walls around pastures tend to have large rocks—the farmers would not bother clearing the smaller stones like they would need to do in making cropland. Pastures were large areas, and building a wall around them was a major enterprise, so the goal was a quick and sturdy boundary. Stone sledges or "boats" were used to drag the large rocks to the edges. If the land was too rocky or steep for crops, it could always be used for pasture, especially if the animals were sheep. As much as possible, the farmer would incorporate existing rock ledges into the wall— the goal being to keep sheep and cattle from straying into other people's cropland and gardens, not necessarily to follow property boundaries. If the wall was built primarily to get rid of stone, it would tend to be low and wide.

As previously noted, the area left open between two ends of a stone wall was called a barway. Rails (bars) or a simple wooden gate could be installed between the ends of the wall. A pasture could be completely enclosed, but it would still need a barway to allow entry of the cows. This opening might not be as big as one needed for wagon access, but it would need to be easily opened and closed.

Any wall ends had to have larger stones to buttress them. A wide opening would be made if access to a hayfield was needed—so the wagons could fit through—or it might indicate the entrance where a main house or a barn might have stood. Smaller barways would be sufficient for animal pens, logging road access, cow paths, vegetable gardens, and other areas that did not need wagon access. If the farmer anticipated never using the barway again—perhaps because the trees were removed and the land converted—the barway area might be filled in with stone (Figure 7.3).

Stone walls sometimes had iron rings inserted to hold the reins for horses. These rings can be seen in urban areas, cemeteries, at commercial sites, and in sections of the wall near the farmhouse or barn. The rings might be pounded into holes drilled in large capstones set on top of the wall, or they may be placed in stones incorporated into the wall. If the iron ring has deteriorated and fallen off, the pin may still be there, or at least you will see staining in the old hole (Figure 7.4). The stone with the ring in it would need to be either a vertical post embed-

Figure 7.3. *The barway in this stone wall has been partially filled in because some change in land use meant there was no longer a need for a logging road or other route through the wall. If trees have sprung up on either side of the barway, you can make an approximation of when it was last used.*

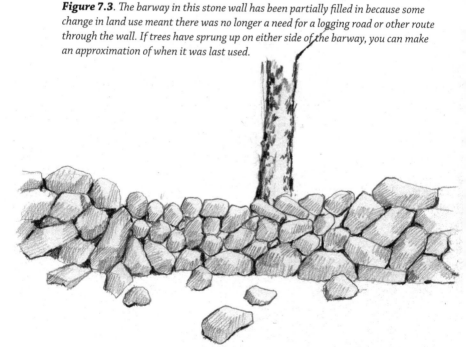

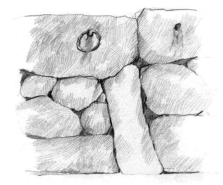

Figure 7.4. *Iron ring in stone wall. Used for tying up horses, the ring was a necessity or at least an expected courtesy. A rust-stained hole may be all that is left. The stone would be large enough to resist the pull of a horse.*

ded in the ground or a large anchoring block of several hundred or more pounds.

Sometimes the stone wall at the farmyard was incorporated into a barn foundation. This was a particularly useful strategy in hilly areas. If the barn is gone, this incorporation can be inferred from the presence of vertical columns of large stones in either end of the foundation where the barn walls would have rested (Figure 7.5). If the walls are gone and just the foundation remains, you may be able to see stones protruding from the sides, indicating where the walls were attached.

If the stone wall was replaced with a barbed-wire fence, or if it bordered a road that was to be widened, any stones in the way would typically be removed and used elsewhere on the farm or sold as a crop to help the farmer cope with rough times. In the late 1800s and before the post–World War II rediscovery of the use of stone walls in landscaping,

Figure 7.5. *Barn foundation incorporated into a stone wall. The corner edges of the barn are supported by a sturdy column of stone.*

the road crew or farmer might even bury an entire row of stones to get them out of the way. This also had the advantage of controlling or directing the drainage of a field. And if the stones were deep enough, the soil on top could be farmed. Over generations, though, frost heaves might bring the stones back to the surface.

The Single Wall

Stone walls are built following the one-over-two/two-over-one rule, which ensured that there would not be more than one layer of common joints in a vertical line between rows. This is the same rule that governs how most brick walls are laid, and increases the strength and stability of the wall. Farmers liked the single-stack wall, also called a "single wall" or "farmer wall" (Figure 7.6). It was basic and quicker to build than double-wall or other forms and was a sufficient deterrent for most herd animals. The farmers had to check perimeters anyway, so they could readily patch up the occasional tumbled-down rock. The single wall varies in thickness from a foot or so at the top to several feet wide at the base, and can be three to five feet tall. On steep slopes with exposed bedrock, the wall is usually blended into any available ledge, which saved work.

A single-stack wall that shows a lot of daylight is called a "lace wall." It might look rickety, but this is deceptive—careful placement of rocks made such walls statements of craft. Itinerant builders might be responsible, perhaps newly emigrated Irish or Welsh wandering the countryside working for food and a place to sleep.[161] The farmers themselves were more likely to throw together quicker, less artistic walls, figuring they could re-dress them during annual fence surveys before the animals were turned out to spring pastures. Enslaved people of African and Native ancestry and free or indentured laborers who were people of color also built stone walls.[162]

A sturdy, thick wall is what you want if you have a grand entrance to the barnyard at a successful farm, or for a town animal pound (discussed later in this chapter), which was used to accommodate stray animals until they could be claimed. Proper containment of animals was serious busi-

Plate 1. *At the center is an old open-growth maple, now almost completely obscured by the emergent woods that surround it.*

Plate 2. *The shapes of a pasture oak (above) and an elm (right) are quite distinctive.*

Plate 3. *The familiar lilac is a hardy survivor that often marks the former site of a home.*

Plate 4. *Another telltale sign of a long-gone house: steps to nowhere.*

Plate 5. *Although subtle, the lines in the grass mark the location of a 1900s house, the foundation of which was filled in years ago.*

Plate 6. *These stones are part of a nineteenth-century house foundation on the Isle of Shoals.*

Plate 7. *An old telegraph pole is nearly disguised by living trees.*

Plate 8. *What appear to be brown logs are actually the ties of an old railway bed.*

Plate 9. *More evidence of a long-departed railway can be found in this structure.*

Plate 10. *Three types of fencing—stone, wood, and wire—are visible at this location.*

Plate 11. *This tree grew around the barbed wire fence.*

Plate 12. *Barbed-wire was an inexpensive and effective fencing material that can be stumbled upon in unexpected places.*

Plate 13. *It's taken 50 years, but this tree has begun swallowing up the remnants of this stone wall.*

Plate 14. *These rock piles are what remains of an animal pound in Buxton, Maine.*

Plate 15. *What at first glance seems to be a trash dump is a stream bulwark constructed of old tires in the mid-twentieth century.*

Plate 16. *A wrought-iron fence poses no barrier to a growing tree.*

Figure 7.6. *Single-stack "lace" stone wall. This type of construction would not be tall enough to be a fence because it has independently perched rocks that are a single layer of thickness—you can see daylight between the stones, and it may even seem delicate. A tall fence needs more stone width at the bottom, which allows it to taper toward the top (about two inches for every foot in height) and thereby be stable. The large boulders would be at the bottom, and smaller stones would be independently laid on top. It took skill to lay up the wall, and it required maintenance, but it was efficient, and a well-built stone wall of this type can remain standing for a surprising length of time. If you see one of these, most likely it was built by a farmer to contain disciplined sheep or cattle. Seeing daylight though the fence, the animal might not trust it as safe to climb over. But it would not suffice for a "breachy cow," according to the Farmer's Almanac.*

ness. In one day, a loose, unruly pig, sheep, or cow could easily destroy the garden a family might need to get through the winter.

The Double-Wall Fence

A double-wall fence is an impressive structure having two separate walls built parallel to each other (Figure 7.7). The interior contains excess smaller stones. If there is no separate placement of inside stones, and if the walls are tied together with large stones placed perpendicular to the front ("through stones"), it is probably a thick single-wall and not a true double-wall. Anything might be in the rubble between the two walls if built on a reclaimed site. The double-wall filled with rubble will not be nearly as strong and durable as the single-wall of the same thickness. A double-wall is more likely to exist where two plowed fields were divided because there was probably twice the amount of stone to be removed from the plow zones.

Figure 7.7. *This double-wall fence was a durable boundary to a 19th-century cow lane that connected the barn and the stony pastures. Both sides of the lane contained fields and cropland, so there was a need to get rid of lots of stones, which filled in between the double walls. The soil buildup on the uphill side reflects erosion from active upland use—probably animals were on both side of this fence. The slight change in the nature of construction in the central part of this fence suggests that it was repaired sometime after its construction. It takes about a generation for the lichen and other growth on the repaired section to match the original, but the change in the actual stone placement pattern is permanent.*

Wire Fences

Wire fences were not used in northern New England until the advent of barbed wire and the demise of ready sources of wood for rail fencing. Barbed wire was patented in the early 1870s and quickly found its way into New England pastures soon after.[163] A barbed-wire fence took less wood than rail fencing, was faster to build and easier to maintain than stone walls, and took up less space. If trees were available, that is where the wire would go. Pieces of barbed wire are often found growing out of the trees on which they were hung, and remnant pieces can be found lying on the ground between the trees. After the wire is gone, circular

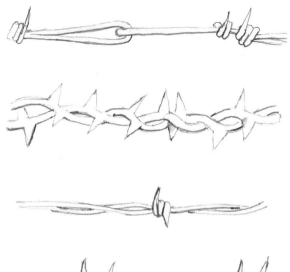

Figure 7.8. *Barbed wire from Rutland County, Vermont.[165] From top to bottom: Crandal's Link Compound, 1881; Crandal's Zigzag, 1879; Schutt's Plate Arrow Point,1876; and Allis's Buckthorn, 1881. These examples include those collected by Jim Philbrook, retired County Forester; you may see other types of wire in the woods, as well.*

bark scars on either side of the tree where the wire hung may still be visible, looking like a small branch bark cover or a closed tap hole.

Certain types of wire were in vogue during particular times (see Figure 7.8). Another way to date the wire is to estimate the age of any trees that might have grown around the wire after it was attached. Old farm records, day books, and store ledgers may detail purchase or use of fencing materials. *(Plates 10–13)*

The Compound Fence

A compound fence has multiple components, some of which may still be visible. Many compound fences are a combination of stone and wood. A popular technique was to cross poles over a stone wall, with a pole base on either side, then set a rail on top of that, making a "crotch" fence. The stone wall portion of this compound fence would endure long after the poles had rotted away, making it hard to tell if the wall was originally a compound fence. However, if there is a low wall and the land was formerly pasture or cropland, most likely a compound fence existed or a double fence—with barbed wire on poles next to the original stone wall.

By the time people got around to putting up barbed wire, many property boundaries and pastures had already been delineated by other fence systems. You might discover the remains of multiple layers of fences. The wire might have been added to posts that replaced an old rail fence or to augment a tumbled stone wall (see Figure 7.9).

Figure 7.9. *This property boundary shows a fence line along former pasture. The tree size and placement suggest the pasture has been abandoned for 50 years or more. Here you can see a succession of fences and the result is a compound fence. The farmer most likely started with stumps or poles. This site is from an 18th-century farm, so probably by the early 19th century, the original fence would have been replaced by the stone wall. On top of the stone wall there would have been poles and rails to raise the barrier where it would have been cumbersome to get that much stone up higher. After a while, the farmer added a barbed-wire fence. The barbed wire is classic twisted-strand wire in use after the Civil War and still available today. Nailed to a small tree, the barbed wire has been engulfed by it. Eventually, the tree died, and now has the wire running through its heart. Another fence system exists—a later one than the barbed wire, because it has single-strand wire on poles, probably added to augment the deteriorating barbed wire. A final fence system exists here, too—the line of trees. On the outer side of the fence, away from the pasture, the vegetation and protection let trees sprout up and they followed the fence line.*

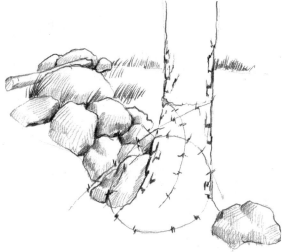

Stone Posts

Stone posts were harder to get and more expensive than wood posts, so they were used for special purposes—gateways perhaps, or to provide a sense of purpose and endurance near the house, cemetery, or property boundary. Occasionally, you can see an entire fence made of stone posts, usually granite (Figure 7.10). Fasteners might have been placed in the post through which wooden or iron poles might bar a gateway, or an iron ring may have been inserted to create a hitching post. Stone posts might be near the barn, serving as gate posts for access to the cow path.

Figure 7.10. *Stone fence post, made from granite. The original owner might have had access to a quarry or gotten a good deal on quarry remnants. There would have been wooden rails or poles connecting the posts. Once one post is taken down by looters ("igneous larceny," as builder/artist Kevin Gardner calls it[164]) or recycled, the others soon follow.*

Cairns

In addition to farmers' piles of stones made to clear agricultural fields or build stone walls, you may find stone monuments, or cairns. Vermont has over a hundred and fifty of them[165]—ranging from 30- by 15-foot structures to six-foot-tall dry-laid structures. Other New England states have their share, too.[166] Some are very basic—a stone on top of a rock on top of a boulder. Some are on the hills, and some are visible in rivers during low-flow conditions. There has been much speculation about the origins of cairns. Surveyors may have established them at property corners if there were no handy trees or other potential markers. Remains of shallow-river fishing weirs might include piles of stone. Artists and others have whimsically piled them. The New England Antiquities Research Association (NEARA, http://www.neara.org/) and Nativestones.com http://www.nativestones.com/cairns.htm have websites and organizations that document structures and explore the possible origins. Some stone features in the southern Appalachians are yielding pre-contact artifacts and human burials, making it interesting to speculate on similarities. See also the section "Root Cellars and Stone Enclosures" in Chapter 4.

Animal Pounds

The cheapest and easiest way to keep animals was off on an island or up in the hills. Or just let them roam about the grounds. However, once there was any kind of settlement density, or any concern about predators, something more had to be done. "Horse-high, bull-strong, and hog-tight," goes the old saying about fences.[167] It made sense to keep animals in impoundments and behind fences. Animals represented a valuable investment by the farmer, but they could cause damage to crops and property—one pig and one evening and a garden is no more. And animals infected with foot-rot or scab could spread disease. The town pound was a rectangular enclosure or pen (Maine does have one *round* pound, in Jefferson) with dry-laid stone walls and a gate. The enclosed area of a town pound is larger than typical houses of the time period, and the stones are larger boulders than those found in houses. *(Plate 14)*

A public pound was an important item in colonial America, and many communities put them up pretty quickly, but also solidly. Originally, they might have been built of wood or stone topped with wood, but it was desirable to get them converted into all stone. Those sturdy, usually chest-high granite walls could make a statement about the town's prosperity, encouraging further settlement, and they would prevent destruction from escaped and hungry animals. Fees were charged for corralling loose animals, and a portion went to the pound-keeper.

Pounds were also built by soldiers along the military roads in the 18th and early 19th centuries, and local farmers put them to good use when they were no longer needed by the militia or army. The Crown Point Military Road in Vermont had stone pounds, and the remnants of one may be visible north of Rutland.

Mary and James Gagne's Stone Structures website at http://www.

stonestructures.org/html/town_pounds.html contains photographs and other documentation about town pounds. They list some pound sites for New Hampshire and Massachusetts, and one in Maine (as of 2013). Table 7.1 shows the Maine Historic Preservation Commission's inventory of town pounds in Maine; primarily these are cattle pounds, which became particularly important with the rise of the milk market and the associated increase in numbers of cows.

Farmers sometimes had their own animal pounds for use as night pens or barnyard walls. The enclosed area around the barn was where the animals could be separated according to species (horse, cattle, and sheep), age (yearlings, heifers, calves, and lambs), gender, or health. The night pen was also where animals could be brought close to the house and protected from predators—particularly important during the birthing times.

The farmer's hog pen would have to be heavy stone or boards. These animals could destroy rail fences and plow through wire fences. They would chew up the boards and get their noses in between to pry them up, too, if they were not properly fed and entertained. Some farmers would put their piglets in a walled garden space, getting more effective soil churning than we do now with a rototiller, and with the added benefit of automatic fertilizing. After the pigs were harvested, the garden would over-winter, then be ready for vegetable planting.

Now that we have addressed stone walls, fences, and other enclosures in the landscape, in the next chapter we will deal with another form of enclosure—water. New England states are rich in surface waters that served farms and industry, and the landscape contains the remains of a history of interactions.

List of Maine Cattle Pounds

Table 7.1. *Conditions of these public animal containment pounds range from ruins to excellent. Some of the pounds are now on private property, and permission should be sought to visit them. The pounds were documented and photographed by Geraldine Thompson (The Town Pounds of Maine), by William and Elizabeth Huntington of Dover-Foxcroft, Maine, or by Maine Historic Preservation Commission staff. (List courtesy of Christi Mitchell, Architectural Historian, Maine Historic Preservation Commission; Buxton pound added by the author—and there are still other pounds out there to be discovered.)*

Town (estimated date of pound)	**Location**
Acton (1831)	East side of Milton Mills Road, South Acton, Route 109.
Albany (c. 1825)	From Bethel, heading south, at junction 5 and 35 (at Town House), take left onto Hunt's Corner Road, head southeast toward Hunt's Corner. At about ¼ mile from the junction on the left next to the road on the east side is the cattle pound.
Alexander	On Cooper's Road off Route 9, left-hand side of road
Alfred	(no location given)
Bethel	From Bethel heading toward Lock Mills (E&W), after the Locke Mills/East Bethel Road on the left, take the next road on the left (Bird Hill Road, now known perhaps as Kimball Hill). At the cemetery, on the left side of the road, is the cattle pound.
Bristol Mills	Route 130
Brooklin	Roadside Route 175 on the left side coming from Blue Hill.
Buxton (c. 1820)	West side of Route 112, about 5 miles from Saco. Inventoried by Nathan Hamilton and the author.

Casco	Latitude & longitude provided by Geraldine Thompson in The Town Pounds of Maine.
Charlotte (1826)	Charlotte Road, ¼ mile off Route 214; cedar logs (Washington County).
Cornish	Take High Street; go past Old Limington Road; puts you on Pound Road.
Deer Isle	On Route 15 to Deer Isle, in village, right side of road across from cemetery.
Durham (1821)	Pound Road
East Corinth	Off Route 15 coming from Bangor, turn left on West Corinth. Pound is just to right after the house on corner.
Edgecomb	Old County Road, just west of intersection with Mt. Hunger Road. Located on private property.
Eliot	Between mailboxes 222 and 224, Goodwin Road (East Eliot); north side of road, 0.3 miles from junction with Depot Road; partial remains.
Falmouth	Hillside Road
Garland	Partial remains about 300 feet down Center Road coming from Garland Village, on right side.
Gorham	Location given as "Near old town green?"
Greenwood	East side of Twitchell Pond Road, 2 miles north of western terminus of Route 219.
Harrison	(no location given)
Harpswell	Harpswell Neck, Harpswell Center, east side of Route 123.
Hartford	(no location given)
Jay	Intersection of Old Jay Hill Road and Macomber Hill Road. On private property.

Jefferson (1829)	Route 126, about 0.3 miles west of the junction with Route 213, on south side of road.
Kittery	Near 117 Haley Road.
Lebanon (1813)	Center Road, 0.2 miles, beside Congregational Church (west side of road)
Lyman	(no location given)
Minot	2 Death Valley Road.
Monroe (1800s)	From junction 139 and 141, heading toward Brooks, go 1½ to 2 miles; at southwest corner of Route 139 and Monroe Center Road, near a tiny brook, about 40 to 50 feet from road. Area is overgrown and lots of trees; still some stones and can make out outline of walls.
Mt. Vernon	(no location given)
Whitefield	At junction of Route 126 and Cooper Road, across from St. Denis Church. Partially buried by road realignment.
Norway	In the woods off Old County Road, North Norway. Route 118 west, then take Morrill Road. Pound is on right just before steep hill.
Orrington (1807)	Route 15, west side of road, 0.6 miles north of Orrington Center, near power transmission line, just south of the railroad tracks; near a small war memorial; rebuilt/cemented.
Otisfield	Bell Hill Road, approx. ½ mile north of Bell Hill Meetinghouse, on west side of road. Take Route 121 south from Route 26, then take Bell Hill Road.
Paris	Paris Hill; by the green, near the old jail.
Parsonsfield (1785)	Middle Road, about 1 mile west of old store. On north side of road, marked.
Pittston	Off Route 194, on left side of Warren Road.

Porter (1825)	Just east of junction Old County Road and Colcord Pond Road. Routes 25/160, South Colcord Pond Road. Turn right. Old Meeting House Road. Pound is just to right.
Pownal	Route 9, Bradbury Mountain State Park, west side of road.
Sedgwick (1821)	Route 172 and Old County Road. Pound is on corner, right-hand side coming down from Blue Hill.
Shapleigh (1790)	Take Hooper Road 1½ miles, turn right on Simon Ricker Road and the pound is just on the left as you turn onto Simon Ricker.
South Bristol	Rote Farm in Walpole.
Sweden	Next to Meetinghouse.
Turner	Intersection of General Turner Hill and Kennebec Trail. Route 219 West, left on Plains Road, goes into General Turner Hill Road. Pound is on right side, across from Bradford Road.
Union	Near original meetinghouse, located off the NE corner of the Commons. Or: From Union on Route 17 west turn Right on Pound Road, ½ mile on left.
Vienna	Traveling west on Route 41, right side of road, 50 feet into woods. Has parts of four sides.
Waldoboro (1819)	Ossipee Hill Road (north side of road), ½ mile west of Route 5.
Waterboro (1824)	(no location given)
Westport Island	Route 144, corner of Spruce Lane.
Weld	Traveling on Route 142 north at Webb Corner, turn left. About 1,000 feet on right, roadside.
Woodstock	(no location given)

8

Water

I hear their scythes cronching[168] the coarse weeds by the river's brink.
—Henry David Thoreau

Always drink upstream from the herd.
—Old farmer's saying

Significant changes in the landscape occurred long before human settlement, and sometimes you can see evidence of this environmental history. For example, if you peer into the water at the Wells National Estuarine Research Reserve in southern Maine, you might be able to see cedar trees from thousands of years ago—the channel has cut through a submerged 4,000-year-old forest bed in a river near the coast. Ancient buried or submerged wood from hardy species can persist for a surprisingly long time under the right circumstances. Old forests get covered up by geological and meteorological events. Rivers are dynamic places. Shifting riverbeds expose clay deposits and other evidence of a different paleo-environment as well as more recent features. Large lakes and rivers may hold submerged logs[169] left over from lumber drives—some of these logs and sawn timbers may be visible in the rivers during low-flow times.

Log drives, dams, canals, beavers, landslides, and flooding all can change the course of rivers. Human changes to the watershed, the coastline, and streambeds may have left a physical record that can be discovered without disturbing the ground—merely by looking.

River, Pond, and Stream Alterations

Aside from weather events and the beavers, for centuries little happened to change the course of surface waters. Native Americans traveled in and along rivers. They built fishing weirs of stone or wood at outlets and in streams, but did little else to change rivers and streams. However, as the nomadic lifestyle gave way to settlements with the advent of agriculture, they placed villages along water corridors, altering the banks and growing food in floodplains. Their preferred agricultural sites were sandy loams and alluvial river plains.[170] The first European settlements in the New World were along the coast and along river corridors, many at the sites of former Indian villages depopulated by smallpox—the epidemic of 1616–1618 cleared many native villages, and there had been waves of epidemics throughout previous (and subsequent) centuries. But riparian landscapes continued to develop. Rivers and streams were altered to accommodate the building of mills, canals, roads, bridges, and railroad tracks. Towns developed around original sawmill sites. The ice trade was launched in the early 1800s by Frederic Tudor,[171] and the era shortly after the Civil War saw a growth in the ice industry. The lifeblood of quite a few townships in 19th-century northern New England was ice and timber. Hundreds of ice ponds were created from impoundments. Many local farmers put up dams so they could make and sell ice. The remnants of most of these dams still exist in some form or another, incorporated into the landscape and permanently changing the watershed drainage patterns. *(Plate 15)*

Canal-building subscription companies were popular in the 18th and early 19th centuries. Canals were constructed with raceways and

locks interconnecting with rivers. Thousands of tons of goods were
shipped annually on canals in northern New England until the railroads
made them obsolete in the middle to late 1800s. The operation of canals
required a managed water supply, as did the generation of power for
sawmills, granaries, and other rural industry. Most states conducted
mid-19th-century power inventories as part of increasing production
for the Civil War or to promote commerce. For example, the *Provisional
Report upon the Water-Power of Maine* provided a description of all known
dams and head-falls, sites of potential power generation for watercourses
in the state (Wells, 1868).

Post–Civil War–era photographs show giant rafts of lumber and
steam-driven sawmills. Even if the route of a river or stream was not
changed, the log drives scoured the banks, affecting vegetation and con-
tributing to erosion. The end of the 19th century saw a shift to pulpwood
and an increase in paper mills. The demand for pulpwood grew after
World War I,[172] though trucks became a favored mode of transport. The
four-foot sections of cordwood used in the pulp industry were smaller
and easier to transport than tree-length logs, whether by river or road.
The logging drives on rivers ended in the mid-1970s, but left lasting
effects. These historical drives left layers of logs in many riverbanks.
In areas along the Presumpscot River in Maine, there are six-foot-deep
buildups of logs in meandering siltation areas below sections of falls.
Giant old log butts may occasionally be seen protruding from riverbeds
where sedimentation made it unprofitable to retrieve them. Slab wood
also escaped downriver from the sawmills and became lodged in mud at
the edges of main flow paths in the river.

Some river channels were widened by the log drives. Old log landing areas may be discernible as flat earthen platforms near the river.
In Berlin, New Hampshire, the pilings that still stand in the river were
attached to a network of floating logs that directed saw logs from the
upstream woods to the mills. Many small dams were built to help provide
enough spring-season runoff water to float the logs to the mill. Some of
these dams are still in place. In addition to "reading" the landscape, old
maps can help identify changes in surface waters—the dams caused new
ponds to appear, large rivers to shrink, and small streams to increase.

Identifying Signs of the Past in the Water

Rivers and other bodies of water store information. Look into the water at any bridge crossing and you may see the remains of previous bridges— old piers, granite blocks, or slabs of concrete. Some signs are more subtle. Ceramics and other things left in the river may suggest whether houses and other structures were there or whether the site was just used for a little illicit dumping. Broken plates, cups, and other ceramics tend to show up well if the water is clear, and will be a common view for water-front property that has been settled for quite some time. If you find old trademarks on the bottoms, you can look those up on the Internet to get dates of manufacture.[173] You can pick the ceramic out of the water, take a digital photograph of the trademark or pattern, and put it back. Or if there are modern ceramics, glass, or trash in the water, and it is safe to get them, take some with you and leave the place looking a little better.

Diversions and Ponds

Surface waters were sources for power and for storage. Streams were diverted as a result of railway construction, for mill races, and for other development. Some streams were backed up to create ice ponds or to power millworks. Hundreds of small dams have become integrated into the land-scape, permanently altering adjacent watercourses. Stonework on the face of a dam may indicate the period in which it was constructed (Figure 8.1).

Some farmers started with riparian or floodplain fields originally cleared by Native Americans, or in old beaver meadows, but soon found it to their advantage to control the water and keep the land workable. Railroad corporations, mill owners, and others also sought control of storm water and flowage. Drainage ditches (swales) were dug to manage the flow of water on farmland, and many of these can still be seen. But not all attempts to drain land are so visible. Rows of stone or tile could be buried underground to intercept and direct water flow. No evidence of these "French drains" would remain today other than the existence

Figure 8.1. *Small impoundment in the woods. The 19th-century builder used old stone from local quarries. The stone was probably available cheap because it had been rejected for higher use in building foundations and other architecture. New England has many such impoundment structures from ice-pond creation, mill dams, logging, and other past uses.*

of a still well-drained field. In Europe, the Romans used such drains a thousand years ago, and some of them are still working today. Thomas Jefferson noted, ". . . of labor on the large scale I think there is no remain as respectable as would be a common ditch for the draining of lands . . ."[174]

In addition to changing fields with drainage ditches, people changed the course of rivers and streams if it was to the advantage of the farm or business. One use of the river that did not require diversion was as

Figure 8.2. *Stone weir discernible as V-shaped pattern in the water. This weir is probably from the 19th century but could be much older. Abundant stone and the absence of mud meant that a stone weir was the most practical structure—and the most likely to survive the ravages of time and current.*

a source of food. A fishing weir could be set up in the river or stream to control the flow of fish within the water. Once set up, a weir could be left alone and functioning for many years. Weirs were used by indigenous peoples as well as early settlers. The locations of early weirs were often in areas of dynamic water flow that later served as sites for dams and crossings that resulted in destruction of the weir, but in small streams and undeveloped sites, it may be possible to detect the remnants of the weir (Figure 8.2). If the river bottom was muddy, sticks alone could be used. Otherwise, there could be a combination of wood and stone, or the weir could be made entirely of stone.

Bridges and River Crossings

In older times there were more bridges than we have today. People were more likely to build small bridges right where they needed them as part

Figure 8.3. *Former bridge abutment grown into a little island. Trees suggest a firm footing, which would be necessary for a stable bridge. This example is on the Presumpscot River in Maine.*

of rural industry or agriculture. Later, centralized transportation corridors and the decline of small cottage industries, together with increased regulations and safety concerns, led to the abandonment of many of these small bridges and the consolidation of crossings. Often the wood was salvaged and used elsewhere, leaving little behind. New England had a variety of different types of bridges—stone arch, wooden covered bridges, steel truss, concrete arch, and simple span bridges to name a few. There were many engineers making local designs, and some designs were named after them and used elsewhere in the country.

But what if the bridge is no longer there? How can we tell if there even was a bridge? Large bridge supports can be easily interpreted, but some of the smaller ones might just look like small humps or mounds at or below the surface level of the water. Figure 8.3 shows what a small

Figure 8.4. *Small bridge header constructed in the early 19th century out of dry-laid stone. This header is likely the work of a local farmer or sawyer who needed access across the stream. The road and bridge are long gone, and trees have grown up on top of the header.*

bridge abutment might look like a hundred or more years after the bridge has been removed. The stones and boulders have held the base together and trees have become established on top, making it look like a tiny island.[175] The regular shape and high profile provide a contrast from the surroundings. Under either end of the bridge, there might be a header wall (Figure 8.4).

Railroad bridges would span the river at whatever angle would keep the tracks straight. Therefore suspect a railroad bridge if you see remains of old bridge materials that lie in the river diagonally or if you see abutments that are not opposite each other on the sides of the river. (Canals would cross in this manner, too, but there were far fewer of them.) Road and foot bridges would only cross the water at a right angle, reducing the length of the span. The remains of former bridges can often be seen in the waters under the bridge location. If the abutments were solid blocks of stone, they may have been incorporated into a new bridge design. Newer road bridges can afford a diagonal crossing if necessary to soften the curve and accommodate faster traffic. Look for the remains of older bridge crossings within the curve at a sharper approach to the river.

Covered bridges are often of particular interest, but New England has historic bridges of all types. If researching bridge histories for Vermont, consult Robert McCullough's *Crossings: A History of Bridges in Vermont*, published by the Vermont Historical Society (2005). Each state has inventoried its historic bridges. These lists are available on the Internet. For example, the Massachusetts Department of Transportation maintains its list at http://www.mhd.state.ma.us/default. asp?pgid=content/environ/brhist&sid=about. A listing of covered bridges in New Hampshire, with photographs and descriptions, is given at http:// www.nh.gov/nhdhr/bridges/. Information about Maine's historic bridges is provided by the Maine Department of Transportation at http://www. maine.gov/mdot/historicbridges/index.htm. *Maine's Covered Bridges* is an assembly of photographs in the *Images of America* book series of historical photos, by Joseph D. Conwill (2003), also the author of *Vermont Covered Bridges* (2004). A list of Massachusetts covered bridges can be found at http://www.dalejtravis.com/cblist/cbma.htm. Glenn A. Knoblock authored *New Hampshire Covered Bridges* (2002). Broader coverage is achieved in Evans and Evans, *New England's Covered Bridges: A Complete Guide* (University Press of New England, Lebanon, NH, 2004). Covered bridge aficionados Hank and Marlee Bickel maintain a website with links to various state covered bridge societies and documentation, including Maine, Massachusetts, New Hampshire, and Vermont (http:// www.coveredbridgesite.com/index.html). Another covered bridge enthusiast, James Walsh, has documented and mapped bridges in the entire United States and parts of Canada (http://www.coveredbridgemap.com/).

Covered bridges are perhaps the most visible and nostalgic images, but river crossings were more often fords or simple footpaths, or even

Figure 8.5. *This simple pile of stone indicates where a pulley system stood a century ago. The stone is from several sources—local rock, plus a secondary (discarded) piece of pink granite, probably left behind at a quarry and transported here for use as an anchor. Look for a stone pile on the opposite bank. The pulley system was a quick way to deliver supplies to a work site or grain to the mill.*

just a haul line to pull materials across (Figure 8.5), perhaps paralleling the footbridge or crossing. Certainly, there were many more different types of river crossings than we have now.

Fords

Some farm roads and minor secondary roads went right across shallow seasonal streams or wide, flat rivers where the cost of a bridge was not warranted for infrequent use. The farmer would be more likely to need these roads in the summer when the water flow was lowest, so he was not bothered by the lack of a bridge. These fords worked best when the streambed consisted of packed gravel or larger stones, but not boulders. If the water was too flooded for horse and carriage, you had to wait or find a shallower spot. If increased settlement led to the need for a bridge, one would be built, but even today you can see the remains of old roads

Figure 8.6. *Ford in central Vermont. The cobble river bottom makes it a bouncy but durable crossing site. Once used by the farmer to reach different fields on fertile river-valley soil, it now entices the occasional off-road recreational vehicle.*

that simply used fords. From a distance, look for the opening in the trees. Some good examples can be seen heading south from Bethel on Route 14 in Vermont (Figure 8.6). Several roads on the right head to the river, then scoot through it. The Saco River in the Fryeburg area of Maine has many old crossings. More examples exist on lowlands and glacial outwashes in all three northern New England states.

Ferries

Ferries were built to cross deep or fast-current rivers that could not be forded and were too wide for a bridge to be readily constructed. If the route was a main road that would take too long to bypass for an upstream or downstream crossing, a ferry landing was built on either side of the river (Figure 8.7). The ferryman, or his animal, would pull the ferry across. Pylons (towers or posts) and footings for ferry crossings may still exist next to the modern bridge. These will be less massive than bridge

Figure 8.7. *Footings for ferry crossing. Ferries were largely used prior to 1820 in northern New England. If large blocks were put together for pylons, and not taken for reuse elsewhere, they may still exist to identify an old ferry site. Small ferries would have just used poles or trees and therefore leave no indication of their existence.*

abutments, and may simply look like the base of a pier or dock, with an anchoring site where the rope would have been attached. By the 1820s, ferries were largely replaced by bridges. The intervening years may have brought many changes, particularly in main travel corridors with several centuries of bridge use, making original ferry locations hard to detect. But local histories and maps may provide clues.

Flumes

Flumes are channels constructed to bring in water to power mills and foundries. The term *raceway* is often used interchangeably with flume. Flumes were also built to expedite the removal of trees down mountains

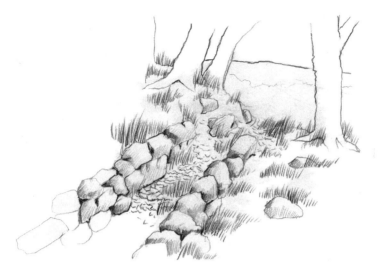

Figure 8.8. *Narrow raceway or flume for sawmill, built by hand from stone. The raceway was designed to provide a source of water to run the mill even when the water level dropped in late summer.*

where water was available and the more traditional means of moving trees were not possible. A natural watercourse might be narrowed and redirected. Figure 8.8 shows a flume for a 19th-century sawmill. These structures only survive in small, out-of-the-way streams, and are signs a mill was once there.

Culverts

Culverts were used on old logging trails, farm roads, turnpikes, highways, town roads, canals, and railroads. Culverts were used for water channels under roads and as outlets for some mill and canal systems. A stone culvert consists of abutments capped by large, flat rocks. The top of the culvert will be covered with gravel and dirt, then the road itself. Stone arch supports provided structure above culverts for railroad tracks. Later, concrete was used, but usually the stone arches endured as long-term culvert systems for tracks built from Civil War times to the early 1900s. Stone-roofed culverts with dry-laid walls made the best, longest-lasting

Figure 8.9. *Culverts like this 19th-century dry-laid example were hand-built in the early 20th century by CCC workers as part of Roosevelt's New Deal to help the country get back on its feet from the Great Depression. The local rock split readily into long slabs and the road went across the top.*

culverts. During the Great Depression, Civilian Conservation Corps crews built many of these dry-laid stone culvert headers in rural roads (Figure 8.9). Sturdy enough to still work fine today, they could give and take with the frost, not crack like wet (mortar) construction, and still retain their load-bearing ability. If the culvert was no longer needed, the header stones were often "borrowed" for other purposes.

Metal culverts gradually replaced stone culverts in the 20th century. But as town roads became abandoned, erosion and lack of maintenance may have caused the old metal culverts to stick out of the ground. They will not last as long as stone culverts will.

The New England states value the sturdy construction and features of their old culverts, and each provides for their assessment when reviewing the effects of proposed construction and road repair. Most states include historic culverts as part of their bridge inventory. New Hampshire has on its website an interesting publication on stone culverts: http://www.nh.gov/dot/org/projectdevelopment/environment/documents/CulvertManagementManual.pdf. Mary and James Gage's Stone Structures is another site with information on culverts: http://www.stonestructures.org/html/culverts.html.

Canals and Towpaths

In many parts of the country, water routes played a key role in getting forest and farm products to market. If there was not a direct river route and if the land was relatively flat, local entrepreneurs evaluated the feasibility of building a canal. Canals were hand-dug channels connecting rivers, lakes, and coastlines with mills, industry, and trade routes.[176] The canal era began in the 1790s and extended until the railroad era that began in the mid-19th century. By late in the 19th century, most canals had been abandoned.

There were canals on or connecting to the Connecticut, Merrimack, Presumpscot, and other rivers. Their towpaths can sometimes be dis-

Figure 8.10. *Towpath segment and submerged canal route visible along the west side of the Presumpscot River in Gorham, Maine. Designated as a Historic Engineering Landmark, and listed on the National Register of Historic Places, the Cumberland and Oxford Canal connected Sebago Lake to Portland. With 26 locks, the canal system was a labor-intensive, 80-mile hand-dug effort. Having the sun behind you makes it easier to pick out the submerged outline of the canal. Other portions of the canal appear above ground as distinctive channels cut through the woods. Look for the canal locks in areas where there is a change in elevation.*

cerned adjacent to the river, and are recognizable by the compacted soils, which reduced tree growth. Any trees that grow between the towpath and the canal would have gotten their start after the canal was abandoned and can be used to estimate how long ago this occurred. Some towpaths became railroad routes or utility-pole line routes. And some became submerged as more dams and flood-control devices were put in rivers to increase power generation.

Until the trains came, canal boats were the best way to haul stone, lumber, and other heavy freight.

Some canals were built in coastal Maine specifically to launch ships, and then were abandoned by the late 1800s. Scarborough Marsh has a good example of a launching canal distinguished by its linear appearance—quite different from the adjacent meandering Dunstan River.

Any significant change in elevation required a canal lock. Originally, these were wooden, but in the later 19th century, granite and cut (dimension) stone was used. Some of the gate materials can still be seen in the canals and off to the side, but most of the wood has rotted away.

Older atlases and historical maps will show canal routes. These may be narrower than you might expect: for example, a Presumpscot canal boat could be 60 feet or more in length, but it was no wider than 10 feet.

Islands

Islands were used as work stations by Native Americans and settlers alike. Islands too small or remote for settlement still had use, particularly for the farmer. They protected livestock from predators and they provided bounded pastures. Sheep could be ferried out to them and kept there, saving the need to build fences or worry about stragglers. After the 19th-century era of sheep herding, young cows—heifers—were more likely to be kept on islands. Hogs were also kept on islands, though they tended to become wild if allowed to reproduce there. The hogs would also root all over the island, and might be put there as part of an intentional effort to break down the vegetation and churn the soil. Goats could do the same thing with less damage to the soil. Poison ivy and other undesirable plants could be kept at bay by the animals. Interpreting the vegetative patterns can help explain the history. Goat or cow paths may still exist. Deer, too, leave paths, and are able to come and go from islands, swimming a mile or more in some cases. Domestic animals can all swim, too, but they will stay where there is food.

Islands in rivers may have had an industrial history, serving as staging areas and manufacturing sites for mills. The flow of water could be regulated on either side of the island, providing power for the mill.

Island place names may give a clue to past usage. Ram Island, Hog Island, Cow Island, Sheep Island, and Goat Island are common names honoring past agrarian use.

Wharfs and Piers

The northern New England states are water-rich, with abundant surface waters. Access to canals and rivers for market transport was useful to the farmer. Water was necessary for the animals and crops. Commonly, a farm would be near a stream or other watercourse. If the surface waters were big enough, the farmer would have a dock of some type for launching a boat to check on the island animals or to transport goods. Since rot-resistant wood was used for the piers to support a dock or wharf, there is a good chance that some piers remain from the last century or two. In coastal areas like Portland, Maine, old piers remain in the Fore River, and in embayments. Piers may also remain from old bridges, footbridges, canals, and other waterside features.

As we come to the end of a series of major landscape features, it is perhaps appropriate that we address the final resting place, the cemetery. Small rural cemeteries provide a permanent local connection between land and people, as discussed in the next chapter.

9

Cemeteries

Thus let me live, unseen, unknown,
  Thus unlamented let me die;
Steal from the world, and not a stone
  Tell where I lie.
—Alexander Pope

The early colonists buried their dead tightly together in village conse-crated ground, but by the end of the 18th century, separate small family plots were equally common. The wide variety of burial sites avail-able included "common" burying grounds, family plots, churchyards, neighborhood cemeteries, "rural" or incorporated cemeteries, military cemeteries, and the unmarked burial grounds of American Indians. Many burial lots have specific orientation on an east–west axis. Some have paired markers (headstone and footstone) and some have family markers. Vinca, oak, yew, and other evergreens are common plantings at burial grounds. Formal cemeteries have manicured trees, trimmed shrub-bery, and neat lawns.

Figure 9.1. *Single grave site in Hubbardton, Vermont. This headstone marks a private cemetery. No fence protects it and no other stones accompany it—just a lone grave in the woods. Such sites are particularly vulnerable to looting. The small trees at the site suggest it has been periodically maintained, probably about every five to ten years.*

Isolation, climate, and the pragmatic nature of New Englanders caused many 18th- and 19th-century farms to have small, private cemeteries on their own land (Figure 9.1). Along river corridors, isolated gravesites might mark the burial of drowned river drivers from the perilous days of the log drives. Crosses or other impromptu markers sometimes document the occurrence of roadside fatalities or other local calamities.

Small cemeteries are powerful sources of information about local properties in old agricultural communities, revealing which families lived in the area. Infectious diseases, accidents, and other calamities can be documented through headstones. Child mortality was high in 1700s and 1800s, and this is often manifested on the grave markers you see. Common death dates may indicate a disaster occurred. Perhaps a plague went through the community. Grave markers also show that if a person survived childhood disease and warfare, a ripe old age could be achieved. Social status and kinship ties can be indicated by the nature and quality of the markers. Locally appreciated, many small historic cemeteries are maintained by cemetery associations.

The Association for Gravestone Studies is a great place to go for information on cemeteries, including how to conserve stones, photograph them, and learn about them.[177] Graveyards existed prior to cemeteries. The difference is that graveyards were a more personal approach, with the burial site viewed as a temporary resting place before the spirit would enter the Promised Land. Cemeteries are considered more of an institutional, urban affair. David Sloane[178] describes four graveyard types: frontier graves, domestic homestead graveyards, churchyards, and potters' fields. Town and city cemeteries existed as formal gardens at city borders. By the 1830s, rural cemeteries came into existence in the suburbs. These cemeteries were picturesque gardens, but not considered practical as populations grew. The lawn-park cemetery marked a change to a more pastoral, park-like appearance, giving way around 1917 to the memorial parks popular in the present era.

Some small cemeteries, sometimes only about 20 feet square, as leftover remnants of rural existence, may have been encroached upon by widened roads. Because of all the paperwork, the importance of tradition, and respect for the dead, such cemeteries are seldom moved. Typical of these small cemeteries is one you can see heading north on Interstate 95 in Maine a few miles after the Wells interchange on the edge of the right-of-way. As urban areas sprawl out into the countryside, more and more of these little roadside cemeteries are encroached upon. They are protected by stone walls, iron fences, and their status as burial sites. Private, secluded areas at one time, they now seem incongruous in their present developed settings (Figure 9.2).

On the other hand, some cemeteries have been completely bypassed by development and are tucked away here and there in the woods. Sometimes trees that marked the entrance of the cemetery may persist.

Figure 9.2. *A small cemetery nestled between "big box stores" and a road widened to improved access to the retail area in South Portland, Maine. The widening and modernization of routes can encroach upon sacred reminders of the past—in this case, a local farming family. Trees in the area are all young, indicating the site has recently been landscaped.*

Evergreens were symbolic of eternity because they are always green and always appear to be living, so they were a common choice—particularly cedars, as was the oak, symbol of strength and endurance. Blackberries and other shrubs that do well in disturbed areas can mark the boundaries of these rural cemeteries.

The Maine Old Cemetery Association has discussion boards organized by county and hosted at http://memoca.proboards.com/. New Hampshire Cemetery Association is at http://www.nhcemetery.org/, but even better, there is a New Hampshire Old Graveyard Association at http://www.rootsweb.ancestry.com/~nhoga/. The Vermont Old Cemetery Association was founded to "encourage the restoration and preservation of neglected and abandoned cemeteries in the State of Vermont." Its

website has stories, resources, and links at http://www.voca58.org/. The
Massachusetts Cemetery Association is at http://www.macemetery.org/.

Gravestones

"Gravestone" originally meant the stone cover on a sarcophagus, but has
come to mean the same thing as a headstone. Historical archaeologist
James Deetz describes the three basic designs used by New England
stone cutters between 1680 and 1820: the grinning winged death's head
with black eyes, the winged cherub, and beginning in the late 18th century, the urn on a pedestal under a willow tree (Figure 9.3).[179] Many other
patterns existed, but most were variants of the death's head. The designs
reflected Puritanism and cultural views. The willow urn reflects the Greek
revival period of architecture.

Earliest graveyard markers prior to 1660 were likely of wood,
because that was common in England. After the mid-17th century,
the stone most commonly selected was a dark gray slate. Sandstone,
marble, limestone, granite, and metal have also been used. Marble[180] and
limestone were used extensively between the Revolutionary War and
the early 20th century, and white was the preferred color. Both types of
stone can be very hard to read when they become worn and covered with
lichen. Limestone and marble are particularly vulnerable to acid rain.
Brownstone, a sandstone quarried in Connecticut, was used from the
mid-17th century until the late 19th century. Granite is very durable and
became the most preferred material by the middle of the 19th century.

The symbols on gravestones have different meanings depending
on the period of time, what the local fashions and values were, and on
religious influences. Over time, general patterns of symbolic meaning
were repeated for particular areas. One cemetery may differ from another
even if the stones are of the same period. However, there are some common meanings for many of the symbols, as indicated in Table 9.1. Some
authors have published photographs, rubbings, and other depictions
of New England graveyard symbols. Noted early examples are Edmund
V. Gillon's *Early New England Gravestone Rubbings* (Dover Publications,

Figure 9.3. *Early New England gravestones had three major stylistic patterns, the winged death's head, the winged cherub, and the willow urn.*

1966; see also his *Victorian Cemetery Art*, Dover Publications, 1972)) and Harriette Merrifield Forbes's *Gravestones of Early New England, and the Men Who Made Them, 1653–1800* (Da Capo Press, 1967, a reprint of the original 1927 publication). The Association for Graveyard Studies has a summary of different symbols on its website, http://www.gravestonestudies.org/). There are many other depictions of headstones and their symbols on other websites.

A gravestone might mark the head or foot of a grave, or it might be off to the side. A headstone should be appreciated for its own sake. There is really no good or easy way to tell what is under the ground and where it is based on a gravestone. Similarly, a rectangular depression in the ground might not indicate a grave; it might be where someone borrowed some soil to put on another grave.

Cemetery Fences and Walls

New England graveyards were often fenced to keep farm animals out and to designate the sacred space. Cemetery walls and fences were made out of granite or other rock material, or iron. Stone walls were common, and stone pillars might be connected by a forged iron chain as more of a symbolic boundary when there were no more cows and sheep to keep out. The iron fences are either wrought (forged) iron or cast iron. Most are from the late 1800s or newer. However, some 18th-century wrought-iron fences and gates exist in a few protected areas. The historical literature makes

(continues on page 182)

Common Symbols on Gravestones

Table 9.1. *Some common symbols on gravestones*[181]

Symbol	Meaning
Acorn	Potential
Alpha (and Omega)	Beginning and the end
Anchor	Eternal life; hope; sailor
Arch	Passage to heaven; victory
Angel	Guidance to heaven. A weeping angel represents mourning. Trumpeting or flying angel means resurrection.
Apples	Salvation; recovery from sin
Arrows	Mortality; martyrdom
Artillery	Military service
Bats	The underworld
Bell	Religion
Bible or book	Reverend, minister, deacon, or other deeply religious person
Bird	Peace; messenger of God
Bones	Death and decay
Boat	Journey
Broken bud or branch	Death in the prime of life
Chicken or rooster	An awakening
Cherub	Angel; anticipated heavenly reward
Circle	Eternity; connectedness
Clasped hands	Finiteness of earthly existence
Clouds	Afterlife; heaven
Coffin	Death; mortality; of the earth

Column	Mortality; especially if draped or broken
Cross	Christianity
Crown	Triumph over death
Drapery	Mourning
Eagle	Veteran, especially of the Civil War. Also associated with various fraternal orders.
Finger pointing	The path to heaven
Flame or torch	Eternity
Flowers	Short-lived human existence. Various types of flowers have specific meanings. Lily is the most well-known as a symbol of resurrection.
Foot	Grounded; humility
Garland	Victory in death
Grapes	Blood of Christ
Hands praying	Devotion
Heart	Spirit or soul, or sacred heart of Christ
Hourglass	Swift passage of time
Ivy	Friendship
Lamb	Child; innocence
Lion	Strength
Moon	Rebirth
Oak leaf	Long-lived
Palm frond, palm tree	Victory over death
Shell	Baptism; rebirth
Sickle	Reaping of life
Skull	Death; mortality. Winged skull means ascension into heaven.

(continues)

Sun	Soul ascending into heaven
Sword	Martyrdom. Crossed sword is cavalry or military officer.
Sleeping child	Death (Victorian symbol)
Star	Five-pointed is Star of Bethlehem. Six-pointed refers to creation.
Urn	Soul
Wheat	Harvest; sheaf of wheat denotes hard worker
Willow	Grief; mourning
Wreath	Victory in death

many references to fences that were probably of the wood picket type. Few survive, but there are some paintings that show them.

Beginning around the mid-19th century, individual plots often received cast-iron fences, with iron posts or stone posts. The gates sometimes have dates on them, incorporated into the scrollwork, on a plaque, or carved into a granite overhead piece. Some iron patterns are datable. Iron rails (sometimes decorated with swags of chain) appeared, linking the posts, and hollow galvanized or bronze rails become popular by the late 1800s. The lawn-park cemetery image gradually displaced that of the rural cemetery, which was viewed by some as cluttered. Fences gave way to curb outlines of plots in some cemeteries. By the dawn of the 20th century, wrought- and cast-iron fences were common around cemeteries, often with tall gateposts and overhead arches.

Cast iron is hard, brittle, and difficult to weld. Galvanized-pipe fences were sometimes used in conjunction with stone posts or walls. The iron posts can be solid (line), panels, or open scroll work. The iron fence will be a hairpin, picket, bow, or some combination of those (Figure 9.4). The gate may have a date on it. In addition to the style of fencing, look for the name of the fence company if you want to research it on the Internet or at the library to determine the approximate period of its manufacture.[182]

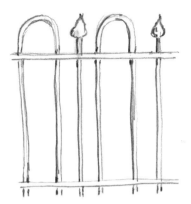 

Figure 9.4. *Hairpin-and-picket wrought-iron fence sections, just two of many common cemetery and yard fence styles of the 19th and 20th centuries. A small agricultural community cemetery or individual household graveyard would have a wrought-iron fence or stone wall if at all possible.*

Cemetery fences of wrought iron or cast iron are collectible and therefore vulnerable to theft if the cemetery is not maintained or inspected regularly. Photographic inventories of cemeteries make it easy to monitor change and help with research. *(Plate 16)*

Researching Cemeteries

For general background, I recommend Edward L. Bell's *Vestiges of Mortality and Remembrance: A Bibliography on the Historical Archaeology of Cemeteries* (Metuchen, NJ: Scarecrow Press, 1994), Lynette Strangstad's *A Gravestone Preservation Primer* (Walnut Creek, CA: Alta Mira, 1995), and her *Preservation of Historic Burial Grounds* (Washington, DC: National Trust for Historic Preservation, 2003). Jenn Marcelais's website called A Very Grave Matter (http://www.gravematter.com/)focuses on colonial cemeteries in Maine, Massachusetts, New Hampshire, and a few places in Vermont. It has pages of headstone photographs. If you find a headstone that has the date obscured or worn off, you might be able to get an appropriate date for it by matching it to the style of another headstone in the cemetery that has a date. *Burial Grounds of Vermont* by Arthur L.

and Frances P. Hyde is available from Vermont Old Cemetery Association (VOVA) and also from the Vermont Historical Society (http://vermonthistory.org/). Another Vermont reference is the *Index to Known Cemetery Listings in VT* by Joann H. Nichols and Patricia L. Haslam, also available from the Vermont Historical Society. Each state's historic preservation office and cemetery association can provide information, as well (See Chapter 10).

The Massachusetts Department of Conservation and Recreation's *Terra Firma #10—Mourning Glory: Preserving Historic Cemeteries* can be downloaded and includes *Preservation Guidelines for Municipally-Owned Historic Cemeteries and Burial Grounds* (2009). It is available at http://www.mass.gov/dcr/stewardship/histland/publications.htm.

When tracking the names on headstones, you may find different spellings. This reflects the common practice of nonstandardized spellings common through the early 19th century. Changes also happened to immigrants at arrival on Ellis Island and other points of entry, and afterwards in response to the process of "Americanization."

Cemeteries are perhaps the strongest visual and cultural reminders of our ties to the land. Laws and customs quickly arose to protect and manage burial grounds. These laws informed a sense of stewardship and protection, the subject of the next chapter, which can be applied broadly to rural preservation and management.

10

Stewardship and Protection

The past is not the property of historians; it is a public possession.
It belongs to anyone who is aware of it and it grows by being shared.
—United States Conference of Mayors, *With Heritage so Rich*[183]

You must do the thing you think you cannot do.
—Eleanor Roosevelt

Why don't we pay more attention to who our farmers are?
We would never be as careless choosing an auto mechanic or
babysitter as we are about who grows our food.
—Michael Pollan

Archaeological and historical resources are cultural because they are
products of people and they belong to society. The settings in which
they occur are also cultural: the landscape is shaped by past and present
human use. Old apple orchards, like daylilies and cellar holes, are cultural
features. The distinction blurs between what is a natural feature and
what is a cultural one. Historical resources and archaeological sites share

characteristics with many natural resources: they can be polluted, and they are nonrenewable. Preservation or conservation of the landscape is necessary to manage and protect these archaeological and cultural resources.

Two very opposite means have served to protect landscapes: neglect and nurture. Neglect can lead to a measure of preservation by default when there is no active maintenance or development pressures, and the countryside persists with very little change. This neglect can occur as a result of little or no economic pressures that would otherwise cause land values to increase and properties to be renovated. But the problem with accidental preservation by neglect is that it is not a true preservation; it does not permanently protect resources from changes, and it does not allow people to make much of a living in the country.

The past can be preserved in the countryside by active nurturing— the conscious care given by communities, special-interest groups, owners, neighbors, and others interested in directly preserving or conserving evidence of the past and in maintaining the conditions under which the countryside is protected. Nurturing can mean formal protection through designation, as in historical districts, museums, and conservation easements. However, we cannot put everything into a museum or buy up the entire countryside to protect it. What else can we do? Another form of nurturing is less formal, but it requires just as much effort. It means finding ways to promote rural living, rural values, and other sustainable aspects of country life—Mark Lapping's notion of a "working landscape" as a means in which farming and other rural life ways are cultivated.[184] The two approaches are not mutually exclusive but in fact are complementary or symbiotic.

The National Park Service website at http://tps.cr.nps.gov/pad/ index.html provides "Strategies for protecting archaeological sites on private land." These strategies include gaining ownership, excavation laws, volunteer approaches, financial support, and management. Just the use of this site is a great way to launch a stewardship and protection campaign. However, in the hope of providing a brief overview, below I summarize a number of approaches, strategies, and organizations that can support historical and archaeological resources associated with agriculture, the landscapes that contain them, and a rural way of life in general.

State and National Registers of Historic Places

If the landowner is a municipality or other public entity, there may be a mandate to manage and protect resources. Historical resources on private property do not belong to the public and are generally not subject to any particular protections. Like significant resources on public property, these resources can be nominated and listed on a state or national register (and thus become "historic" rather than merely "historical"), but privately owned properties may be listed only with the permission and cooperation of the landowner. Listing a property does not guarantee its protection. The listing of buildings, other structures, and sites on the National Register of Historic Places does not prevent them from being removed or destroyed. It merely means their historic nature has been investigated and documented. However, the process of investigation and documentation raises awareness and can improve appreciation for the historical site. Generally, relic features are not sufficient to get a site listed on the national or state registers. Sites need to have "integrity" and meet "Criteria of Eligibility" (36 CFR Part 60). This means they have to be connected to either a famous person or event, embody a particular architectural period or style worthy of documentation, or have the ability to answer important research questions.[185]

The process of nominating a building or site for listing on a state or national register involves documentation, including photographs, maps, measurements, descriptions, and historical research. Comparing the building or site with other known structures helps in the assessment of potential importance. A representative selection of historical structures and features is available in the Historic American Engineering Records at the Library of Congress. Photographs, drawings, and other details of

these sites can be accessed at http://www.loc.gov/pictures/collection/
hh/. Farm museums and farm sites that demonstrate historical crafts
associated with rural life can provide inspiration for local conservation. A
list of New England educational farm sites can be found at http://www.
newenglandgrown.com/pages/educationalfarms.html.

Linking Farmers to Land

Farms and farm land have undergone significant fragmentation due to
development pressures and the late-20th-century decline of the family
farm. Hence many aspiring farmers need access to land. The Forever
Farmland Organization documents farm preservation in Massachusetts,
listing a variety of programs and resources (http://foreverfarmland.
org/). Maine Farmland Trust (MFT) works actively to promote farming in
Maine. MFT lists events, strategies, and resources on its website http://
www.mainefarmlandtrust.org/. The Vermont Land Trust functions
similarly for Vermont: http://www.vlt.org/. The University of Vermont
(UVM) provides advice on lease agreements to connect landowners
with farmers who need access to land (http://www.uvm.edu/~susagctr/
Documents/leaseagreementguide.pdf). Farmers also need tolerance of
farm vehicles on roads that connect lands, which means communities
need to be able to put up with that slow-moving tractor transporting hay
and equipment. Wide shoulders are needed on roads that connect farms
to fields and markets. Fortunately, all states have "right to farm" laws.

The New England Small Farm institute (NESFI) in Belchertown, MA,
is a land-based, nonprofit organization dedicated to encouraging sustainable regional agriculture. It promotes small farm development by providing information and training for aspiring, beginning, and transitioning
farmers. It provides publications, resource links, and workshops. It seeks
collaborative program-delivery partnerships with service providers—
associates, on-farm mentors, organizations, and agencies—throughout
the Northeast and nationwide (http://www.smallfarm.org).

The Farmland Information Center is a clearinghouse for information
about farmland protection and stewardship. It is a partnership between

the USDA Natural Resources Conservation Service (NRCS) and American Farmland Trust (http://www.farmlandinfo.org/).

The Farm and Ranch Land Protection Program (FRPP) provides matching funds to help purchase development rights to keep productive farm and ranchland in agricultural uses. Working through existing programs, USDA partners with state, tribal, or local governments and nongovernmental organizations to acquire conservation easements or other interests in land from landowners. USDA provides up to 50 percent of the fair market easement value of the conservation easement.

To qualify, farmland must: be part of a pending offer from a state, tribe, or local farmland protection program; be privately owned; have a conservation plan for highly erodible land; be large enough to sustain agricultural production; be accessible to markets for what the land produces; have adequate infrastructure and agricultural support services; and have surrounding parcels of land that can support long-term agricultural production. Depending on funding availability, proposals must be submitted by the eligible entities to the appropriate NRCS state office during the application window (http://www.nrcs.usda.gov/programs/frpp/).

Perhaps the most effective means of preserving farming and farmland is "current use"[186] taxation programs where land is taxed according to its use rather than according to its development potential (which is normally a much higher rate).

Cooperative Extension Services

Each state has a cooperative extension service associated with its land-grant academic institution. The University of Vermont's Extension Service website is http://www.uvm.edu/extension/. University of New Hampshire Cooperative Extension offers publications on forestry practices, landscaping, preserving old barns, and other rural-related topics: http://extension.unh.edu/resources/. Similar publications and services for Maine can be found at http://extension.umaine.edu/. In Massachusetts, see the Center for Agriculture at the University of Massachusetts Amherst (http://ag.umass.edu/).

Caring for Stone Walls, Cellar Holes, Roads, and Other Features

Anything built of stone may seem durable, but it still needs maintenance. Replacing fallen stone helps the wall or other structure look like someone takes care of it, and might discourage passersby from helping themselves to neglected stone. However, any tall or unstable structure may require safety precautions and expertise in restoration. New Hampshire Division of Historical Resources publishes an electronic newsletter, "The Old Stone Wall," for those interested in conserving historical resources: http://www. nh.gov/nhdhr/publications/osw.htm. New Hampshire's General Court first protected stone walls in 1791, decreeing that "...if any person shall dig up or carry away any stones, ore, gravel, clay or sand belonging to the proprietors of any common land, or to any particular person or persons, every such offender shall forfeit and pay treble damages to the party or parties injured thereby, and also a sum not exceeding five pounds" (New Hampshire Division of Historical Resources http://www.nh.gov/nhdhr/ publications/documents/stone_wall_legislation.pdf). This law has continued on the books with various amendments, including a 2009 change to add "stone from stone walls."

The origin of the presently worded Massachusetts General Laws, Chapter 266, §113 dates to 1698:

Whoever wilfully cuts down or destroys timber or wood standing or growing on the land of another, or carries away any kind of timber or wood cut down or lying on such land, or digs up or carries away stone, ore, gravel, clay, sand, turf or mould from such land, or roots, nuts, berries, grapes or fruit of any kind or any plant there being, or cuts down or carries away sedge, grass, hay or any kind of corn, standing, growing or being on such land, or cuts or takes therefrom any ferns, flowers or shrubs, or carries away from a wharf or landing place any goods in which he has no interest or property, without the license of the owner thereof, shall be punished by imprisonment for not more than six months or by a fine of not more than five hundred dollars; and if the offence is committed on Sunday, or in disguise, or secretly in the night time, the imprisonment shall not be for less than five days nor the fine less than five dollars.

Stone on private land is not subject to the above protection and is left to the discretion of the individual landowner. In the case of a working farm, it may be necessary for the farmer to sell off accumulated stones as a way to help keep farming viable. However, vigilance on the part of neighbors can help prevent unauthorized taking of stone.

For old family graveyards, check to see if they are being maintained—usually this will be by local representatives of the state's old graveyard association, as mentioned in Chapter 9. The graveyard may be on private or public land. Preserving rural cemeteries can be done through land trusts, local historic commissions, and cemetery associations. If there is a veteran buried there, veterans' groups may be interested in assisting. Lynette Strangstad's *A Graveyard Preservation Primer* (Walnut Creek, CA, Alta Mira Press, 1995) is a good reference point and strategizing guide.

The Terra Firma series, issued by the Massachusetts Department of Conservation and Recreation, has bulletins for stone walls, roads, trees, and other resources at http://www.mass.gov/dcr/stewardship/histland/publications.htm.

A good place to start for anyone interested in historic roads is Dan Marriot's *The Preservation Office Guide to Historic Roads: Clarifying Preservation Goals for State Historic Preservation Offices, Establishing Expectations for State Transportation Offices* (Washington, DC, 2010), which can be downloaded for free at http://www.historicroads.org/documents/GUIDE.pdf. The sponsoring organization, Historic Roads, was founded by Mr. Marriot, and maintains information and resources about such roads nationwide.

Conserving the Working Landscape

Mechanisms dating back to colonial times have existed to promote rural agriculture. These can be quite specific—damaging fences (including stone walls) has been prohibited in Massachusetts law at least since 1726 (the current law, Massachusetts General Laws, Chapter 266, §105, allows an arrest without warrant). Resources and lifestyles become sustainable by being functional. An effective working landscape is a landscape that can sustain itself socially, economically, and ecologically. Anything that supports forestry or farming promotes maintaining a working landscape. Since this is such a broad topic and many sources of information exist, I have presented only a general summary of some of the major ones.

The American Farmland Trust has detailed descriptions of the various approaches to protecting farmland. Its 1997 publication, *Saving American Farmland: What Works,* covers federal, state, and local approaches and tools, and considers the advantages and disadvantages of each. The descriptions include case studies, as well as an outline of the steps involved in creating a farmland protection program. *Holding Our Ground, Protecting America's Farms and Farmland* (Daniels and Bowers, 1997) is another general source of farmland protection methods such as agricultural zoning, state and federal programs, purchase and transfer of development rights, and land trusts. Particularly useful is its extensive appendix of sample forms and agreements that can be used by those working to protect farmland and farmscapes.

The Land Trust Alliance (http://www.landtrustalliance.org/) represents over 1700 land trusts. It provides assistance in working with land trusts to conserve land resources, including historical properties. Historic New England (formerly known as Society for the Preservation of New England Antiquities) is the oldest regional preservation organization in the United States. It owns and operates historic properties throughout New England. It also sponsors events and provides guidance on preservation issues: http://www.historicnewengland.org/.

Resources more specific to the individual states exist through the state universities and departments of agriculture. Nongovernment organizations (NGOs) like Maine Rural Partners (http://www.mainerural. org/) and Yellow Wood Associates in Vermont are working to change rural development and working-landscape management from "attraction, extraction, and supply-based approaches to a demand-driven, wealth-based approach" (http://www.yellowwood.org/). The Vermont Council on Rural Development offers numerous reports and resources to promote working landscapes (http://vtrural.org/) and is linked to The Vermont Working Lands Partnership (http://vtworkinglands.org/).

Land trusts are a key resource for involvement in conserving landscapes. Community and regional land trusts in each state do much more than acquire and manage land. They also provide information on conservation strategies and they work to preserve rural life. Such efforts have been around for decades. Briggs and Kakitis, 1980, assembled approaches to land use and planning, including legal controls, preservation techniques, agricultural districts, zoning and development rights in the 1980 League of Women Voters publication *Farmland Preservation in Maine*, which is still relevant today.

A Richer Heritage (2003) provides a collection of essays on the history and politics of historic preservation in America, including logistical and ethical considerations for both professional and volunteer preservationists. The first section discusses the federal, state, and local approaches to preservation, and their legal administrative and fiscal facets. A particularly relevant essay by Genevieve and Timothy Keller discusses the preservation of entire historic landscapes (as opposed to the more traditional approach of preserving buildings) and how this movement presents both opportunities and conflicts for working with environmental conservation projects. Other sections discuss the creative acquisition of funds for preservation projects along with how to effectively use these funds, and the growing interest in protecting less "tangible" cultural heritage found in rural folk life and various ethnic groups.

In addition to participation in land trusts, conservation groups, and other organized efforts, the way in which we go about our daily lives can enhance the preservation of farmland and rural resources. We can support local farms by buying locally produced farm products. We can support forestry by buying sustainable forest products. We can tolerate the things associated with farming—such as the smell of manure spread as fertilizer, the occasional slow-moving tractor on rural roads, the infrequent escaped cow or fallen bale of hay by the road. Similarly, forestry means having trees that are managed, including being cut down and new ones planted. This can mean early-hour sounds of chain saws, skidders, and logging trucks on the roads.

For people interested in promoting local sustainability and working landscapes, a good place to begin is to assess your own community. New Hampshire has a checklist for sustaining rural agriculture: "Is Your Town Farm Friendly?" at http://cecf1.unh.edu/sustainable/farmfrnd. cfm. This checklist, developed by Gary Matteson for the NH Coalition for Sustaining Agriculture and UNH Cooperative Extension, contains questions and indicators useful for states interested in rural agriculture. The land trusts, other NGOs, local and regional planning boards, and state planning offices all can assist.

Creative Zoning and Land Use

The old-time farm had many different activities, not all of them directly related to farming, but all of them together helped the farmer make a living. One way to help farmers stay in business is to support agricultural zoning that allows multiple uses related to farming. A farmer has a better chance of keeping the farm if allowed creative opportunities such as farm host programs or renting the barn out for special events. Farming requires community support; for example, there need to be commercial enterprises such as feed stores in the area. In addition to supporting multiple agriculturally related uses, zoning can encourage larger setbacks of development from property lines in deference to the operation of adjacent farms, as is the case in Gorham, Maine.

The New Hampshire Division of Historical Resources recommends local ordinances to protect stone walls and other historic resources. A 2008 memorandum from the Division provides a sample ordinance: "No person shall deface, alter the location of, or remove any stone wall which was made for the purpose of marking a boundary of, or which borders, any road in the town of [name], except upon written consent of the Planning Board and the Board of Selectmen."

Londonderry, New Hampshire, uses this model ordinance and has the following requirements in its municipal Site Plan Regulations:

The Heritage Commission will use the following guidelines for making recommendations to the Planning Board for the reconstruction of stone walls disturbed by construction activity:

a. Reconstruction should be done in a fieldstone farm-style wall.

b. Use of existing boulders and fieldstone already in place is strongly recommended.

c. Walls should be dry-stacked with a rustic level topline.

d. The center of the wall should be filled with smaller native stone.

e. Stone should be used from the property and mixed as needed with native New England fieldstone.

f. Walls should be no higher than 3 feet in height, and approximately 3–6 feet deep.

g. The Heritage Commission recommends applicants refer to Chapter 8 of "The Granite Kiss," by Kevin Gardner, Susan Allport, and Guillermo Nunez (ISBN# 0881505463, © 2003, Countryman Press). ii. The Applicant shall take photographs of existing stone walls that are proposed to be disturbed by development. These photographs will be made part of the project file, and can be utilized by the Heritage Commission as they make recommendations on stone wall disturbances.

(http://www.nh.gov/oep/resourcelibrary/referencelibrary/s/stonewalls/documents/londonderry.pdf)

Make Sure People Know About Historical Resources

Not every historical feature or archaeological resource has been inventoried. It cannot be considered for listing on a state or national register if it is not known or evaluated. If you encounter something that you think should be known, be sure to contact the state historic preservation office (listed below) and/or the town historic society. The historic preservation office people will appreciate your help in their attempts to inventory the resources of the state. Most New England states have a process underway to inventory and conserve historical barns and farmsteads. But think how wonderful it would be if each state had a complete listing of its animal pounds, muster fields, water impoundments, cellar holes, and other archaeological and historical architectural features.[187] The first step to conservation is simply knowing that a resource is there.

If you see a newly exposed site or feature, it may be necessary for historic preservation staff to come in and help stabilize it. Research local history and make this information available. Knowing about the past makes it easier for people to appreciate it. A local connection to the past enriches the meaning of community.

Document Landscapes and Compare Them to Historical Photographs and Artwork

Historical resources can be mapped and photographed. The mapping activities might just consist of taking GPS coordinates or orienting the feature to a known point such as a road marker, property corner, or survey pin.

Match photographs of the past with current views. Many local historical societies have compiled local comparisons of "then and now." There are many formal and informal sources of photographs. Photographic compilations such as Bunting's *A Day's Work: A Sampler of Historic Maine Photographs 1860–1920* (2000) show rural landscapes, as do paintings (see Patoni's *Abandoned New England: Landscape in the Works of Homer, Frost, Hopper, Wyeth, and Bishop* [2003] for perspectives on the meaning of landscape). There are many community-based or theme-based historic photograph collections assembled in the Images of America series, Post Card History series, and other series issued by Arcadia Publishing, http://www.arcadiapublishing.com/. A Google images search will reveal historical photographs, and can be narrowed down to search for those pertaining to an individual community. The University of Vermont's Landscape Change Program (http://www.uvm.edu/land-scape/) is exactly the sort of thing for this and is searchable by topic and location. It also has movies, videos, and other resources on the subject of landscape history.

The Maine Historical Society has set up a virtual museum at http://www.mainememory.net/ with contributions from over 200 organizations, searchable by topic and location. New Hampshire History and

Genealogy's online site includes photographs and images at http://www.
nh.searchroots.com/history.html. As mentioned above under "State and
National Registers of Historic Places," photographs and other documentation of known historic sites and features can be accessed online from
the Library of Congress at http://www.loc.gov/pictures/collection/hh/.

The Massachusetts Historic Landscape Preservation Initiative
at http://www.mass.gov/dcr/stewardship/histland/bibliography.htm
provides a bibliography and extensive resources.

Local historical societies and libraries have collections that have not
yet been uploaded to the Internet, not to mention all the photographs
in individual collections. Vermont's Landscape Change Program (http://
www.uvm.edu/landscape/) is designed to encourage uploading and
sharing of images, a great way to conserve aging, fading photographs
that would otherwise be unseen. New photographs, too, will eventually become part of the historical record. Maine Farmland Trust is also
compiling photographs. Each state's historic barns initiative includes
photographic collections and continues to develop.

One of the more difficult things to do is to link historical photographs with maps and address locations. Fortunately, some of this was
done as people prepared for the bicentennial in 1976, producing many
small-town histories, often written by retired teachers, librarians, and
others with long ties to the community. These were often labors of love
leading to a wealth of local historical information. Some 19th-century
atlases and histories commercially produced for larger communities have
"vanity biographies" in which the publisher adds detail about particular
families. These biographies often give clues to events and places, and
there may be an etching of the honoree's estate. Names associated with
foundations can be matched with USGS maps, local histories, and the
19th-century maps such as those by Beers that have the names of householders and businesses on them. Christopher Lenney's *Sightseeking: Clues
to the Landscape History of New England* (2003) is a major resource for
anyone interested in place names and in interpreting landscapes. Some
of the US Department of Agriculture's 19th-century annual reports have
been digitized and are available at Google Books; these can be searched
for information about farm buildings and rural landscapes.

The Trust for Public Land

The Trust for Public Land (TPL, at http://www.tpl.org/) is a national nonprofit land conservation organization that conserves land for people to enjoy as parks, community gardens, historic sites, rural lands, and other natural places, ensuring livable communities for generations to come. TPL projects range from small city lots for a playground, community park, or garden to hundreds or even thousands of acres for addition to a national park or forest. Because TPL does not own or manage land over the long term, there must be a government agency or organization willing and able to assume ownership of the land. In some instances, TPL may help landowners place conservation easements on their property. In such cases, the landowners continue to hold title to their property but forgo development rights. "Greenprinting" is TPL's proactive approach to conservation. Through greenprinting, TPL can:

Help identify lands the community wants to protect.

Develop an acquisition strategy for targeted lands.

Identify sources of public and private funding for conservation.

Independently acquire land from private owners for later purchase by public agencies.

Mobilize public support for land protection.

Assist state organizations.

The Stone Wall Initiative (SWI)

The SWI is a web-based resource for stone wall enthusiasts, an informal regional coalition of property owners, local historians, nature lovers, officers of federal and state agencies, historical and archaeological societies, cultural resource managers, museums, land trusts, architects, scientists, and teachers. The SWI is regional, but housed within the Connecticut State Museum of Natural History within the College of Liberal Arts and Sciences at the University of Connecticut. Though coordinated by Robert M. Thorson, the content of the website represents the collective work of many individuals. SWI offers suggestions and resources for the preservation of stone walls as a cultural resource, including outlines and considerations of who the stakeholders might be, what regulations do and could exist, how and why to inventory the resource, and other recommendations for stone-wall and cellar-hole preservation: http://www.stonewall.uconn.edu/index.htm.

The National Trust for Historic Preservation

The National Trust for Historic Preservation provides leadership, education, advocacy, and resources to save America's diverse historic places and revitalize our communities. The National Trust for Historic Preservation is a private nonprofit membership organization that provides legal, funding, public policy, technical assistance, and training resources: http://www.preservationnation.org/about-us/regional-offices/northeast/.

State and Local Resources

The states and many cities and towns also have preservation resources that can be useful.

Maine Historic Preservation

The Maine Historic Preservation Commission and State Historic Preservation Office is at 55 Capitol Street, Station 65, Augusta, Maine 04333. Phone: 207.287.2132; fax: 207.287.2335; website: www.state.me.us/mhpc/.

A statewide nonprofit organization called Maine Preservation seeks to conserve and preserve historic places. It is located at 500 Congress Street, Portland, Maine 04101. Phone: 207.775.3652; fax: 207.775.7737; e-mail: maineprs@gwi.net; website: http://www.mainepreservation.org/.

New Hampshire Historic Preservation

The New Hampshire Division of Historical Resources and State Historic Preservation Office is at 19 Pillsbury Street, 2nd Floor, Concord, New Hampshire 03301-3570. Phone: 603.271.8850; fax: 603.271.3433; website: www.nh.gov/nhdhr/. Its resources include a guide to researching town histories at http://www.nh.gov/nhinfo/guide.html, and its "Tools for Preserving Barns and Farms" at http://www.nh.gov/nhdhr/programs/barns.html provides many links to online resources, including grant programs and tax programs.

A notable tool is Annette Lorraine's *Conserving the Family Farm: A Guide to Conservation Easements for Farmers, Other Agricultural Professionals, Landowners and Conservationists*, which can be downloaded for free from http://extension.unh.edu/resources/representation/Resource000020_Rep20.pdf.

The New Hampshire Preservation Alliance is a statewide organization "dedicated to preserving New Hampshire's historic buildings, landscapes, and communities through leadership, advocacy, and education." It can be reached at P.O. Box 268, Concord, New Hampshire 03302. Phone: 603.224.2281; e-mail: admin@nhpreservation.org; website: www.nhpreservation.org.

The Society for the Protection of New Hampshire Forests provides references, links, and expertise. Its publications include *Saving Special Places: Community Funding for Land Conservation*. http://www.forestsociety.org/pdf/savingplaces.pdf.

Vermont Historic Preservation

The Vermont Division for Historic Preservation and State Historic Preservation Office is at the National Life Building, Drawer 20, Montpelier, Vermont 05620-0501. Phone: 802.828.3211; website: http://accd.vermont.gov/strong_communities/preservation/.

The nonprofit Preservation Trust of Vermont is the statewide partner. It "provides assistance to other groups and individuals who are involved in historic preservation, undertakes educational programs, holds easements on individual properties, and accepts gifts of property."

Address: 104 Church Street, Burlington, Vermont 05401. Phone: 802.658.6647; website: www.ptvermont.org.

Massachusetts Historical Commission

The Massachusetts Historical Commission is located at 220 Morrissey Boulevard, Boston, Massachusetts 02125. Phone: 617-727-8470. It has programs for preservation planning, grants, and technical services. Website: http://www.sec.state.ma.us/mhc/.

Preservation Massachusetts is a statewide NGO that "actively promotes the preservation of historic buildings and landscapes as a positive force for economic development and the retention of community character." Website: http://preservationmass.org/.

Certified Local Government (CLG)

Municipalities can participate in a program to conserve and manage architectural and historical resources by partnering with the State Historic Preservation Office and the National Park Service (http://www.nps.gov/history/hps/clg/). If a community adopts a historic preservation ordinance that creates a local historic preservation commission and implements a formal review process, it can apply for designation as a CLG. Once designated, a community becomes eligible for federal funding for preservation planning and cultural resource conservation.

Forestry and Historic Resources

If the land has a forest, it should be under a forest management plan that is sensitive to historic resources. The forest itself is of cultural and natural resource value as part of a working landscape. It may have historic logging roads and other features in it. The state forest service or consulting forester can recommend practices to protect these features and resources during logging.[188] Similar to farming, forestry should be approached as a small-scale industry in the context of a working landscape. A "current use" program can reduce the tax burden for qualifying land.

If you do not have a forest and just have some historic trees that you want to save, collaboration with a forester and the local historical society may still be recommended.

If you think a historical resource will be destroyed, you may wish to photograph it first. In fact, documenting the historical resources on your property can be a fascinating activity regardless of your land management intentions. You can find advice online or from your state historic preservation office.

This chapter has scratched the surface of a vast array of resources available for people interested in landscape history, but the biggest resource of all is people themselves. The act of caring for the land brings us closer to the past and to where we are headed for the future.

End Notes

Chapter 1

1 Interest is growing; the Vernacular Architecture Forum (VAF), a nonprofit organization focusing on common architecture and landscapes, now has regional chapters, including one for New England. See http://www.vernaculararchitectureforum.org/. The publications of the authors in the remaining footnotes, below, also reflect and encourage this trend.

2 For example, Eric Sloane, *An Age of Barns* (New York: Ballantine Books, 1974); Allen G. Noble & Richard K. Cleek, *The Old Barn Book: A Field Guide to North American Barns and Other Farm Structures* (New Brunswick, NJ: Rutgers University Press, 1995); Thomas Durant Visser, *Field Guide to New England Barns & Farm Buildings* (Hanover, NH: University Press of New England, 1997); and Thomas C. Hubka, *Big House, Little House, Back House, Barn: The Connected Farm Buildings of New England.* (Hanover, NH: University Press of New England, 1984).

3 Susan Allport, *Sermons in Stone: The Stone Walls of New England and New York* (New York: W.W. Norton, 1990). This book is a must-have for lovers of stone walls, as is Robert Thorson's *Stone by Stone: The Magnificent History in New England's Stone Walls* (New York: Walker & Co., 2002).

4 Robert Sanford, et al., *Stone Walls and Cellar Holes: A Guide for Landowners on Historic Features and Landscapes in Vermont's Forests* (Waterbury, VT: Department of Forests and Parks, Agency of Natural Resources, 1994). You can download a free copy of this from http://accd.vermont.gov/sites/accd/files/images/strongcommunities/historic/stonewall%20and%20cellarhouse_pub_screen.pdf.

5 There is a great tradition in academic geography of broadly "reading the landscape," as evidenced in the works of D. W. Meinig, Pierce Lewis, J. B. Jackson, and Y-Fu Tuan. John R. Stilgoe's books on urban, coastal, and rural landscapes reawaken a desire for a "seeing" of the everyday environment—especially his *Common Landscape of America, 1580–1845* (New Haven, CT: Yale University Press, 1982), *Alongshore* (Yale University Press, 1994), *Outside Lies Magic: Regaining History and Awareness in Everyday Places* (New York: Walker Publishing, 1998), and *Landscape and Images* (Charlottesville, VA: University of Virginia Press, 2005). Many state and regional or local natural and cultural history books include broad interpretations of landscapes. Kerry Hardy's *Notes on a Lost Flue: A Field Guide to the Wabanaki* (Rockport, ME: Down East Books, 2009) is an eclectic and delightful example for Maine.

6 A good source for northern New England weeds is France Royer and Richard Dickinson's *Weeds of the Northern U.S. and Canada* (Edmonton, Alberta, Canada, University of Alberta Press: 2006). This is one of the books I like to keep with me when I go out to "read" the landscape.

7 Anthony W. D'Amato, David A. Orwig, and David O. Foster, 2006. "New Estimates of Massachusetts Old-Growth Forests: Useful Data for Regional Conservation and Forest Reserve Planning." *Northeastern Naturalist* 13(4)495:506. See also Bruce Kershner and Robert T. Leverett, *The Sierra Club Guide to the Ancient Forests of the Northeast* (San Francisco, CA: Sierra Club Books, 2004).

8   May Theilgaard Watts, *Reading the Landscape of America* (New York: Macmillan Publishing, 1972).

Chapter 2

9   Pliny the Elder spells it Publilius in his *Natural History*; others commonly use Publius.

10 Sheep had been in the New World since Columbus, although England discouraged the wool industry in the colonies. Merino sheep were introduced in 1811 and spread widely in the 1830s. As a result, some farms switched from subsistence farming and produced large flocks.

11 Susan Freinkel, *American Chestnut: The Life, Death, and Rebirth of a Perfect Tree* (Berkeley, CA: University of California Press, 2007).

12 Samuel de Champlain noted large cleared fields and Indian villages during his voyages up and down the coast in the early 17th century. His 1613 map of Saco (Maine) shows cornfields. *The Works of Samuel de Champlain*, edited by H. H. Langton and W. F. Ganong. 6 vols. (Toronto, Ontario: Champlain Society, 1922.)

13 For a history of the Maine forest, see Andrew Barton, Allan S. White, and Charles V. Coggbill, *The Changing Nature of the Maine Woods* (Lebanon, NH: University of New Hampshire Press, 2012). It covers everything from the Ice Age to the present.

14 The historical marker (erected 1982) in Fremont, NH, at Brentwood Road (111A) and Rt. 107: "Mast Tree Riot of 1734. Local lumbermen illegally cut Mast Trees reserved for the King's Royal Navy. When David Dunbar, Surveyor General, visited nearby Copyhold Mill to inspect fallen lumber, local citizens assembled, discharging firearms and convinced Dunbar to leave. Returning with 10 men, Dunbar's group was attacked and dispersed at a local tavern by citizens disguised as 'Indians.'" (http://afkabob.com/nhhistmk/nhhist142.htm)

15 In 1784, a Massachusetts colonial law proscribed a $100 fine per tree. William D. Williamson, *The History of the State of Maine: From its first discovery, A.D. 1602, to the separation, A.D. 1820, inclusive*, Vol. 1. (Hallowell, ME: Glazier, Masters & Co., 1832). Williamson, the second governor of Maine, was a founding member of the Maine Historical Society, and is frequently cited in subsequent histories of Maine. His book can be read online at Google Books.

16 Howard S. Russell, *A Long, Deep Furrow: Three Centuries of Farming in New England* (Hanover, NH: University Press of New England, 1976), p. 173.

17 Upright, straight saws (sash) were in use exclusively until about 1830, when circular blades were introduced. It took another 70 years for the circular blades to fully replace the vertical ones. The "chattering" of the upright blade biting back and forth is straighter on the cut timber than the curved marks on a circular-cut wood. If the lumber has not been planed, as in the underside of floor joists or in barns, you may be able to tell how it was sawn. With a sharp blade, turbines and steam-driven saws create a steady cutting "signature" on the wood by reducing "chatter." Beginning in the mid-19th century, steam engines granted independence from water power for small, movable sawmills, which could then be brought to the lumberyard rather than the other way around. But water was still the way to transport wood, and in some rivers, the logging drives continued through the early to mid-20th century. Retired forester Bill Gove's *Log Drives on the Connecticut River* (2003) portrays what these logging drives were like.

18 US Department of Agriculture, *Report of the Commissioner of Agriculture 1886* (Washington, DC: US Government Printing Office, 1887), p. 169.

19 Maine Tree Foundation, http://www.mainetreefoundation.org/.

20 *Forest Landscape Baseline No. 14*, 1996, http://www.ancientforest.org/flb14.html.

21   The New Hampshire Natural Heritage Inventory report "Black Gum (*Nyssa sylvactica* Marsh) in New Hampshire," is available online at http://www.nhdfl.org/library/pdf/BlackGumReport.pdf. Its cover depicts two of the oldest black gums.

22   http://www.ldeo.columbia.edu/~adk/oldlisteast/

23   Maine trees are listed at http://www.maine.gov/doc/mfs/projectcanopy/pages/resource/pubs.htm. New Hampshire trees are listed at http://extension.unh.edu/forestry/bigtree.htm. Vermont big trees are listed at http://www.vtfpr.org/urban/vt_big_trees.cfm. This list of big trees for Massachusetts was compiled in 1999: http://www.nativetreesociety.org/fieldtrips/mass/big_trees_ma_1999.htm; newer lists can be found online and some are listed at the American Forests list (see footnote 17).

24   American Forests maintains a national list of big trees at http://www.americanforests.org/resources/bigtrees/.

25   For example, see Wisconsin Department of Natural Resources, http://dnr.wi.gov/org/land/forestry/treeid/comnameindx.htm.

26   C. L. Brockman, *Trees of North America* (New York: Golden Press, 1968).

27   Michael Wojtech, *Bark: A Field Guide to Trees of the Northeast* (Hanover, NH: University Press of New England, 2011). A particularly useful feature about this book is that it enables identification of trees during the lengthy part of the year in which many of them do not have leaves. If you get right up next to a tree, the bark may quickly become the most distinguishing characteristic.

28   Allen J. Coombes, *The Book of Leaves* (Chicago, IL: University of Chicago Press, 2010).

29   May Theilgaard Watts, *Master Tree Finder: A Manual for the Identification of Trees by Their Leaves* (Berkeley, CA: Nature Study Guild, 1985).

30   Tree identification materials are available for free at the National Arbor Day Foundation website: http://www.arborday.org/trees/treeid.cfm.

31   Based on W. M. Harlow and E. S. Harrar's *Textbook of Dendrology*, 5th ed. (New York: McGraw-Hill, 1969), and Lucy E. Braun, *Deciduous Forests of Eastern North America* (New York: McGraw-Hill, 1950).

32   Tom Wessels, *Reading the Forested landscape: A Natural History of New England* (Woodstock, VT: Countryman Press, 2004).

33   Blowdowns occur when one or more shallow-rooted trees are knocked down by intense high winds. Blowdowns open up the forest canopy and churn the soil—the resultant "wind-throw" damage is a significant change agent. Soil exposed by blowdowns can be examined for artifacts and to reveal history in its stratigraphy.

34   If it is severe enough, fire can remove all the vegetation and destroy all the soil, leading to a primary succession as revegetative colonization begins with the chemical breakdown of rock and development of new soil. Secondary succession, where some soil remains and revegetation or recolonization can occur, is much more common.

35   Andrew Barton, Alan S. White, and Charles V. Cogbill, *The Changing Nature of the Maine Woods* (Lebanon, NH: University of New Hampshire Press, 2012), p. 132. This book is a great background for an ecological perspective on forest history.

36   The urban landscape was also irrevocably changed by invading weeds. See Peter Del Tredici, *Wild Urban Plants of the Northeast: A Field Guide*, (Ithaca, NY: Cornell University Press, 2010), and Zachary J. S. Falck, *Weed: An Environmental History of Metropolitan America* (Pittsburgh, PA: University of Pittsburgh Press, 2010).

37   Clarence A. Day, *A History of Maine Agriculture, 1604–1860*, University of Maine Bulletin 56 (1954), p. 174.

38   Spurr, p. 185.

39   There are over 1,500 species in the goosefoot family, which includes spinach, beets, and chard. Many of these annuals have been introduced, but many are native. *Chenopodium* was an important part of the diet of many native peoples. Archaeologists have speculated that its members' ability to pioneer in disturbed areas helped bring it to the attention of early gatherers and horticulturalists, leading to the propagation of these nutritious plants. *Chenopodium album* (in addition to goosefoot, also called lamb's quarters, fat hen, or pigweed) was a common foraged dish on my family table as a kid. It was one of the first spring weeds in disturbed areas. We liked it better than spinach.

40   The popularity of sheep was immortalized in Boston with the 1830 publication of New Hampshire native and Boston resident Mrs. Sarah Josepha Hale's *Mary had a little lamb*, which was based on a true story.

41   Russell, p. 352.

42   Russell, p. 291.

43   F. L. Harvey, "Three Troublesome Weeds." In *Fortieth Annual Report of the Secretary of the Board of Agriculture for the Year 1897*. (Augusta, ME: Maine Board of Agriculture, 1898): 17.

44   US Department of Agriculture, *Report of the Commissioner of Agriculture 1886*, (Washington, DC: Government Printing Office, 1887), p. 92.

45   Harvey, pp. 13–19.

46   Oliver Wendell Holmes Sr., noted physician and poet and father of the jurist Oliver Wendell Holmes, was fond of measuring elms (in his younger days, he "never traveled without a measuring-tape in [his] pocket"), observed that the average elm was 16 feet in diameter. He found one in Springfield, Massachusetts, that was 24 feet, 6 inches in 1837. Oliver Wendell Holmes, *Our Hundred Days in Europe* (Boston: Houghton, Mifflin & Co., 1889), p. 290.

47   http://www.rootsweb.ancestry.com/~mosmd/champlain.jpg

48   Howard S. Russell, *Indian New England Before the Mayflower* (Hanover, NH: University Press of New England, 1980).

49   For example, see Christopher Lenny, *Sightseeking: Clues to the Landscape History of New England* (Hanover, NH: University Press of New England, 2003), especially Chapter 2.

50   Greenleaf, 1829, pp. 182–183. Available online for no cost at Google Books.

51   Fred Lape, *Apples & Man* (New York: Van Nostrand Reinhold, 1979), p. 18.

52   There are many online sources of information about New England orchards. The "Heirloom Orchardist" is a particularly interesting website with quotes posted from farm ledgers and other firsthand sources pertaining to rural life and orchards. http://www.heirloomorchardist.com/

53   Perhaps that explains why the apple orchard was just about a stone's throw away from our front yard on the family farm. Pressing apples was a memorable fall activity, as was feeding the fermented apple "drops" to the animals.

54   Day, p. 7.

55   Thomas Jefferson to John Jay, July 7, 1785, *Respectfully Quoted: a Dictionary of Quotations*, Suzy Platt, ed. (New York: Barnes & Noble, 1993), p. 7. See also *The Quotable Jefferson*, John P. Kaminski, ed. (Princeton, NJ: Princeton University Press, 2006).

56   Hayward, 1839 (this edition has no page numbers).

57   If necessary, a wet field could be improved through installing tiles or stones in underground trenches (French drains), which permanently solved some drainage problems—see Chapter 8, "Diversions and Ponds."

58   William Cronon, *Changes in the Land: Indians, Colonists, and the Ecology of New England* (New York: Hill and Wang, 1983), p. 120. A cord of wood is four feet tall, four feet deep, and eight feet long. It took about an acre of hardwood forest to meet the yearly firewood needs of one farmhouse. Closed metal stoves were available in the middle of the 18th century—Benjamin Franklin designed his stove in 1742—but did not come into popular use in rural northern New England until around the middle of the 19th century.

59   James Elliot Defebaugh,. *The Lumber Tariff in its Relation to the Value of Farms and to the Property Interests of Farmers and other Small Timber Owners.* Report to the Ways and Means Committee of the US House of Representatives. (Washington, DC: The American Lumberman, 1909). Available online at Google Books.

60   Cronon, p. 145.

Chapter 3

61   Cornell University describes "The Life of a Sugar Maple" at http://maple.dnr. cornell.edu/pubs/trees.htm. Even an old tree, if it is still healthy, can support a tap or two. A rule of thumb is to use one tap per foot of diameter and never more than three. However, if the tree is being used in a vacuum tubing system, no more than one tap should be used regardless of diameter. University of Maine Extension Bulletin #7036, "How to tap maple trees and make maple syrup," is available online at http://www.umext.maine.edu/onlinepubs/pdfpubs/7036.pdf.

62   The Lombardy poplar originated in Italy around 1700, spread to France and England, and was in the New World by the late 1700s. Its manicured appearance and rapid growth made it popular for street use. However, its relatively short-lived nature and weak wood brought it out of favor. It enjoyed resurgence in the mid-20th century, perhaps as a result of the rapid housing boom to accommodate returning GIs and their families pursuing the American Dream. Christina D. Wood, "A Most Dangerous Tree: Lombardy Poplar in Landscape Gardening." *Arnoldia* 54.1 (1994): 24–30.

63   Most farms had a cider press to utilize excess apple for cider and vinegar (Lape, p. 17). Cider had the advantage of being fermentable, among other things. Apple cider vinegar was touted as a folk remedy for everything from sterility to sore throat due to its potassium content (D. C. Jarvis, *Folk Medicine: A Vermont Doctor's Guide to Good Health*. New York: Henry Holt and Company, 1958). Cider vinegar was the basis of the old-time farmer's drink, switchel (sometimes known as "haymaker's punch"—perhaps its powerful fermented version is an alternative explanation for the origin of the boxing term "haymaker" for a wild punch, usually attributed to an imitation of the wide swing of a scythe), an important restorative for long, dry workdays.

64   Russell, *A Long, Deep Furrow.*

65   Howard A. Meeks, *Time and Change in Vermont: A Human Geography* (Chester, CT: The Globe Pequot Press, 1986), p. 285. These apples were a "snow apple" variety (*Fameuse*). The first apple orchard in North American was planted in Boston in 1625. Cultivated apples were introduced; crabapples are native to North America.

66   There are many excellent sources of information on restoring old apple trees. The University of Maine Cooperative Extension fruit tree specialist, James R. Schupp, authored an online guide, "Renovating Old Apple Trees" (Bulletin #2409, 2002), at http://umaine.edu/publications/2409e/. See also http://www.mainelyapples.com/pruning.html (Maine-ly Apple Orchard, Dixmont, ME) for additional depictions of proper apple tree pruning and management.

67   Lawns have been around since the ancient Greeks, who had small plots of mixed grasses, weeds, and wildflowers, and the Persians had swaths of green grass to bal-

ance their flower gardens. Lawns can be seen in tapestries from the Middle Ages. Sometime in the 18th century, lawns started to become fashionable among the elite, scythed by servants or shorn by sheep. They became established household fixtures with the growing popularity in the 19th century of outdoor lawn games, the desire to escape urban industrialism, and the development of lawn mowers. British textile plant foreman Edwin Budding patented a rotary shearing machine in 1830. By the 1880s, these had become affordable and widely used as push mowers. Colonel Edwin George stuck the gasoline motor from his wife's washing machine on top of his mower in 1919. This, coupled with improved weed-free grasses, made it much easier to have a manicured lawn. When I was a child, we experimented with staking the horse in the yard to keep the grass shorn. As long as we moved her regularly, we could keep the lawn from looking like alien crop circles.

68   Hubka, p. 70.

69   Not to be confused with the more toxic pasture weed, tansy ragwort (*Senecio Jacobea*).

70   See Virgil J. Vogel, *American Indian Medicine* (Norman, OK: University of Oklahoma Press, 1970), Anthony J. Cichoke, *Secrets of Native American Herbal Remedies: A Comprehensive Guide to the Native American Tradition of Using Herbs and the Mind/Body/Spirit Connection for Improving Health and Well-being* (NY: Penguin Putnam, 2001), and Alma R. Hutchens, *Indian Herbalogy of North America: The Definitive Guide to Native Medicinal Plants and Their Uses* (Boston, MA: Shambhala Publications, 1973). There are many other guides and encyclopedias for native medicinal and herbal plants, but the books listed here are a good start.

71   Maine Board of Agriculture, 1866, pp. 54–55.

72   In 1851, Maine became the first "dry state" with the passage of the Maine Liquor Law. The primary goal was the reduction of alcohol consumption in villages and urban areas. But prohibition did not have an easy time of it. What happened on the farm stayed on the farm, and that was okay—"just keep it there" seemed to be the prevailing sentiment. For more on prohibition in Maine see Frank L. Byrne, *Prophet of Prohibition: Neal Dow and His Crusade* (Gloucester, MA: Peter Smith, 1969).

73   Archaeologists (including the author) who worked on the late-19th-century Malaga Island site in coastal Maine successfully experimented with making beer— for research purposes, of course—flavored with hops that still thrive on the island.

74   From *hemera*, meaning "day," and *kallos*, meaning "beauty." There are many different species of this common European import. The early species had blooms that only lasted one day, hence the name. The tawny daylily (Hemerocallis fulva) arrived in the 17th century and is a common sight along roadsides and near former settlements.

75   In many parts of New England, periwinkle (*Vinca minor*) is sometimes called myrtle or creeping myrtle, although myrtle normally refers to the *Myrtus* species.

76   A. W. Chase, *Dr. Chase's Recipes, or Information for Everyone* (Ann Arbor MI: R. A. Beal, 1872).

77   Russell, pp. 91–92.

78   Known by many names, this hardy, fast-growing invasive was brought over in the late 19th century, supposedly to help with erosion control and bee production.

79   Susceptibility to poison ivy has increased, as have human reactions to many other environmental toxins. A smaller percentage of the population appears to have been affected by the oil(urushiol) in past centuries. Native Americans had some medicinal uses for the plant. Animals are unaffected by poison ivy.

Chapter 4

80   Day, *A History of Maine Agriculture, 1604–1860*, p. 171.

81   Day, p. 20.

82   Stephen W. Silliman, "Change and Continuity, Practice and Memory: Native American Persistence in Colonial New England." *American Antiquity* 74(2): 211–230.

83   Bureau of Indian Affairs, http://www.bia.gov/WhoWeAre/BIA/OIS/TribalGovernmentServices/TribalDirectory/index.htm. Of course, many other Native American peoples and descendants live in the northern New England States, in addition to the tribes and bands I have listed. The Native Languages of the Americans website provides a good source of links: http://www.native-languages.org/.

84   For example, Jonathan Periam, *The Home & Farm Manual: A Pictorial Encyclopedia of Farm, Garden, Household, Architectural, Legal, Medical, and Social Information* (New York: Greenwich House, 1984), and Byron D. Halsted (ed.) *Barns, Sheds and Outbuildings* (Brattleboro, VT: The Stephen Greene Press, 1977. Reprint of the 1881 edition published by O. Judd, New York).

85   Hubka, *Big House, Little House, Back House, Barn*, p. 180.

86   James Walter Goldthwait, "A Town that has Gone Downhill." *The Geographical Review*, Vol. 17(4), October 1927, pp. 527–552. Dr. Goldthwait was a noted geology professor at Dartmouth College with an obvious sense of humor.

87   See Blake A. Harrison, *The View from Vermont: Tourism and the Making of an American Rural Landscape* (Lebanon, NH: University Press of New England, 2006). This book also includes the relationship between the abandonment of farms and the development of the tourism industry. Also see Ronald Jager and Grace Jager, *The Granite State New Hampshire: An Illustrated History* (Franklin, TN: American Historical Press, 2000), and Donna Garvin (ed.), *Historical New Hampshire: Consuming Views: Art and Tourism in the White Mountains, 1850–1900* (Lebanon, NH: University Press of New England for New Hampshire Historical Society, 2006).

88   Urban equivalents include almshouse, workhouse, town home, and town infirmary. See David Wagner, *The Poorhouse: America's Forgotten Institutions* (Lanham, MD: Rowman & Littlefield, 2005) for an excellent discussion on poorhouse history in New England. Professor Wagner provides a context for comparing the roles of the work-farm and the poorhouse in the social history of New England with current social issues. See also Suzanne M. Spencer-Wood, "Feminist Theoretical Perspectives on the Archaeology of Poverty: Gendering Institutional Lifeways in the Northeastern United States from the Eighteenth Century through the Nineteenth Century," in *Historical Archaeology* 44(4) (2010): 110–135.

89   James Deetz, *In Small Things Forgotten: The Archaeology of Everyday Life* (Garden City, NY: Anchor Books, 1977), p. 109. This classic work might be owned by every historic archaeologist in New England.

90   The average house size in square feet at the start of the 21st century was double that of the 1950s.

91   Kenneth L. Feder, *A Village of Outcasts: Historical Archaeology and Documentary Research at the Lighthouse Site* (Mountain View, CA: Mayfield Publishing, 1994). The investigations of archaeologist Nathan D. Hamilton of the University of Southern Maine on Malaga Island in Casco Bay support this finding. Feder and Hamilton represent a growing number of archaeologists who deal with the "vernacular" (common) everyday people and landscape history in New England archaeology. We know much more about how famous people and

the elite lived than we do about small householders and workers who formed the bulk of the population. The big, sturdy houses of the wealthy might be more likely to endure and thus be around for people to study them. But our predilection to do so might also be a reflection of social dominance influencing what we have tended to value in the early days of the historic preservation movement. Now we have greater appreciation for all aspects of history. Fred B. Kniffen, Henry Glassie, Thomas Hubka, and many others, especially the Vernacular Architecture Forum, have done much to promote interest in vernacular buildings and landscapes.

92   Buildings that had posts in the ground are known as "earthfast" structures. With a durable wood, these were quick, practical structures that made sense for New England architecture and agriculture. Emerson W. Baker, Robert L. Bradley, Leon Cranmer, and Neill DePaoli, 1992: "Earthfast Architecture in Early Maine." Paper presented at the Vernacular Architecture Forum annual meeting, Portsmouth New Hampshire. Available online at a variety of sites including http://www.maine.gov/doc/parks/parksinfo/colonialpemaquid/dwellings/Earthfast%20Architecture%20in%20Maine.pdf.

93   The ground-up shells made good grit for chicken feed, and Whaleback, the largest one in Damariscotta, Maine, was largely removed for processing by a feed factory in the late 1880s; http://www.maine.gov/doc/parks/history/whaleback/. Undoubtedly many others were repurposed for this use.

94   The Dalziel Barn web page provides a display and summary of North American barns at http://www.dalzielbarn.com/pages/TheBarn/NorthAmericanBarns.html.

95   In addition to excavating sites for artifacts and features, archaeologists can examine the soil for pollen and seeds to determine what grains were used and what type of work was done in what areas of the site. For an example in New England, see Gerald K. Kelso, Frederica R. Dimmick, David H. Dimmick, and Tonya B. Largy, 2006: "An Ethnopalynological Test of Task-Specific Area Analysis: Bay View Stable, Cataument, Massachusetts." *Journal of Archaeological Science* 33:953–960.

96   Purdue University, School of Veterinary Medicine: http://www.vet.purdue.edu/toxic/plant46.htm.

97   Concrete dates back to Roman times, but it was more a form of cemented rubble. Reinforced concrete was not patented until after the Civil War. See *Reinforced Concrete: Preliminary Design for Architects and Builders*, by Ronald E. Shaeffer, New York: McGraw-Hill, 1992.

98   Clarence A. Day, *Farming in Maine 1860–1940*. University of Maine Studies, Second Series, No. 78, Orono, ME: 1963.

99   Two examples of these popular press books are Warren Dexter and Donna Martin, *America's Ancient Stone Relics: Vermont's Link to Bronze Age Mariners* (Rutland: Academy Books, 1995); and Barry Fell, *America B.C.: Ancient Settlers in the New World* (New York: Demeter Press, 1976). See also Kenneth L. Feder, *Frauds, Myths, and Mysteries: Science and Pseudoscience in Archaeology, 7ᵗʰ Edition.* (New York: McGraw-Hill, 2011).

100   Giovanna Neudorfer, *Vermont's Stone Chambers: An Inquiry into Their Past* (Montpelier: Vermont Historical Society, 1980). Giovanna (now Peebles) is the State Archaeologist for Vermont. Her book was the definitive treatment on the origins and uses of root cellars and other small, rural stone buildings in Vermont, and her findings are applicable to other New England states. Other references on this subject include Alan Leveillee (1997): "When Worlds Collide: Archaeology in the New Age—The Conant Parcel Stone Piles" in *Bulletin of the Massachusetts Archaeological Society* 58 (1):24–30; http://library.bridgew.edu/exhibits/BMAS/

pdf/MAS-v58n01.pdf; John R. Cole (1980): "Cult Archaeology and Unscientific Method and Theory" in *Advances in Archaeological Method and Theory*, 3:1–23; John R. Cole (1980): "Enigmatic Stone Structures in Western Massachusetts" in *Current Anthropology* 21(2):269–270; Dena F. Dincauze (1982): "Monks' Caves and Short Memories" in *Quarterly Review of Archaeology* 3(4):1, 10–11. [This is a review of Giovanna's book on Vermont Stone Chambers, but Dena also discusses John Cole's work, and how transformed, reforested landscapes ordinary to our farmer ancestors have become foreign and mysterious to modern eyes.] Also, Brian Fagan (1987): "Archaeology and Pseudo-archaeology" in *Expedition Magazine* 29(2):2–3. A good source of articles on critical thinking and pseudoscience is the Committee for Skeptical Inquiry, which publishes *Skeptical Inquirer*; see http://www.csicop. org/.

101 *Barn Plans and Outbuildings* by Byron D. Halsted (Orange Judd Co., 1881) shows various configurations of root cellars and other farm structures. It was reprinted as *Barns, Sheds and Outbuildings* (Brattleboro, VT: Stephen Greene Press, 1977), and most recently as *Barns and Outbuildings and How to Build Them* (Guilford, CT: Lyons Press, 2008). See also James Gage, *Root Cellars in America: Their History, Design and Construction 1609–1920* (Amesbury, MA: Powwow River Books, 2009).

102 Native people in New England dug small pits for food storage; these might be covered with a rock, but in general, stone was not a typical element used in indigenous food-storage feature technologies in New England. Archaeological evidence of native storage pits tends to be deeply buried because New England soil development quickly covers occupation surfaces and associated features. Rocky cultural features visible on the ground in New England may be estimated to date from recent (historical) times, not ancient times, because soil development in this region tends to be rapid.

103 Douglas S. Frink, "Evidence of Last Use for New England's Stone Structures." Paper presented at the New England Antiquities Association Fall Conference, White River Junction, Vermont, 1987; also Neudorfer, 1980, and Periam, 1984.

104 Allport, p. 77.

105 Snow, 2001.

106 Naturally, there are many factors that could interfere with this dating technique, including the species of lichen, influence on growth by the physical and chemical properties of the stone, the exposure to sun, acid rain, climate, and physical disturbance to the stone. Eric Steen Hanson (2008) provides a good summary of lichenometry in "The Application of Lichenometry in Dating of Glacier Deposits" in *Danish Journal of Geography*, 108(1):143–151, available at http://rdgs.dk/ djg/pdfs/108/1/10.pdf. A broader review of the effects of lichen on stone is by Marcello Liscia, Michela Monteb, and Ettore Pacinia (2003): "Lichens and Higher Plants on Stone: A Review" in *International Biodeterioraton and Biodegradation*. 51(1):1–17. This article can be read online at http://www.aseanbiodiversity.info/ abstract/51004276.pdf. There are many field guides to lichen. A quick way to get started is F. May, Irwin M. Brodo, and Theodore L. Esslinger (2000): "Identifying North American Lichens: A Guide to the Literature" (Farlow Herbarium, Harvard University, Cambridge, Massachusetts); available online at http://www.huh. harvard.edu/collections/lichens/guide/index.html. This website provides general lichen references, works for beginners, lichen keys online, and a lichen bibliography by genus.

107 Some spring house designs are shown in Halsted, 1881.

108 Photographs and documents of the history of water and sewer lines from around the world can be found at http://www.sewerhistory.org/.

109 The water pipe might also be made of staves of wood (constructed similar to a barrel) bound with iron. London's water system had miles of elm. Portland, Oregon, used Douglas fir, and cedar was used in Chicago. Hemlock, tamarack, pine, and spruce were also choices.

110 Some schools in northern Maine (Aroostook County) still have a midsemester break to allow students to participate in the potato harvest.

111 I speak from personal experience, having attended such a school for the first four years of my education, shortly before the rural school consolidation movement of the 1960s.

112 Periam, p. 403.

113 See Eric Sloane's *The Little Red Schoolhouse* (Garden City, NY: Doubleday & Company, Inc., 1972) for a picturesque treatment of old school houses.

Chapter 5

114 Society for Industrial Archeology: http://www.siahq.org/.

115 Harold A. Meeks, *Time and Change in Vermont: A Human Geography* (Chester, CT: The Globe Pequot Press, 1986), p. 172. For a history of butter, see WebExhibits, an Interactive Museum of Science, Humanities and Culture, "Butter through the ages" at http://www.webexhibits.org/butter/history-dairy.html.

116 Maurice M. Whitten, *The Gunpowder Mills of Maine* (Gorham, ME: Whitten, 1990), p. 53. Dr. Whitten, a retired professor of chemistry, produced this fine local history as a labor of love. He was instrumental in raising awareness of this historic site. His book includes stories of how the sound of an explosion resulted in job seekers flocking to the company offices for a risky chance at earning two to three times the pay of other, safer work.

117 Whitten, p. 27.

118 Paul E. Rivard, *Made in Maine: From Home and Workshop to Mill and Factory* (Charleston SC: The History Press, 2007).

119 Gary Kulik (1985), "Dams, Fish, and Farmers: Defense of Public Rights in Eighteenth-Century Rhode Island" in Steven Hahn and Jonathan Prude (eds.), *The Countryside in the Age of Capitalist Transformation* (University of North Carolina Press, Chapel Hill), pp. 25–50.

120 James Elliot Defebaugh's *History of the Timber Industry of America*, Vol. 2 (Chicago: The American Lumberman, 1907) includes a state-by-state history of sawmills and lumbering. This book can be viewed online for free at Google Books. It has fascinating descriptions of logging processes, along with a great deal of statistics. Defebaugh was the editor of *The American Lumberman*, a leading weekly trade publication issued between 1899 and 1960.

121 Defebaugh, *The Lumber Tariff in its Relation to the Value of Farms and to the Property Interests of Farmers and Other Small Timber Owners* (1909), p. 8.

122 Victor Rolando, *200 Years of Soot and Sweat: The History and Archeology of Vermont's Iron, Charcoal, and Lime Industries* (Burlington, VT: Archaeological Society of Vermont, 1992), p. 24. This impressive book reflects a massive inventory of furnaces and kilns in Vermont, and includes numerous photographs of old kilns and their ruins found in the woods. It is also available on CD in Volume 8 (2009) of the *Journal of Vermont Archaeology*, which may be ordered at http://vtarchaeology.org/publications.

123 Slag comes in a variety of forms; some is colorful and glass-like, and some is coarse-textured like pumice as a result of air bubbling through it. An industrial site will often have more than one type of slag.

124 Rolando, p. 37.

125 Rolando. See also Roger L. Grindle, "Quarry and Kiln: The Story of Maine's

Lime Industry" in *The Business History Review*, Vol. 47, No. 4 (Winter, 1973), pp. 529–530.

126   Lime was transported by ship. This was a dangerous business because the lime could spontaneously combust and burn fiercely if it got wet. By the mid-19th century, over 500 ships were engaged in transport of lime or wood to fuel lime kilns in Maine. William H. Rowe, *The Maritime History of Maine: Three Centuries of Shipbuilding and Seafaring* (NY: W. W. Norton, 1948).

127   Rolando, p. 225.

128   United States Patent and Trademark Office: http://www.uspto.gov.

129   Keith Richard Barney, *The History of Springfield, Vermont 1885–1961* (William L. Bryant Foundation, 1972). A wave of local history publications swept through the nation on the occasion of its bicentennial, capturing many stories that might otherwise have been lost. Most are labors of love worth perusing for their local details and sense of community.

130   Rolando, p. 147.

131   Industrial minerals of Vermont are summarized at http://www.anr.state.vt.us/ DEC/geo/industrialmins.htm, which has many useful links pertaining to quarries.

132   W. B. Thompson, et al., *A Collector's Guide to Maine Mineral Localities*, Bulletin 41, 3rd Ed. (Augusta: Maine Geological Survey, 1998). This useful guide has maps, directions, and descriptions of mines and deposits. It can be used to plan rockhound trips around the state.

133   New Hampshire Department of Environmental Services: http://www.des.state. nh.us/geo1link.htm.

134   Vermont Geological Survey: http://www.anr.state.vt.us/DEC/GEO/rockkits.htm.

135   A website with quarry location maps and quarry information for various states including those in New England can be found at Peggy B. Perazzo's *Stone Quarries and Beyond*: http://quarriesandbeyond.org/index.html. Her site has many historic maps scanned and reproduced, showing locations of quarries and types of stone. Another source is the Stonecutters and Quarry Workers of North America Preservation Group, http://www.stonecuttersonline.org/.

136   Roy Underhill, *The Woodwright's Companion: Exploring Traditional Woodcraft* (Chapel Hill, NC: The University of North Carolina Press, 1983), pp. 62–63. Mr. Underhill was the master craftsman at Colonial Williamsburg, and hosted the PBS show, *The Woodwright's Shop*. He now operates The Woodwright's School in North Carolina. His books are must-haves for anyone interested in traditional woodworking.

137   Mary Gage and James Gage, *The Art of Splitting Stone: Early Rock Quarrying Methods in Pre-Industrial New England 1630–1825* (Amesbury, MA: Powwow River Books, 2002).

138   John Hayward, *The New England Gazetteer*, 2nd Ed. (Boston: Boyd & White, 1857). He also wrote *A Gazetteer of New Hampshire* (Boston: J. P. Jewett, 1849). These works can be read online at Google Books.

139   Stephen G. Pollock, N. D. Hamilton, and R. Bonnichsen (1999): "Chert from the Munsungun Lake Formation (Maine) in Palaeoamerican Archaeological Sites in Northeastern North America: Recognition of its Occurrence and Distribution." *Journal of Archaeological Science*, 26(3):269–293.

Chapter 6

140   Sarah Orne Jewett (1849–1909), *Country of the Pointed Firs* (1896). A native of South Berwick, Maine, she was a novelist and prolific contributor to *The Atlantic Monthly*.

141   Chester B. Price, "Historic Indian Trails of New Hampshire" in *The New Hampshire Archaeologist*, 14 (1967). Price includes a map showing the location of Native American trails and villages.

142 *The Vermont Atlas and Gazetteer* (Freeport, ME: DeLorme Mapping, 1988, 8th Edition). This atlas is updated regularly. See especially Maps 40, 47, 48, and 55.

143 Sloane, p. 58.

144 Frederic J. Wood, *The Turnpikes of New England, and Evolution of the Same through England, Virginia, and Maryland* (Boston: Marshall Jones Co., 1919), abridged by Ronald Dale Carr, and reprinted as *The Turnpikes of New England* (Pepperell, MA: Branch Line Press, 1997).

145 An example of the controversy between shunpikes and turnpikes can be found at http://www.hampton.lib.nh.us/hampton/history/holman/shunpike.htm, where historian John M. Holman relates the case taken up by the selectmen of Hampton, New Hampshire, between 1821 and 1826. Periam, pp. 573–574.

146 See Roadside America at http://www.roadsideamerica.com/story/9784. This site can be searched by state or town to locate "offbeat tourist attractions."

147 A rare example of a corduroy road built in 1750 in Fairfield, Connecticut, still exists and can be seen in a photograph showing a tilted row of logs protruding into the air along the shoreline of Ash Creek at http://www.fairfieldcitizenonline.com/news/article/Corduroy-road-a-bumpy-pathway-back-to-Colonial-646040.php. This road linked a grist mill to the town center and was designated a State Archeological Preserve in 2009. A photograph of a 1790s corduroy road in Marsh Norwell, Massachusetts, can be seen online at http://www.flickr.com/photos/notaonetrickpony/6124948032/.

148 C. Francis Belcher, *Logging Railroads of the White Mountains* (Boston: Appalachian Mountain Club, 1980), p. 133.

149 Stone embankments from the Cumberland and Oxford Canal can be seen on the Little River in Gorham, about a quarter mile east of the Route 237 bridge. The canal crossed at an angle, connecting Sebago with Portland, and was fed by the Presumpscot River.

150 Bill Gove, *Logging Railroads of the Saco River Valley* (Littleton, NH: Bondcliff Books, 2001). Gove has authored a number of other railroad histories and his works are valued local histories.

Chapter 7

151 Cronon, p. 120. Cronon is quoting from *Sketches of Eighteenth-Century America*, a 1925 collection of the colonial writer's works published under the name of St. John de Crevecoeur.

152 Quoted in Eric Sloane, *Our Vanishing Landscape* (New York: Ballantine Books, 1955), p. 28.

153 *The Farmer's Almanac* (Boston: Hickling, Swan & Brewer, 1858), p. 37.

154 George A. Martin, *Fences, Gates and Bridges: A Practical Manual* (Brattleboro, VT: The Stephen Greene Press, 1974). Reprint of the 1887 edition published by O. Judd, New York.

155 Clifton Johnson, *Highways and Byways of New England* (New York: The Macmillan Co., 1915), pp. 97–98.

156 Sanford, et al., *Stone Walls and Cellar Holes*, p. 26.

157 Robert M. Thorson, *Stone by Stone: The Magnificent History in New England's Stone Walls* (New York: Walker & Co., 2002), p. 153. This terrific book is required reading for anyone interested in stone walls.

158 Jonathan Periam, *The Home & Farm Manual: A Pictorial Encyclopedia of Farm, Garden, Household, Architectural, Legal, Medical, and Social Information* (New York: Greenwich House, 1984), p. 437. This Classic Edition is a reprint of the original 1884 manual.

159 Cited in David McCullough, *John Adams* (New York: Simon & Schuster, 2001), p.
     590. Originally in L. Butterfield (ed.), *Letters of Benjamin Rush*, Vol. II (Princeton,
     NJ: American Philosophical Society, 1951).

160 The individual nature of stone calls forth the artist in us. Examples of masterful
     stonework abound in the landscape of New England, but if you want a book show-
     ing beautiful dry-laid stone construction, see Dan Snow's *In the Company of Stone:
     The Art of the Stone Wall* (New York: Workman Publishing, 2001). The photographs
     are amazing, and Mr. Snow is one of the very few Americans certified by the Dry
     Stone Walling Association of Great Britain. *The Salt Book* (edited by Pamela Wood
     (Garden City, NY: Anchor Press/Doubleday, 1977) contains photographs and
     descriptions of 20th-century Maine stone wall construction.

161 Lace walls have been known as "Kerry Walls," reflecting their Old World influence.

162 The Cowee-Smith Site (listed in the Massachusetts State Register of Historic
     Places) in northern Worcester County, Massachusetts, has massive stonework that
     created the foundations of agricultural buildings and associated stone walls. These
     are likely to have been constructed by the enslaved African Americans documented
     to have been at that property. See http://www.freedomsway.org/towns/westmin-
     ster/westminster.html.

163 Robert Clifton, *Barbs, Prongs, Points, Prickers, & Stickers: A Complete and Illustrated
     Catalogue of Antique Barbed Wire* (Norman, OK: University of Oklahoma Press, 1970).

164 Based on Sanford, et al., *Stone Walls and Cellar Holes*, p. 29.

165 Gardner, p. 25.

166 For example, cairns in the northeastern states are addressed in http://www.ston-
     estructures.org/html/cairns.html, which includes terminology, drawings, and links
     to other Internet sources/sites. Maine cairns are illustrated in http://rockpiles.
     blogspot.com/2012/04/cairns-from-maine.html.

167 William F. Robinson, *Abandoned New England: Its Hidden Ruins and Where to Find
     Them* (Boston: Little, Brown & Co., 1976, for New York Graphic Society), p. 57.

Chapter 8

168 Thoreau used "cronching" more than once in his writings, so it is safe to call it new
     word coinage (neologism) rather than a misspelling of "crunching."

169 Deep in the bottom of lakes, the cold water and lack of oxygen preserves the wood,
     which can be reclaimed. One company in Maine, DeadHead, named after the col-
     loquial term for these submerged logs, retrieves hardwood ("deadheading") from
     Moosehead Lake. Other companies operate throughout New England and in the
     Great Lakes. Lake Winnipesaukee in New Hampshire and Lake Chaplain between
     New York and Vermont are also likely sources. Submerged timber is particularly
     valued for furniture-making and for building wooden instruments.

170 Howard S. Russell, *Indian New England Before the Mayflower* (Hanover, NH:
     University Press of New England, 1980), p. 119.

171 Carl Seaburg and Stanley Patterson (Alan Seaburg, ed.), *The Ice King: Frederick
     Tudor and His Circle* (Boston: Massachusetts Historical Society, 2003).

172 In Maine, the Penobscot River drive peaked in 1915 with 1.8 million logs trans-
     ported.

173 One book particularly handy for identifying ceramic trademarks is Gordon Lang,
     Miller's Pottery & Porcelain Marks (London: Octopus Publishing, 1995). Online
     introductions to ceramic trademarks can be seen at http://www.thepotteries.org/
     mark/general.htm and http://www.studiosoft.it/antiqueporcelainmarks.htm.

174 Thomas Jefferson, *Notes on the State of Virginia* (1781). It was subsequently revised

several times. It can be read online at http://etext.virginia.edu/toc/modeng/public/JefVirg.html.

175 Old cairns—anchoring stations in the river for log drives—can be mistaken for bridge abutments. These anchoring stations were used to hold chains for log booms and therefore will be in wide sections of the river where it would not make much sense to build a bridge.

176 See Wikipedia (http://en.wikipedia.org) on canals in the United States, including a list of abandoned canals.

Chapter 9

177 Association for Gravestone Studies, 278 Main St., Greenfield, MA 01301 (413-772-0836): http://www.gravestonestudies.org/.

178 David Charles Sloane, *The Last Great Necessity: Cemeteries in American History* (Baltimore: The Johns Hopkins University Press, 1991).

179 James Deetz, *In Small Things Forgotten: An Archaeology of Early American Life* (Garden City, NY: Anchor Books, 1977). Deetz led excavations at the Plymouth Colony and is considered one of the founders of historical archaeology in America. Pretty much all historical archaeologists in the United States own a copy of this highly readable classic work. It is recommended for anyone interested in folk culture and history.

180 Marble is a harder metamorphic version of limestone.

181 Although I provide some common interpretations, not all symbols are interpreted the same way and there is room for a wide variety of interpretation. See Gaylord Cooper, *Stories Told in Stone: Cemetery Iconography* (Louisville, KY: Mote, 2004), and Douglas Keister, *Stories in Stone: A Field Guide to Cemetery Symbolism and Iconography* (Layton, UT: Gibbs Smith, 2009).

182 Chicora is a public, nonprofit heritage preservation organization that, although focused on the southeastern United States, has significant experience with cemetery history and preservation. It also has valuable information on its website about fences: http://chicora.org/index.html.

Chapter 10

183 United States Conference of Mayors, *With Heritage so Rich* (Washington, DC: Heritage Press, 1966), p. 130. This quote by Professor Walter E. Havighurst is cited by Carl Feiss. The recommendations of the mayors at this conference helped lead to the passage of the National Historic Preservation Act.

184 An impressive example of independence and innovation in saving family farms and preserving rural life can be seen in 2012 documentary film *Betting the Farm*, about eight dairy farms in Maine that collaborated to form their own milk company after being dropped by a national milk company (http://www.bettingthefarmfilm.com/). There are many books and sources available to help in understanding the connection between agriculture and community. In addition to your own municipal offices, a good place to start is Kathy Ruhf, Matthew Hora, Sue Ellen Johnson, and Kathy Lawrence, *Northeast Farms to Food: Understanding Our Region's Food System* (Northeast Sustainable Agricultural Working Group, 2004); and Elizabeth Henderson and Robyn Van En, *Sharing the Harvest: A Citizen's Guide to Community Supported Agriculture* (White River Junction, VT: Chelsea Green, 2007). For general land use planning, see Brian Hart and Dorothy Tripp Taylor, *Saving Special Places: Community Planning for Land Conservation* (Concord,

NH: Society for Protection of New Hampshire Forests, 2002), available online at www.forestsociety.org.

185 "Significance" has particular meaning in the application of law to archaeological and historic resource assessments; see Donald L. Hardesty and Barbara J. Little, *Assessing Site Significance: A Guide for Archaeologists and Historians*, 2nd Edition (Lanham, MD: AltaMira Press, 2009). In the Federal "Section 106 Process," a property must have "significance" to be eligible for listing on the National Register of Historic Places. In 36 CFR 60.4, "the quality of significance" means having "integrity" while also being associated with events, people, or information considered "important." More broadly and in somewhat looser usage, "significance" has come to mean being eligible for listing on the National Register, since a cultural resource eligible for such listing has the "quality of significance." Another good reference is John S. Wilson, "We've Got Thousands of These! What Makes an Historic Farmstead Significant?" in *Historical Archaeology* 24(2):23–33 (1990).

"Integrity" is a complex concept linked to significance and the condition of the site. Broadly, it means remaining as physically true as possible to the reasons why (under 36 CFR 60.4 [a-d]) the property is eligible for listing on the National Register. Thomas W. Neumann, Robert M. Sanford, and Karen G. Harry, *Cultural Resources Archaeology* (Lanham, MD: AltaMira Press, 2010), pp. 32–39. See also Advisory Council on Historic Preservation, *Treatment of Archeological Properties: A Handbook* (Washington, DC: National Park Service, 1991); National Park Service, *How to Apply the National Register Criteria*, National Register Bulletin (Washington, DC: National Park Service, 1995): http://www.nps.gov/nr/publications/bulletins/nrb15/; National Park Service, *Guidelines for Evaluating and Registering Archeological Properties*, National Register Bulletin (Washington, DC: National Park Service, 2000): http://www.nps.gov/nr/publications/bulletins/arch/; Patricia L. Parker and Thomas F. King, *Guidelines for Evaluating and Documenting Traditional Cultural Properties*, National Register Bulletin (Washington, DC: National Park Service, 1995): http://www.nps.gov/nr/publications/bulletins/nrb38/; and Thomas F. King, *Federal Planning and Historical Places: The Section 106 Process* (Walnut Creek, CA: AltaMira Press, 2000).

186 All New England states have current use taxation laws. Vermont's current use program is entitled "use value appraisal."

187 Hubka's *Big House, Little House, Back House, Barn: The Connected Farm Buildings of New England* (University Press of New England, Hanover, NH. 1984) is the "bible" for farmland/rural architecture. Original research for this book was conducted in Maine and New Hampshire in particular, and throughout New England.

188 Recommendations are contained in Sanford et al., *Stone Walls and Cellar Holes: A Guide for Landowners on Historic Features and Landscapes in Vermont's Forests* (Department of Forests and Parks, Agency of Natural Resources, Waterbury, VT, 1994; available online at no cost). The Society for the Protection of New Hampshire Forests has similar recommendations (see http://www.forestsociety.org/Default.asp).

Glossary

anadromous: Fish that travel from salt water to fresh water to spawn. Examples include salmon, smelt, shad, and sturgeon.

arch: Structure used in the production of maple syrup. The arch holds the evaporator pans in which the maple sap is boiled.

assemblage: The total set of artifacts from a site.

barways: Openings in a stone fence or wall used to provide access. The way is blocked with rails or poles when not in use. When it is abandoned or in long-term disuse, it may be blocked with stone.

berm: Mound of earth.

blowdown: A landscape in which the trees have been knocked down by wind, as from a **microburst**.

bog: Wetland characterized by past or present nonflowing water and dominated by sedges and shrubs.

borrow pit: Site where gravel, fill, or other earth resource is (or was) extracted for local use.

cairn: Pile of stones or boulders. Cairns can mark property boundaries, anchor features, be memorials, serve as aesthetic statements, or have other purposes. They can be prehistoric, historic, built by native peoples, or be recent.

canopy: In reference to forests, the uppermost layer of leaves; the sun-lit vegetation in and above the crown of trees.

clear-cutting: Commonly, the removal of all trees in a particular forest stand or area. As an even-aged silvicultural system, this involves harvesting trees to start a new forest and generally favors early-successional species like aspen, birch, and pine.

clinker: Commonly, burned coal from a stove or furnace, but can refer to any byproduct or leftover material from a fire or furnace. See also **klinker**.

collier: Person who makes charcoal.

coppice (also **copse**): Small cluster or thicket of trees or bushes. To coppice a tree means to cut it back to just above ground level, thereby encouraging sprouts to make a thicket.

copse: Small cluster or thicket of trees or bushes.

corduroy road: Road built out of logs laid side by side perpendicular to the path of the road, and resembling corduroy cloth. Locust was the preferred choice in New England, due to its durability. Hemlock, tamarack, cedar, and other softwoods were also used.

cultural resource: A generic term for historical, archaeological, and built-environment properties. It is sometimes used as a synonym for the formal term "property" referenced in historic preservation regulations.

cupola: Small structure on top of a roof. It is often rounded, and provides ventilation or an observation point.

datum: A fixed, permanent, and readily relocated position used in mapping, be it an archaeological site or a project area.

debitage: Waste materials, often used by archaeologists in reference to chips (flakes) from the processing of stone tools.

diameter at breast height (dbh): The diameter of a tree taken at 4.5 feet above average ground level around the base of the tree.

dimension stone: Large quarried stone cut to similar shapes for use in buildings, curbs, and other construction.

dugway: Originally, a road built into a mountainside as a main haul road for mining or logging. It also refers to an older road that, through the forces of erosion over time, has had its surface "lowered" below that of the surrounding land on both sides. You can see it where there are stone walls on either side of the road and the surface of the road is several feet below the base level of those adjacent walls.

effect: An impact or alteration to a cultural resource. If adverse, it changes the nature of the resource.

feature: A nonportable human alteration of an archaeological site, such as a pit, foundation, or hearth. A feature cannot be removed without loss of physical **integrity**.

fen: Wetland site characterized by flowing water and dominated by shrubs.

flume: A raceway or water channel constructed for transport of water or movement of materials, usually at a mill site, but also in steep forested locations.

forb: A broad-leafed plant that is not a grass and that lacks woody tissue. It usually grows in a meadow or other open area.

ford: An at-grade river or stream crossing. There is no bridge; just wade or drive through.

freestone: A comparatively soft stone, often sandstone or limestone, which can be shaped with hand tools.

French drain: System of buried tile or stone in a trench used to move water in a field so that it is neither too waterlogged nor too dry.

gable: The upper end section of the outer wall of a building with a pitched roof. This is usually a triangular space between the two slopes of the roof.

gray water: Waste water not contaminated with septic waste, as in waste water from a sink, bath, or laundry.

ground truth: Verification of remotely sensed data by on-site measurements. Also generally refers to verification of externally supplied site data.

gundalow: Flat-bottomed long, narrow cargo boat used in canals, rivers, and calm coastal waters.

high grading: In reference to timber harvesting, this is an exploitative practice that removes only the biggest, highest-quality trees from a forest, and has a negative connotation because it weakens the health and value of the forest over time (see McEvoy, 1995). High grading is also used in other contexts such as mineral extraction.

Historic Property: In capital letters, this is a regulatory term meaning a property that is eligible for listing on the National Register of Historic Places. In lower-case letters, it is a general term for an old property.

integrity: Degree to which a site, structure, feature, or collection is undisturbed or unaltered relative to currently known examples.

klinker: Rejected and discarded brick from a brick factory or kiln. Originally, the term referred to a type of Dutch brick. See also **clinker**.

limestone: A sedimentary rock usually formed of calcium carbonate fossils and popular as a building material.

lithic: Of or pertaining to stone tools.

marble: A rock which originated as sedimentary limestone, then was subjected to heat and pressure in a metamorphic process. Popular for gravestones, statuary, and as a building material.

matrix: The surrounding material in which archaeological or related materials are found.

microburst: Sudden, high downdraft of wind. It usually lasts only a few minutes and affects a small area of a few acres. It can have wind speeds in excess of 100 mph and do great damage.

midden: A pile of discarded material in the landscape, such as a shell midden or trash midden.

mitigate: To offset the effects of.

National Register of Historic Places: Defined in CFR Part 61.2 as the national list of districts, sites, buildings, structures, and objects significant in American history, architecture, archaeology, engineering, and culture, maintained by the Secretary of the Interior under authority of Section 101(a)(1)(A) of the **NHPA**.

NHPA: National Historic Preservation Act of 1966 as amended (16 USC 470-470t, 110) and subsequent modifications. The basic historic preservation legislation requiring agencies to check for properties eligible for the National Register before any federally enabled undertaking proceeds. Takes precedence over the National Environmental Policy Act.

old growth: Refers to a primary or virgin forest that is past its mature state, often hundreds of years old. This is the original forest, with snags, fallen trees, and no evidence of significant human disturbance. (See also **secondary growth**.) The forests encountered by the colonists were old-growth forests. McEvoy (1995) defines it as a self-perpetuating forest community that has reached a dynamic steady state (i.e., changes occur in the community only when gaps are formed as old trees die out, but the changes do not affect the overall character of the community) in the absence of silvicultural treatments. The dominant vegetation is considered to be "climax," with all age classes represented.

overburden: Earth material that lies on top of a deposit of archaeological (culture-bearing) material. May include consolidated or unconsolidated material intentionally placed on top of a culturally sensitive layer or site.

peat swamp: Wetland area characterized by peat deposits and water-tolerant trees (red maple, black spruce, larch).

primary succession: The development of the vegetation sequence on a landscape that begins from bare rock or other condition in which the soil is gone. Primary succession starts with lichen, algae, and fungi and progresses, depending on conditions and the development of new soil, to an eventual climax species composition. It takes a severe disturbance to initiate primary succession.

puncheon: Heavy, rough slab split from a durable wood post and dressed on top by a broadax or adz. Used in house or barn construction when sawmills were not available or affordable.

riparian: Adjacent to or associated with a river, stream, or similar surface water body.

rod: Unit of linear land measurement equal to sixteen and a half feet, commonly used in reference to road widths.

secondary succession: The regeneration and colonization of a disturbed landscape in which some components of the original soils and substrate remain, as opposed to **primary succession**, which begins when there is no remaining soil or substrate.

secondary growth: The second generation of a forest; a new forest that grows after a major disturbance such as logging or fire.

seres: Pattern sequences recognizable over time, often used to describe vegetation.

shunpike: A road used as an alternative to turnpikes and other roads that charged a toll. Shunpike has also become a verb meaning to avoid main roads.

significance: The quality of significance, set out in 36 CFR 60.4, means that the archaeological site or element of the built environment can be listed on the National Register of Historic Places.

sill: Horizontal beam that supports the base of a house, barn, or other structure. Sills are usually made of wood. The base of a window and the threshold of a doorway can also be sills.

silviculture: The "art and science of controlling the establishment, growth, composition, health and quality of forests and woodlands to meet the diverse needs and values of landowners and society on a sustainable basis," according to the US Forest Service (http://www.fs.fed.us/forestmanagement/silviculture/index.shtml). McEvoy (1995) puts it more simply as the art and science of growing forests for timber and other values.

single-tree selection: The least invasive forest regeneration tool in an uneven-aged silvicultural system in which individual mature trees are harvested, but for the first few cutting cycles some trees are removed from almost all diameter classes to create a more nearly even succession of mature trees over time. This system favors shade-tolerant tree species like beech, maple, and hemlock (see McEvoy, 2004).

skidder: A tractor used to haul logs out of the woods.

slag: Byproduct of industrial furnaces consisting of glass-like material from the processing of ore. It can take on a variety of appearances ranging from glass to

slash: Branches, small trees, and other wood remnants from logging activity.

sluiceway: A narrow, artificial channel to convey water for a mill, mining, agriculture, or similar use. Most sluiceways have a gate to control the flow of the water.

soapstone: A talc–schist metamorphic rock, also known as steatite. It is soft, easy to carve, and a stable material for sinks, countertops, and other architectural uses, as well as for decorative carving.

spile: A spout or tubular metal device inserted into a maple tree. The sap comes out of it and drips into the sap bucket or is collected by plastic tubing. Originally, spiles were made of wood and referred to as cask plugs.

staddle: Wooden pole crib placed by farmers to hold salt hay harvested in salt marshes.

stand: The trees in a given area distinguishable from adjacent forest because of their characteristics of age, species composition, and site characteristics.

State Historic Preservation Officer (SHPO): The official within each state who has been appointed by the governor to administer the state's historic preservation program.

subsistence farming: Most of the food produced on the farm is consumed by the farming family itself.

substrate: The layer upon which other things subsist. Soil is a substrate for plants. Substrate can be wood, rock, sand, or other earthy material, singly or in combination.

succession: The orderly transition of one plant community (landscape vegetative state) to another. The transition may be predictable if sites are left undisturbed and the environmental factors are understood.

survey: An archaeological reconnaissance of an area. See also Phase I.

swale: A drainage area or ditch.

talc: The softest of the minerals, with a smooth soap-like feel to it. Quarried for use in cosmetics, ceramics, and in general manufacturing. **Soapstone** is largely composed of talc.

understory: The vegetation that occupies an area between the forest floor and the main canopy of the stand (McEvoy, 1995).

upper: A secondary road built to haul materials from mining or logging.

vernacular: Common, locally available, everyday; usually in reference to language, but also to architecture, landscapes, and other features or characteristics.

References

Advisory Council on Historic Preservation, 1991. *Treatment of Archeological Properties: A Handbook*. Advisory Council on Historic Preservation, Washington, DC.

Albers, Jan, 2000. *Hands on the Land: A History of the Vermont Landscape*. Orton Family Foundation/MIT Press: Cambridge, MA.

Allport, Susan, 1990. *Sermons in Stone: The Stone Walls of New England and New York*. W. W. Norton: New York.

American Farmland Trust, 1997. *Saving American Farmland: What Works*. American Farmland Trust: Northampton, MA.

Ancient Forest Exploration & Research, 1996. *Forest Landscape Baseline No. 14*. Available at http://www.ancientforest.org/flb14.html.

Anderson, Hayden L. V., 1982. *Canals and Inland Waterways of Maine*. Maine Historical Society Research Series No. 2. Maine Historical Society, Portland, ME.

Anger, Paul Tudor, 2001. "Who Built New England's Megalithic Monuments?" *Planet Vermont Quarterly*. Summer 2001, Vol. 9(2). Available online at http://planetvermont.com/pvq/v9n2/megaliths.html.

Baker, Emerson W., Robert L. Bradley, Leon Cranmer, and Neill DePaoli, 1992. "Earthfast Architecture in Early Maine." Paper presented at the Vernacular Architecture Forum annual meeting, Portsmouth, NH, May 1992. Available online at various sites.

Barney, Keith Richard, 1972. *The History of Springfield, Vermont 1885–1961*. William L. Bryant Foundation, Springfield, VT.

Barrett, John W. (ed.), 1994. *Regional Silviculture of the United States*, 3rd Edition. New York: John Wiley & Sons.

Bartlett, John, 1923. *Familiar Quotations* (10th ed.). Boston: Little, Brown, & Co. Searchable online at http://www.bartleby.com/100/.

Barton, Andrew, Alan S. White, and Charles V. Cogbill, 2012. *The Changing Nature of the Maine Woods*. Lebanon, NH: U. of New Hampshire Press.

Bastin, Edson S., and Charles A. Davis, 1909. *Peat Deposits of Maine*. US Geological Survey Bulletin #376. Washington, DC: Government Printing Office. Available at http://pubs.usgs.gov/bul/0376/report.pdf.

Beaudry, Mary C., 2003. "Trying to Think Progressively About 19th-Century Farms." *Northeast Historical Archaeology* 30–31 (2001–2002):129–142; http://www.academia.edu/199071/Trying_to_Think_Progressively_about_19th-Century_Farms.

Beaudry, Mary C., 1986. "The Archaeology of Historical Land Use in Massachusetts." *Historical Archaeology* 20 (2):38–46.

Belcher, C. Francis, 1980. *Logging Railroads of the White Mountains*. Boston: Appalachian Mountain Club.

Bell, Edward L., 1994. *Vestiges of Mortality and Remembrance: A Bibliography on the Historical Archaeology of Cemeteries*. Metuchen, NJ: Scarecrow Press.

Bennett, Dean B., 1996. *The Forgotten Nature of New England: A Search for Traces of the Original Wilderness*. Rockport, ME: Down East Books.

Bourque, Bruce J., 2001. *Twelve Thousand Years: American Indians in Maine*. Lincoln, NB: University of Nebraska Press.

Braun, E. Lucy., 1950. *Deciduous Forests of Eastern North America*. New York: McGraw-Hill.

Briggs, Gwynne and Sally Kakitis, 1980. *Farmland Preservation in Maine*. Augusta, ME: League of Women Voters of Maine.

Brockman, C. L., 1968. *Trees of North America*. New York: Golden Press.

Bruchac, Margaret M., 2005. "Earthshapers and Placemakers: Algonkian Indian Stories and the Landscape," in Claire Smith and H. Martin Wobst (eds.), *Indigenous Archaeologies: Decolonizing Theory and Practice*, pp. 56–80. London: Routledge.

Bunting, W. H., 2000. *A Day's Work: A Sampler of Historic Maine Photographs 1860–1920*. Gardiner, ME: Tilbury House, Publishers.

Burk, John C., and Marjorie Holland, 1979. *Stone Walls and Sugar Maples: An Ecology for Northeasterners*. Boston: Appalachian Mountain Club.

Byrne, Frank L., 1969. *Prophet of Prohibition: Neal Dow and His Crusade*. Gloucester, MA: Peter Smith.

Caldwell, D. W., 1998. *Roadside Geology of Maine*. Missoula, MT: Mountain Press.

Cenkl, Pavel, 2006. *This Vast Book of Nature: Writing the Landscape of New Hampshire's White Mountains*. Iowa City, IA: University of Iowa Press.

Chase, A. W., 1872. *Dr. Chase's Recipes, or Information for Everyone*. Ann Arbor, MI: R. A. Beal.

Cichoke, Anthony J., 2001. *Secrets of Native American Herbal Remedies: A Comprehensive Guide to the Native American Tradition of Using Herbs and the Mind/Body/Spirit Connection for Improving Health and Well-being*. New York: Penguin Putnam.

Clifton, Robert T., 1970. *Barbs, Prongs, Points, Prickers, & Stickers: A Complete and Illustrated Catalogue of Antique Barbed Wire*. Norman, OK: University of Oklahoma Press.

Cole, John R., 1980, "Cult Archaeology and Unscientific Method and Theory." *Advances in Archaeological Method and Theory* 3:1–23.

———, 1980. "Enigmatic Stone Structures in Western Massachusetts." *Current Anthropology* 21 (2):269–270.

Conwill, Joseph D., 2003. *Maine's Covered Bridges*. Charleston, SC: Arcadia Publishing.

Cook, David S., 1985. *Above the Gravel Bar: The Indian Canoe Routes of Maine*. Milo, ME: Milo Printing Company.

Coombes, Allen J., 2010. *The Book of Leaves: A Leaf-by-Leaf Guide to Six Hundred of the World's Great Trees*. Chicago: Chicago University Press.

Cornell University Department of Natural Resources. "The Life of a sugar maple tree" at http://maple.dnr.cornell.edu/pubs/trees.htm.

Cooper, Gaylord, 2004. *Stories Told in Stone: Cemetery Iconography*. Louisville, KY: Mote.

Cronon, William, 1983. *Changes in the Land: Indians, Colonists, and the Ecology of New England*. New York: Hill and Wang.

Daniels, Tom, and Deborah Bowers, 1997. *Holding Our Ground, Protecting America's Farms and Farmland*. Washington, DC: Island Press.

D'Amato, Anthony W., David A. Orwig, and David O. Foster, 2006. "New Estimates of Massachusetts Old-Growth Forests: Useful Data for Regional Conservation and Forest Reserve Planning." *Northeastern Naturalist* 13 (4)495:506.

Day, Clarence A., 1954. *A History of Maine Agriculture, 1604–1860*. University of Maine Bulletin 56.

———,1963. *Farming in Maine, 1860–1940*. University of Maine Bulletin, Vol. 65 (20).

Deetz, James, 1977. *In Small Things Forgotten: The Archaeology of Everyday Life*. Garden City, NY: Anchor Books.

Defebaugh, James Elliot, 1907. *History of the Timber Industry of America*, Vol. 2. Chicago: The American Lumberman. Available online at Google Books.

———, 1909. *The Lumber Tariff in Its Relation to the Value of Farms and to the Property Interests of Farmers and Other Small Timber Owners*. Report to the Ways and Means Committee of the US House of Representatives. Washington, DC: The American Lumberman. Available online at Google Books.

Del Tredici, Peter, 2010. *Wild Urban Plants of the Northeast: A Field Guide*. Ithaca, NY: Cornell University Press.

Dexter, Warren, and Donna Martin, 1995. *America's Ancient Stone Relics: Vermont's Link to Bronze Age Mariners*. Rutland, VT: Academy Books.

Dincauze, Dena F., 1982. "Monks' Caves and Short Memories." *Quarterly Review of Archaeology* 3(4):1,10–11.

Drury, W. H., and I. C. T. Nisbet, 1973. "Succession." *Journal of the Arnold Arboretum* 54:333–367.

The Dry Stone Conservancy: http://www.drystone.org/.

Dry Stone Walling Association of Great Britain: http://www.dswa.org.uk/.

Dwight, Timothy, 1969. *Travels in New England and New York*. Cambridge, MA: Harvard University Press. (First published in 1821–1822, various early editions may be viewed online at Google.docs.)

Elliott, Douglas B., 1976. *Roots: An Underground Botany and Forager's Guide*. Old Greenwich, CT: The Chatham Press.

Evans, Benjamin D., and June R. Evans, 2004. *New England's Covered Bridges: A Complete Guide*. Lebanon, NH: University Press of New England.

Fagan, Brian, 1987. "Archaeology and Pseudo-archaeology." *Expedition Magazine* 29(2):2–3.

Falck, Zachary J. S., 2010. *Weed: An Environmental History of Metropolitan America*. Pittsburgh, PA: University of Pittsburgh Press.

The Farmer's Almanac for 1858. Boston: Hickling, Swan & Brewer.

Feder, Kenneth L., 1994. *A Village of Outcasts: Historical Archaeology and Documentary Research at the Lighthouse Site*. Mountain View, CA: Mayfield Publishing.

———, 2011. *Frauds, Myths, and Mysteries: Science and Pseudoscience in Archaeology* (7th ed.). New York: McGraw-Hill.

Fell, Barry, 1976. *America B.C.: Ancient Settlers in the New World*. New York: Demeter Press.

Forbes, Harriette Merrifield, 1927. *Gravestones of Early New England, and the Men Who Made Them, 1653–1800*. Boston: Houghton Mifflin. Reprints from 1955, 1967, 1973, and newer dates may be available online.

Foster, David R., and John F. O'Keefe, 2000. *New England Forests through Time: Insights from the Harvard Forest Dioramas*. Cambridge, MA: Harvard University Press.

Freinkel, Susan, 2007. *American Chestnut: The Life, Death, and Rebirth of a Perfect Tree*. Berkeley, CA: University of California Press.

Frink, Douglas S., 1987. "Evidence of Last Use for New England's Stone Structures." Paper presented at the New England Antiquities Association Fall Conference, White River Junction, VT.

Gage, James, 2009. *Root Cellars in America: Their History, Design and Construction 1609–1920* (2nd ed.). Amesbury, MA: Powwow River Books.

Gage, Mary, and James Gage, 2002. *The Art of Splitting Stone: Early Rock Quarrying Methods in Pre-Industrial New England 1630–1825*. Amesbury MA: Powwow River Books.

Gardner, Kevin, 2001. *The Granite Kiss: Traditions and Techniques of Building New England Stone Walls*. Woodstock, VT: The Countryman Press.

Garvin, Donna (ed.), 2006. *Historical New Hampshire: Consuming Views: Art and Tourism in the White Mountains, 1850–1900*. New Hampshire Historical Society, Lebanon, NH: University Press of New England.

Garvin, James L., 2002. *A Building History of Northern New England*. Hanover, NH: University Press of New England.

——, 2002. "Notes on the origins of arched stone bridges in the Contoocook River Valley of New Hampshire." New Hampshire Division of Historic Resources. Available at http://www.nh.gov/nhdhr/publications/documents/contoocook_stone_arch_bridges.pdf.

Gillon, Edmund V., 1966. *Early New England Gravestone Rubbings*. New York: Dover Publications.

——, 1972. *Victorian Cemetery Art*. New York: Dover Publications.

Glassie, Henry H., 1969. *Pattern in the Material Folk Culture of the Eastern United States*. Philadelphia: University of Pennsylvania Press.

——, 2000. *Vernacular Architecture*. Bloomington, IN: Indiana University Press.

Goldthwait, James Walter, 1927. "A Town that has Gone Downhill." *The Geographical Review*. Vol. 17(4), October 1927, pp. 527–552.

Gove, Bill, 2001. *Logging Railroads of the Saco River Valley*. Littleton, NH: Bondcliff Books.

——, 2003. *Log Drives on the Connecticut River*. Littleton, NH: Bondcliff Books.

Greenleaf, Moses, 1829. *A Survey of the State of Maine in Reference to Its Geographical Features, Statistics, and Political Economy*. Portland, ME: Shirley and Hyde. Maine State Museum Reprint, Augusta, Maine, 1970.

Grindle, Roger L., 1973. "Quarry and Kiln: The Story of Maine's Lime Industry." *The Business History Review*, Vol. 47, No. 4 (Winter 1973), pp. 529–530.

Gurcke, Karl, 1987. *Bricks and Brickmaking: A Handbook or Historical Archaeology*. Moscow, ID: University of Idaho Press.

Halsted, Byron D. (ed.), 1977. *Barns, Sheds and Outbuildings*. Brattleboro, VT: The Stephen Greene Press. Reprint of the 1881 edition published by Orange Judd, New York. Most recently reprinted as *Barns and Outbuildings and How to Build Them*, Guilford, CT: Lyons Press, 2008.

Hardy, Kerry, 2009. *Notes on a Lost Flute: A Field Guide to the Wabanaki*. Rockport, ME: Down East Books.

Hare, Sid J., and S. Herbert Hare, 1921. *The Cemetery Handbook*. Chicago: Allied Arts Publishing Company.

Harlow, W. M., and E. S. Harrar, 1969. *Textbook of Dendrology*, (5th ed.). New York: McGraw-Hill.

Hanson, Eric Steen, 2008. "The Application of Lichenometry in Dating of Glacier Deposits." *Danish Journal of Geography* 108(1):143–151; http://rdgs.dk/djg/pdfs/108/1/10.pdf.

Hardesty, Donald L., and Barbara J. Little, 2009. *Assessing Site Significance: A Guide for Archaeologists and Historians* (2nd ed.). Lanham, MD: AltaMira Press.

Harrison, Blake A., 2006. *The View from Vermont: Tourism and the Making of an American Rural Landscape*. Lebanon, NH: University Press of New England.

Harrison, Blake A., and Richard W. Judd (eds.), 2011. *A Landscape History of New England*. Cambridge, MA: MIT Press.

Hart, Brian, and Dorothy Tripp Taylor, 2002. *Saving Special Places: Community Planning for Land Conservation*. Concord, NH: Society for Protection of New Hampshire Forests. Available online at www.forestsociety.org.

Haviland, William A., and Marjory W. Power, 1994. *The Original Vermonters: Native Inhabitants, Past and Present* (revised and expanded edition). Hanover, NH: University Press of New England.

Hayward, John, 1839. *The New England Gazetteer: Containing Descriptions of all the States, Counties, and Towns in New England* (6th ed.). Boston: Boyd & White. Available online at Google Books.

———, 1849. *A Gazetteer of Massachusetts: Containing Descriptions of all the Counties, Towns, and Districts in the Commonwealth*. Boston: J. P. Jewett. Available online at Google Books.

———, 1849. *A Gazetteer of New Hampshire: Containing Descriptions of all the Counties, Towns, and Districts in the State*. Boston: J. P. Jewett. Available online at Google Books.

———, 1849. *A Gazetteer of Vermont: Containing Descriptions of all the Counties, Towns, and Districts in the State*. Boston: J. P. Jewett.

———, 1857. *The New England Gazetteer* (2nd ed.). Boston: Boyd & White.

Heald, Bruce D., 2007. *A History of the Boston & Maine Railroad*. Charleston, SC: The History Press.

Heath, Kingston William, 2001. *The Patina of Place: The Cultural Weathering of a New England Industrial Landscape*. Knoxville, TN: University of Tennessee Press.

Henderson, Elizabeth, and Robyn Van En, 2007. *Sharing the Harvest: A Citizen's Guide to Community Supported Agriculture*. White River Junction, VT: Chelsea Green.

Henry D. and Frances T. McCallum, 1972. *The Wire That Fenced the West*. Norman, OK: University of Oklahoma.

Historic Documentation Company, 2009. *Historic Stone Highway Culverts in New Hampshire Asset Management Manual*. New Hampshire Department of Transportation. Available at http://www.nh.gov/dot/org/projectdevelopment/environment/documents.

Holmes, Oliver Wendell, 1889. *Our Hundred Days in Europe*. Boston: Houghton, Mifflin & Co.

Hubble, William, 2006. *Good Fences: A Pictorial History of New England's Stone Walls*. Camden, ME: Down East Books.

Hubka, Thomas C., 1984. *Big House, Little House, Back House, Barn: The Connected Farm Buildings of New England*. Hanover, NH: University Press of New England.

Huden, John C., 1962. *Indian Place Names of New England*. New York: Museum of the American Indian, Heye Foundation.

Hutchens, Alma R., 1973. *Indian Herbalogy of North America: The Definitive Guide to Native Medicinal Plants and Their Uses*. Boston, MA: Shambhala Publishers.

Images of America Series by Arcadia Press: http://www.arcadiapublishing.com/.

Jackson, John Brinkerhoff, 1984. *Discovering the Vernacular Landscape*. New Haven, CT: Yale University Press.

Jager, Ronald, and Grace Jager, 2000. *The Granite State New Hampshire: An Illustrated History*. Franklin, TN: American Historical Press.

Jarvis, DeForest Clinton, 1958. *Folk Medicine: A Vermont Doctor's Guide to Good Health*. New York: Henry Holt and Company.

Jefferson, Thomas, 1781. *Notes on the State of Virginia*. Available online at http://etext.virginia.edu/toc/modeng/public/JefVirg.html.

———. Letter to John Jay, 1785, in *Respectfully Quoted: a Dictionary of Quotations* (Suzy Platt, ed.), p. 7. New York: Barnes & Noble, 1993.

Jerome, John, 1996. *Stone Work: Reflections on Serious Play and Other Aspects of Country Life*. Hanover, NH: University Press of New England.

Johnson, Charles W., 1980. *The Nature of Vermont: Introduction and Guide to a New England Environment*. Hanover, NH: University Press of New England.

Johnson, Clifton, 1915. *Highways and Byways of New England*. New York: The Macmillan Co.

Johnson, Eric S., 2012. *Roads, Rails, and Trails: Transportation-related Archaeology in Massachusetts*. Boston: Massachusetts Historical Commission.

Jorgensen, Neil, 1977. *A Guide to New England's Landscape* (2nd ed.). Chester, CT: Globe Pequot Press.

Judd, Richard W., Edwin A. Churchill, and Joel Eastman (eds.), 1995. *Maine: The Pine Tree State from Prehistory to the Present*. Orono, ME: University of Maine Press.

Keister, Douglas, 2009. *Stories in Stone: A Field Guide to Cemetery Symbolism and Iconography*. Layton, UT: Gibbs Smith.

Kelso, Gerald K., Frederica R. Dimmick, David H. Dimmick, and Tonya B. Largy, 2006. "An Ethnopalynological Test of Task-Specific Area Analysis: Bay View Stable, Cataument, Massachusetts." *Journal of Archaeological Science* 33:953–960.

Kershner, Bruce, and Robert T. Leverett, 2004. *The Sierra Club Guide to the Ancient Forests of the Northeast*. San Francisco: Sierra Club Books.

King, Thomas F., 2000. *Federal Planning and Historical Places: The Section 106 Process*. Walnut Creek, CA: AltaMira Press.

———, 2003. *Places that Count, Traditional Cultural Properties in Cultural Resource Management*. Lanham, MD: AltaMira Press.

Klamkin, Charles, 1973. *Barns: Their History, Preservation, and Restoration*. New York: Hawthorn Books.

Klyza, Christopher, and Stephen Trombulak, 1994. *The Story of Vermont: A Natural and Cultural History*. Hanover, NH: University Press of New England.

Knoblock Glenn A., 2002. *New Hampshire Covered Bridges*. Charleston, SC: Arcadia Publishing.

Kulik, Gary, 1985. "Dams, Fish, and Farmers: Defense of Public Rights in Eighteenth-Century Rhode Island," in Steven Hahn and Jonathan Prude (eds.), *The Countryside in the Age of Capitalist Transformation*, pp. 25–50. Chapel Hill, NC: University of North Carolina Press.

Lang, Gordon, 1995. *Miller's Pottery & Porcelain Marks*. London: Octopus Publishing.

Lape, Fred, 1979. *Apples & Man*. New York: Van Nostrand Reinhold.

Lapping, Mark B., 2011. "Stone Walls, Woodlands, and Farm Buildings: Artifacts of New England's Agrarian Past," in B. Harrison and R.W. Judd (eds.), *A Landscape History of New England*, pp. 129–132. Cambridge, MA: MIT Press.

Larkin, Jack, 1994. "From 'Country Mediocrity' to 'Rural Improvement': Transforming the Slovenly Countryside in Central Massachusetts, 1775–1840," in Catherine E. Hutchins (ed.), *Everyday Life in the Early Republic*, pp. 175–200. Winterthur, DE: Henry Francis du Pont Winterthur Museum.

Lehman, Tim, 1995. *Public Values, Private Lands: Farmland Preservation Policy, 1933–1985*. Chapel Hill, NC: University of North Carolina Press.

Lenney, Christopher J., 2003. *Sightseeking: Clues to the Landscape History of New England*. Hanover, NH: University Press of New England.

Leveillee, Alan, 1997. "When Worlds Collide: Archaeology in the New Age—The Conant Parcel Stone Piles." *Bulletin of the Massachusetts Archaeological Society* 58 (1):24–30; http://library.bridgew.edu/exhibits/BMAS/pdf/MAS-v58n01.pdf.

Lipke William C., and Philip N. Grime, 1976. *Vermont Landscape Images 1776–1976.* Burlington, VT: Robert Hull Fleming Museum.

Liscia, Marcello, Michela Monteb, and Ettore Pacinia, 2003. "Lichens and Higher Plants on Stone: A Review." *International Biodeterioraton and Biodegradation* 51(1):1–17; http://www.aseanbiodiversity.info/abstract/51004276.pdf.

Lorraine, Annette, 2002. *Conserving the Family Farm: A Guide to Conservation Easements for Farmers, Other Agricultural Professionals, Landowners and Conservationists.* NH Coalition for Sustaining Agriculture and UNH Cooperative Extension; available at http://extension.unh.edu/resources/representation/Resource000020_Rep20.pdf.

MacWeeney, Alan, and Richard Conniff, 1986. *Irish Walls.* New York: Stewart, Tabori and Chang.

Maine Archaeological Society: http://www.mainearchsociety.org/.

Maine Board of Agriculture. Fourteenth Annual *Report of the Secretary of the Board of Agriculture for the Year 1869.* Augusta, ME: Maine Board of Agriculture, 1870.

———. Fortieth Annual *Report of the Secretary of the Board of Agriculture for the Year 1897.* Augusta, ME: Maine Board of Agriculture, 1898.

———. Forty-fifth Annual *Report of the Secretary of the Board of Agriculture for the Year 1901.* Augusta, ME: Maine Board of Agriculture, 1901.

Maine Forest Service. *Forest Trees of Maine,* Centennial Edition. Augusta, ME: Maine Forest Service, Department of Conservation, 2008.

Maine Historic Preservation Commission: http://www.state.me.us/mhpc/.

Maine Olmsted Alliance for Parks and Landscapes: http://www.maineolmsted.org.

Maine Preservation: http://www.mainepreservation.org.

Marchand, Peter J., 1987. *North Woods: An Inside Look at the Nature of Forests in the Northeast.* Boston: Appalachian Mountain Club.

Marriot, Paul Daniel, 2010. *The Preservation Office Guide to Historic Roads: Clarifying Preservation Goals for State Historic Preservation Offices, Establishing Expectations for State Transportation Offices.* Washington, DC: http://www.historicroads.org/documents/GUIDE.pdf.

Martin, George A., 1974. *Fences, Gates and Bridges: A Practical Manual.* Brattleboro, VT: The Stephen Greene Press. Reprint of the 1887 edition published by O. Judd, New York.

May, F., Irwin M. Brodo, and Theodore L. Esslinger, 2000. *Identifying North American Lichens: A Guide to the Literature.* Farlow Herbarium, Harvard University, Cambridge, MA. Available online at http://www.huh.harvard.edu/collections/lichens/guide/index.html.

McCullough, David, 2001. *John Adams.* New York: Simon & Schuster.

McCullough, Robert, 1995. *The Landscape of Community. A History of Communal Forests in New England.* Hanover, NH: University Press of New England.

McCullough, Robert. 2005. *Crossings: A History of Bridges in Vermont.* Barre, VT: Vermont Historical Society.

McEvoy, Thom J., 1995. *Introduction to Forest Ecology and Silviculture.* UVM Extension System booklet BR 1387. Burlington, VT: University of Vermont.

———, 2004. *Positive Impact Forestry: A Sustainable Approach to Managing Woodlands.* Washington, DC: Island Press.

McMurry, Sally, 1995. *Transforming Rural Life: Dairying Families and Agricultural Change, 1820–1885 (Revisiting Rural America).* Baltimore, MD: Johns Hopkins University Press.

McVarish, Douglas C., 2008. *American Industrial Archaeology: A Field Guide*. Walnut Creek, CA: Left Coast Press.

Meeks, Harold A., 1986. *Time and Change in Vermont: A Human Geography*. Chester, CT: Globe Pequot Press.

Mehrhoff, L. J., J. A. Silander, Jr., S. A. Leicht, E. S. Mosher, and N. M. Tabak, 2003. *IPANE: Invasive Plant Atlas of New England*. University of Connecticut Department of Ecology & Evolutionary Biology, Storrs, CT; http://www.ipane.org.

Meinig, D. W. (ed.), 1979. *The Interpretation of Ordinary Landscapes: Geographical Essays*. New York: Oxford University Press.

Muir, Diane, 2000. *Reflections in Bullough's Pond: Economy and Ecosystem in New England*. Hanover, NH: University Press of New England.

National Park Service, 1995. *How to Apply the National Register Criteria*. National Register Bulletin. Washington, DC: National Park Service; http://www.nps.gov/nr/publications/bulletins/nrb15/.

———, 2000. *Guidelines for Evaluating and Registering Archeological Properties*. National Register Bulletin. Washington, DC: National Park Service; http://www.nps.gov/nr/publications/bulletins/arch/.

Neudorfer, Giovanna, 1980. *Vermont's Stone Chambers: An Inquiry into Their Past*. Montpelier, VT: Vermont Historical Society.

Neumann, Thomas W., and Robert M. Sanford, 1987. "The Use of Vegetation Successional Stages in Cultural Resource Assessments." *American Archeology* Vol. 6(2):119–127.

Neumann, Thomas W., Robert M. Sanford, and Karen G. Harry, 2010. *Cultural Resources Archaeology: An Introduction* (2nd ed.). Lanham, MD: AltaMira Press.

New England Antiquities Research Association: http://www.neara.org/.

New Hampshire Archaeological Society: http://www.nhas.org/.

New Hampshire Department of Environmental Services: http://www.des.state.nh.us/geo1link.htm.

New Hampshire Division of Historical Resources (DHR): http://webster.state.nh.us/nhdhr/; New Hampshire DHR, State Conservation and Rescue Archaeology Program: http://www.mv.com/ipusers/boisvert/; State of New Hampshire, Department of Cultural Resources: http://webster.state.nh.us/nhculture/.

New Hampshire Historical Society, The Tuck Library, 30 Park Street, Concord, NH 03301-6384.

Nichols, Joann H., and Patricia L. Haslam. "Index to Known Cemetery Listings in VT." Vermont Historical Society: http://www.vermonthistory.org/.

Noble, Allen George, 1984. *Wood, Brick, and Stone: The North American Settlement Landscape*. Amherst, MA: University of Massachusetts Press.

Noble, Allen G., and Richard K. Cleek, 1995. *The Old Barn Book: A Field Guide to North American Barns and Other Farm Structures*. New Brunswick, NJ: Rutgers University Press.

Nylund, Megan, 2006. *A Study of Lichens and Lichenometry*. Primary Research: http://www.primaryresearch.org/stonewalls/nylund/index.php.

Offwell Woodland and Wildlife Trust, 2009. *Lichens*. Available at http://www.countrysideinfo.co.uk/fungi/lichens.htm.

Parker, Patricia L., and Thomas F. King, 1995. *Guidelines for Evaluating and Documenting Traditional Cultural Properties*. National Register Bulletin. Washington, DC: National Park Service; http://www.nps.gov/nr/publications/bulletins/nrb38/.

Patoni, Priscilla, 2003. *Abandoned New England: Landscape in the Works of Homer, Frost, Hopper, Wyeth, and Bishop.* Hanover, NH: University Press of New England.

Perazzo, Peggy B. *Stone Quarries and Beyond.* Available at http://quarriesandbeyond.org/index.html.

Periam, Jonathan, 1984. *The Home & Farm Manual: A Pictorial Encyclopedia of Farm, Garden, Household, Architectural, Legal, Medical, and Social Information.* Reprint of classic 1884 edition. New York: Greenwich House.

Peterson, R. T., and M. McKinny, 1968. *A Field Guide to Wildflowers of Northeastern and Northcentral North America.* Boston: Houghton Mifflin.

Pollock, Stephen G., Nathan D. Hamilton, and Robson Bonnichsen, 1999. "Chert from the Munsungun Lake Formation (Maine) in Palaeoamerican Archaeological Sites in Northeastern North America: Recognition of Its Occurrence and Distribution." *Journal of Archaeological Science* 26(3), March 1999, pp. 269–293.

Price, Chester B., 1967. "Historic Indian Trails of New Hampshire." *The New Hampshire Archaeologist* 14.

Rivard, Paul E., 2007. *Made in Maine: From Home and Workshop to Mill and Factory.* Charleston, SC: The History Press.

Robinson, William F., 1976. *Abandoned New England: Its Hidden Ruins and Where to Find Them.* Boston: Little, Brown & Co. for New York Graphic Society.

Rolando, Victor, 1992. *200 years of Soot and Sweat: The History and Archeology of Vermont's Iron, Charcoal, and Lime Industries.* Burlington, VT: Archaeological Society of Vermont. Available on CD from the Archaeological Society of Vermont.

Rossen, Jack, 1994. *The Archeology of the Farm Project. Improving Cultural Resource Protection on Agricultural Lands: A Vermont Example.* Demonstration Report No. 3, Lake Champlain Basin Program, Grand Isle, VT.

Rowe, William Hutchinson, 1948. *The Maritime History of Maine: Three Centuries of Shipbuilding and Seafaring.* New York: W. W. Norton.

Royer, France, and Richard Dickinson, 2006. *Weeds of the Northern U.S. and Canada.* Edmonton, Canada: University of Alberta Press.

Ruhf, Kathy, 1999. *Farmland Transfer and Protection in New England.* Belchertown, MA: The New England Small Farm Institute.

Ruhf, Kathy, Matthew Hora, Sue Ellen Johnson, and Kathy Lawrence. 2004. *Northeast Farms to Food: Understanding Our Region's Food System.* Northeast Sustainable Agricultural Working Group.

Russell, Emily B., 1998. *People and the Land through Time: Linking Ecology and History.* New Haven, CT: Yale University Press.

Russell, Howard S., 1980. *Indian New England Before the Mayflower.* Hanover, NH: University Press of New England.

——, 1976. *A Long, Deep Furrow: Three Centuries of Farming in New England.* Hanover, NH: University Press of New England.

——, abridged by Mark Lapping, 1982. *A Long, Deep Furrow: Three Centuries of Farming in New England.* Hanover, NH: University Press of New England.

Rutherford, Phillip H., 1970. *The Dictionary of Maine Place Names.* Portland, ME: Cumberland Printers.

Ryden, Kent C., 2001. *Landscape with Figures: Nature & Culture in New England.* Iowa City, IA: University of Iowa Press.

Sanford, Robert, T. W. Neumann, and G. Salmon, 1997. "Reading the Landscape: Inference of Historic Land Use in Vermont Forests." *Journal of Vermont Archaeology* 2:1–12.

Sanford, Robert, N. Huffer, D. Huffer, T. Neumann, G. Peebles, M. Butera, G. Anderson, and D. Lacy, 1994. *Stone Walls and Cellar Holes: A Guide for Landowners on Historic Features and Landscapes in Vermont's Forests.* Department of Forests and Parks, Agency of Natural Resources, Waterbury, VT. Revised in 1995 and now available online at http://accd.vermont.gov/sites/accd/files/images/strongcommunities/historic/stonewall%20and%20cellarhouse_pub_screen.pdf.

Schupp, James R., 2002. *Renovating Old Apple Trees.* University of Maine Cooperative Extension Bulletin #2409; available at http://umaine.edu/publications/2409e/.

Seaburg, Carl, Stanley Patterson, and Alan Seaburg (eds.), 2003. *The Ice King: Frederick Tudor and His Circle.* Boston, MA: Massachusetts Historical Society.

Searls, Paul M., 2006. *Two Vermonts: Geography and Identity 1865–1910.* Hanover, NH: University Press of New England.

Shaeffer, Ronald E., 1992. *Reinforced Concrete: Preliminary Design for Architects and Builders.* New York: McGraw-Hill.

Silliman, Stephen W., 2009. "Change and Continuity, Practice and Memory: Native American Persistence in Colonial New England." *American Antiquity* 74(2):211–230.

Skehan, James W., 2001. *Roadside Geology of Massachusetts.* Missoula, MT: Mountain Publishing.

Sloane, David Charles, 1991. *The Last Great Necessity: Cemeteries in American History.* Baltimore, MD: Johns Hopkins University Press.

Sloane, Eric, 1955. *Our Vanishing Landscape.* New York: Ballantine Books.

———, 1965. *A Reverence for Wood.* New York: Ballantine Books.

———, 1974. *An Age of Barns.* New York: Ballantine Books.

———, 1972. *The Little Red Schoolhouse.* Garden City, NY: Doubleday & Company, Inc.

Snow, Dan, 2001. *In the Company of Stone: The Art of the Stone Wall.* New York: Workman Publishing.

Society for Industrial Archeology: http://www.siahq.org/.

Spencer-Wood, Suzanne M., 2010. "Feminist Theoretical Perspectives on the Archaeology of Poverty: Gendering Institutional Lifeways in the Northeastern United States from the Eighteenth Century through the Nineteenth Century." *Historical Archaeology* 44(4):110–135.

Spencer-Wood, Suzanne M., and Christopher N. Matthews, 2011. "Impoverishment, Criminalization, and the Culture of Poverty." *Historical Archaeology* 45(3):1–10.

Sperduto, Daniel D., William F. Nichols, Katherine F. Crowley, and Douglas A. Bechtel, 2000. *Black Gum (Nyssa sylvatica Marsh) in New Hampshire.* Concord, NH: The New Hampshire Natural Heritage Inventory: http://www.nhdfl.org/library/pdf/BlackGumReport.pdf.

Spurr, Stephen H., 1964. *Forest Ecology.* New York: The Ronald Company Press.

Starbuck, David A., 2006. *The Archaeology of New Hampshire: Exploring 10,000 Years in the Granite State.* Hanover, NH: University Press of New England.

Stilgoe, John R., 1982. *The Common Landscape of America, 1580–1845.* New Haven, CT: Yale University Press.

———, 1994. *Alongshore.* New Haven, CT: Yale University Press.

———, 1998. *Outside Lies Magic: Regaining History and Awareness in Everyday Places.* New York: Walker Publishing Company.

———, 2005. *Landscape and Images.* Charlottesville, VA: University of Virginia Press.

Stipe, Robert (ed.), 2003. *A Richer Heritage.* Chapel Hill, NC: University of North Carolina Press.

Stilphen, George Albert, 1993. *The Apples of Maine*. Bolster's Farm/Harrison, ME: Stilphen's Crooked River Farm.

Strangstad, Lynette, 1995. *A Graveyard Preservation Primer*. Walnut Creek, CA: Rowman AltaMira.

———, 2003. *Preservation of Historic Burial Grounds*. Washington, DC: National Trust for Historic Preservation.

Stonecutters and Quarry Workers of North America Preservation Group: http://www. stonecuttersonline.org/.

The Stone Wall Initiative: http://www.stonewall.uconn.edu/.

"Stone Quarries and Beyond": http://quarriesandbeyond.org/ (6 August, 2010).

Thompson, W. B., D. L. Joyner, R. G. Woodman, and V. T. King, 1988. *A Collector's Guide to Maine Mineral Localities*, Bulletin 41 (3rd ed.). Augusta, ME: Maine Geological Survey.

Thoreau, Henry David, 1963 reprint. *The River*. New York: Bramhall House.

———, 1988 reprint. *The Maine Woods*. New York: Penguin Nature Classics.

Thorson, Robert M., 2002. *Stone by Stone: The Magnificent History in New England's Stone Walls*. New York: Walker Publishing Company. See also Thorson's website: http:// web.uconn.edu/stonewall.

———, 2005. *Exploring Stone Walls: A Field Guide to New England's Stone Walls*. New York, Walker Publishing Company.

Underhill, Roy, 1983. *The Woodwright's Companion: Exploring Traditional Woodcraft*. Chapel Hill, NC: University of North Carolina Press.

US Department of Agriculture, 1887. *Report of the Commissioner of Agriculture 1886*. Washington, DC: Government Printing Office. Full text available online at Google Books.

———, 1908. *23rd Annual Report of the Bureau of Animal Industry for the year 1906*. Washington, DC: Government Printing Office. Full text available online at Google Books.

Upton, Dell, and John Michael Vlach (eds.), 1986. *Common Places: Readings in American Vernacular Architecture*. Athens, GA: University of Georgia Press.

Van Diver, Bradford B., 1987. *Roadside Geology of Vermont and New Hampshire*. Missoula, MT: Mountain Press.

Vermont Archaeological Society, P.O. Box 663, Burlington, VT 05402-0663: http://www. vtarchaeology.org/.

The Vermont Atlas and Gazetteer. Freeport, ME: DeLorme Mapping, 1988 (8th ed.).

Vermont Division for Historic Preservation (DHP), Agency of Development and Community Affairs. National Life, Drawer 20, Montpelier, VT 05620-0501: http:// accd.vermont.gov/strong_communities/preservation.

———, 2002. *Vermont Historic Preservation Office's Guidelines for Conducting Archaeology in Vermont*. Division for Historic Preservation, Montpelier, VT. Available at http:// accd.vermont.gov/strong_communities/preservation/review_compliance/archeol-ogy_tools.

Vermont Geological Survey: http://www.anr.state.vt.us/DEC/GEO/rockkits.htm.

Vermont Historical Society. Vermont History Center, 60 Washington Street, Barre, VT 05641-4209: http://www.vermonthistory.org/.

Visser, Thomas Durant, 1997. *Field Guide to New England Barns & Farm Buildings*. Hanover, NH: University Press of New England.

Vogel, Virgil J., 1970. *American Indian Medicine*. Norman, OK: University of Oklahoma Press.

Wagner, David, 2005. *The Poorhouse: America's Forgotten Institutions*. Lanham, MD: Rowman & Littlefield.

Walewski, Joe, 2007. *Lichen of the North Woods*. Duluth, MN: Kollath & Stensaas Publishing.

Watts, May Theilgaard, 1985. *Master Tree Finder: A Manual for the Identification of Trees by Their Leaves*. Berkeley, CA: Nature Study Guild.

———, 1972. *Reading the Landscape of America* (revised and expanded edition). New York: Macmillan Publishing.

Wells, Walter, 1868. *Provisional Report upon the Water-Power of Maine*. Augusta, ME: Hydrographic Survey.

Wessels, Tom, 2010. *Forest Forensics: A Field Guide to Reading the Forested Landscape*. Woodstock, VT: Countryman Press.

———, 2004. *Reading the Forested Landscape: A Natural History of New England*. Woodstock, VT: Countryman Press.

White, E. B., 1997. *One Man's Meat*. Gardiner, ME: Tilbury House, Publishers.

Whitten, Maurice M., 1990. *The Gunpowder Mills of Maine*. Gorham, ME: Whitten.

Williams, Eric (ed.), 2008. *Innovative Land Use Planning Techniques: A Handbook of Sustainable Development*. Concord, NH: NH Department of Environmental Services.

Williamson, William D., 1832. *The History of the State of Maine: From Its First Discovery, A.D. 1602, to the Separation, A.D. 1820, Inclusive*, Vol. 1. Hallowell, ME: Glazier, Masters & Co.

Wilson, Chris, and Paul Erling Groth, 2003. *Everyday America: Cultural Landscape Studies After J. B. Jackson*. Berkeley, CA: University of California Press.

Wilson, John S., 1990. "We've Got Thousands of These! What Makes an Historic Farmstead Significant?" *Historical Archaeology* 24(2):23–33.

Wojtech, Michael, 2011. *Bark: A Field Guide to Trees of the Northeast*. Hanover, NH: University Press of New England.

Wood, Christina D., 1994. "A Most Dangerous Tree: Lombardy Poplar in Landscape Gardening." *Arnoldia* 54.1:24–30.

Wood, Frederic J., and Ronald Dale Carr, 1997. *The Turnpikes of New England*. Pepperell, MA: Branch Line Press. Revised edition of Wood's *The Turnpikes of New England, and Evolution of the Same through England, Virginia, and Maryland*. Boston: Marshall Jones Co., 1919.

Wood, Pamela (ed.), 1992. *The Salt Book: Lobstering, Sea Moss Pudding, Stone Walls, Rum Running, Maple Syrup, Snowshoes, and Other Yankee Doings*. Garden City, NY: Anchor Press/Doubleday.

Yazzie, Victoria, 2007. "The Tribal Perspective of Old Growth in Frequent-fire Forests—Its History." *Ecology and Society* 12(2):21. Available at http://www.ecologyandsociety.org/vol12/iss2/art21/.

Zelinsky, Wilbur, 1992. *The Cultural Geography of the United States*, revised ed. Englewood Cliffs, NJ: Prentice Hall.

Index

About the Author

Robert M. Sanford lives in Gorham, Maine. A former Registered Professional Archaeologist and environmental regulator, he is a professor of environmental science & policy at the University of Southern Maine. His books include *Cultural Resources Archaeology*, *Practicing Archaeology*, and *Site Plan and Development Review: A Guide for Northern New England*.

About the Illustrator

Michael Shaughnessy lives in Portland, Maine. A sculptor who works primarily in hay, he is a professor of art at the University of Southern Maine. He once drove across the USA and back with a giant hay ball on the top of his car—he brought his landscape with him. More about him and his work can be found at http://www.shaughnessyart.com/.